Divine Transcendence
and the Culture of Change

Divine Transcendence
and the Culture of Change

David H. Hopper

WILLIAM B. EERDMANS PUBLISHING COMPANY

GRAND RAPIDS, MICHIGAN / CAMBRIDGE, U.K.

© 2011 David H. Hopper

Published 2011 by
Wm. B. Eerdmans Publishing Co.
2140 Oak Industrial Drive N.E., Grand Rapids, Michigan 49505 /
P.O. Box 163, Cambridge CB3 9PU U.K.
www.eerdmans.com

Printed in the United States of America

16 15 14 13 12 11   7 6 5 4 3 2 1

Library of Congress Cataloging-in-Publication Data

Hopper, David H. (David Henry), 1927-
Divine transcendence and the culture of change / David H. Hopper.
        p.   cm.
Includes bibliographical references and index.
ISBN 978-0-8028-6505-2 (pbk.: alk. paper)
1. Transcendence of God. 2. Christianity and culture.
3. God (Christianity)   I. Title.

BT124.5.H67   2011

231'.4 — dc22

2010015110

Unless otherwise noted, Scripture quotations are taken from the Revised Standard Version of the Bible, copyright 1952 [2nd edition 1971] by the Division of Christian Education of the National Council of the Christian Churches of Christ in the United States of America. Used by permission. All rights reserved.

The author and publisher gratefully acknowledge permission to reprint materials granted by the institutions listed on p. viii.

To service in charity, yes;
but also to edification in the
community of faith — and beyond

With thanks to all who made this work possible
and contributed to it:
Julia, Kate, Roy, Kari, John, Martin, Karl, Søren,
Macalester colleagues, friends, students

Thanks also to the Newberry Library (Chicago)
for hosting me for research and teaching
in 1992-93

Contents

Acknowledgments   viii

Introduction   ix

1. Theology and Multiculturalism:
   A Reappraisal of the "Christ and Culture" Question   1

2. The Idea of Progress and the Culture of Change   23

3. Divine Transcendence and the Critique
   of Otherworldliness: Luther   61

4. Divine Transcendence and Corporate Historical
   Existence: Bucer and Calvin   119

5. The English Reformation: The Ripple Effect of
   Reformation in Francis Bacon   167

6. Theological Summary and Discussion/Interpretation   221

   Index of Names   257

   Index of Subjects   261

Acknowledgments

The author and publisher gratefully acknowledge permission granted to reprint material from the following sources:

The Heavenly City of the Eighteenth-Century Philosophers by Carl Becker, published and copyrighted in 1932. Used by permission of The Yale University Press.

The Idea of Progress by J. B. Bury, originally published and copyrighted by Macmillan & Co. (London) in 1920, republished by the Macmillan Co. in an American edition in 1932 with an introduction by William Beard. Dover reprint editions in 1955 and 1987 published by special arrangement with St. Martin's Press. Used by permission of Dover Publications Inc.

Instruction in Christian Love: 1523 by Martin Bucer the Reformer, translated with an introduction by Paul T. Fuhrmann, copyright © Martin Bucer, 1953. Used by permission of Hymns Ancient & Modern Ltd. and John Knox Press.

Luther's Works, Volume 31, copyright © 1957 Fortress Press. Used by permission of The Augsburg Fortress Publishers.

A Reformation Debate: John Calvin and Jacopo Sadoleto, edited with an introduction by John C. Olin. Copyright © John C. Olin. Copyright renewed 1994 John C. Olin. Reprinted by permission of Harper-Collins Publishers.

Introduction

A recent survey by the Pew Forum on Religion and Public Life reported that "70 percent of Americans affiliated with a religion or denomination said they agreed that 'many religions can lead to eternal life,' including majorities among Protestants and Catholics."[1] The report concluded that there was a "broad trend toward tolerance and an ability among many Americans to hold beliefs that might contradict the doctrines of their professed faiths."[2] By way of explanation, one outside observer commented that it is difficult to hold narrow sectarian beliefs while working side by side with people of other faith persuasions or parenting children with similar involvements in schools or on playgrounds. It can hardly be doubted that shared efforts and experiences make for greater understanding and sympathy among both adults and children.

Tolerance is widely and properly viewed as an essential condition for an increasingly interdependent world. Almost a hundred years ago, however, the Swiss theologian Karl Barth raised questions about the sufficiency of tolerance for providing direction for faith. After citing divisiveness among Christian groups and the varied rationalizations that were offered to "justify" the divisions, Barth, in a 1916 address, asked rhetorically: "Then shall we take the position that fundamentally we are all right? Shall we dip our hands into that from which the spirit of the

---

1. "Survey of Religion in U.S. Finds a Broad Tolerance for Other Faiths," *New York Times*, June 24, 2008, p. 15, sec. A.
2. "Broad Tolerance," *New York Times*, June 24, 2008.

Bible silently turns away, the dish of tolerance which is more and more being proclaimed . . . as the highest good?"[3] Barth turned away from commonplace tolerance to "the strange new world within the Bible," a strange new world in which God's transcendence was/is inescapably the overriding reality. Barth averred: "The fact is that we must seek our answer in this direction — 'Yea, let God be true, but every man a liar.'"[4]

The present work seeks to explore reservations about the sufficient, sustaining nature of tolerance for the faith community in an altered, "global" world, yet in such a spirit as not to reject the pragmatic necessity of tolerance for getting on with things in the world. What follows is an argument that the sources and motivations for tolerance in the faith community arise out of needs and understandings — and histories — that go beyond the prudential necessity of simply "getting on in the world." The following analysis thus focuses upon a second scholarly observation in the *New York Times* report on the Pew study, the suggestion that many who embrace a bland tolerance of religious belief "are not very well educated and they are not expressing mature theological points of view."[5] The ensuing analysis rejects the sort of tolerance expressed in such common assertions as "It doesn't matter what a person believes just so long as he/she is sincere," or "after all, we're all trying to get to the same place."

A major challenge in addressing the problem of neglected understandings of faith is that of offering edification without condescension. The challenge is to reclaim dimensions of faith that have collapsed into the cultural milieu. I take this to be the point of Barth's jarring comment about God being true but all men liars. So-called "biblical religion" inevitably finds God's transcendence at the center, a transcendence that stands athwart all human presumption, even — perhaps especially — that of teacher and theologian. Humility needs to be a presence even amidst sharp theological rejoinders. Because of its subject matter rejoinders need not be excluded if they induce reflection and self-reappraisal even when, and if, they call forth occasional responses of defensiveness and offense.

The work that follows, I expect, will theologically provoke and will

3. Karl Barth, *The Word of God and the Word of Man*, trans. Douglas Horton (New York: Harper Torchbooks, 1956), p. 42.

4. Barth, *The Word of God and the Word of Man*, p. 42.

5. "Broad Tolerance," *New York Times*, June 24, 2008.

also elicit correction and counterargument from various quarters. It is intended to engage. Whether it succeeds in engaging and especially in edifying will be at question, but if it can stir doubt about a lazy and thoughtless tolerance, that will be counted gain by the author.

What follows in argument is that truth — "truth" to the present writer — and our general thought processes are, in Francis Bacon's words, "the daughter of time." Truth is not a timeless mental achievement. In the faith community it is a witness, a testimony, rooted in its own life and historical existence, an existence sharpened and made exigent by its transcendent Author and Subject. While it is not expected that all, or even most, members of the faith community will aspire to become "lay" theologians — there are a variety of gifts in the "communion of saints" — Scripture enjoins us "to give a reason for the hope that is within you" (1 Peter 3:15). We cannot abandon our own thought processes — a gift too — while opting graciously for those of charity, service, and ministration to people in need.

In utilizing at the start an exposition of H. Richard Niebuhr's persistently thought-provoking study, *Christ and Culture*,[6] I make use of a text often used over the years in college courses as an introduction to Christian thought and often as a takeoff point for discussions of diversity in Christian ethics. It provides a useful typology, in no way rigid, for grasping important differences of Christian viewpoint and commitment. In the preface to the fiftieth-anniversary edition of *Christ and Culture* (2001), James M. Gustafson commented that the book "deepens our understanding . . . of its subject matter. Indeed its pedagogical effectiveness probably accounts for its continued use in classrooms, and is the principal motivation for an appreciative interpretation of it."[7] Gustafson also noted, that in a 1999 discussion of the book by a study group at the Harvard Kennedy School of Government, "What deeply impressed me was that some of the participants who had never before read a book by a theologian grasped Niebuhr's purpose and reveled in the access it gave them to comparing theological differences that affect[ed] the subject and agenda of the seminar."[8]

6. H. Richard Niebuhr, *Christ and Culture* (New York: Harper & Row, 1951).
7. Niebuhr, *Christ and Culture*, with new preface by James M. Gustafson (New York: HarperCollins, 2001), p. xxxi. See p. 2, n. 2, below.
8. Niebuhr, *Christ and Culture* (2001 ed.), p. xxiv.

Niebuhr's work offers a typology for identifying major forms of Christian interaction with the social and cultural situation. It offers examples of types of interaction but not histories or major theological analyses. The latter are directions that reflection often pursues in the aftermath of a Niebuhr reading. And these are directions that the present work also explores. As will be discussed below, two of Niebuhr's types involve ongoing interaction with history, one especially, viewed in a "transformative" role. The two historically oriented types offer critiques of the status quo on the basis of fresh awareness of divine transcendence as discovered and understood on a scriptural basis. Both of these types, the paradoxical and the transformative, are discussed below in a theological/historical context, but only after sketching in the origins and nature of the "progress idea," an idea that profoundly influences the way people in the Western cultural tradition have come to think about history and purpose in history, a belief that has come in recent centuries to inspire and direct human energies in social and political change. It will be argued below that it was not alone the scientific revolution of the sixteenth and seventeenth centuries but also the religious revolution of the same centuries that have contributed to a commitment to change that has distinctively characterized the intellectual/cultural tradition of the West. The idea of progress has, as well, come to find accommodation, perhaps hesitantly and in lesser degree, in other major cultural traditions of our time.

As framers of the break with the medieval ecclesiastical system of salvation, the sixteenth- and seventeenth-century figures of Martin Luther, Martin Bucer, John Calvin, and the English church reformers — but also the lay philosopher/theologian Francis Bacon — contributed to a theological review and restatement of divine transcendence that moved with, and supplemented, in various ways processes of change stimulated by the fourteenth and fifteenth centuries' Renaissance and earlier technological innovations. What emerges from reappraisal of these cited theological figures and their historical involvements is the likely contentious thesis that their recovery of a sense for God's transcendence helped break open formerly closed systems of thought and life.

Luther was an initiating figure of new theological reflection. What is characterized below as his critique of "otherworldliness," beginning with his attack on the sale of indulgences, a criticism that developed into an increasing rejection of what he came to see as the medieval church's "perforation of heaven," its overreach into life beyond death and its neglect of the unconditional proclamation of the unconditional gospel of forgiveness and grace. In the gospel of grace Luther saw the substance and what he came to see as the authentic nature of God's transcendence, manifested chiefly in the cross and only secondarily in the order of nature or creation.

Provoked and stimulated by Luther's affirmations, which were greatly facilitated by the innovative technology of the printing press, Bucer, Calvin, and especially Francis Bacon among the English, furthered the theological recovery of the sense of God's transcendence and an appreciation for its expression in varied venues — for example, in affirmation of the political goal of "greatest good for the greatest number," in church life as a participatory, non-hierarchical "communion of saints," and in the need to break through stultifying modes of thought so that the world might be seen ever again with new eyes (Bacon's critique of intellectual idolatry).

Edification as a goal of both a mature spiritual and intellectual life seeks interchange. Thus, what is sought in what follows is consideration, engagement, correction, alternative statement. If, in what follows, appreciation is garnered for the somewhat alien thought that history, rather than nature, is the critical sphere for apprehending God's transcendence, that certainly will be counted a gain.

Chapter 1

Theology and Multiculturalism: A Reappraisal of the "Christ and Culture" Question

R ecent decades have seen more and more talk about "culture," the
conflict of cultures and/or civilizations, and the assertion of cultural and ethnic "identities." This talk goes on in the pages of our leading newspapers and journals and in our educational institutions. It is increasingly a matter of foreign policy considerations in the troubled
developments of a post–Cold War, post-9/11 world. On most college and
university campuses "multiculturalism" is the lodestar of curriculum development, a common selling-point in the recruitment of new students.
Amidst our new "global" modes of thought it is to be expected that we
should ponder the cultural differences that divide as well as attract.[1]
Certainly there is an objective historical basis for all of this discourse.
But whether the talk has the concreteness it tries to project will demand
ongoing scrutiny and analysis. Much of the discussion carries ideological suppositions, and there is a need to maintain a critical perspective.

In these discussions of "culture" it is generally the case — and this is
readily understandable — that religion comes up for analysis primarily
as an aspect of the assumed larger term. Religion has most often been
understood as one, but only one, of the determining and conserving fac-

---

1. It has not yet been determined what the impact of the September 11, 2001, attack on
the World Trade Center towers will be in the long term. In the Western world, it seems to
have raised only limited questioning about the underlying relativism of the earlier multicultural disposition among intellectual advocates of a "postmodern" world. On the other
hand, on the political level, there was assertion of absolutist, "black/white" moral and ethical advocacy and, in the minds of others, a reaffirmation of the precepts of "natural law"
and timeless "truth."

tors in a culture, along with history, crafts, folklore, literature, and varied ritual celebrations. In the contemporary embrace of multiculturalism, the quest for meaning is frequently presented as a quest for "identity" within a cultural, tribal, ethnic tradition. This often entails the effort to experience and relive neglected religious traditions. The two terms, "experience" and "identity," figure large in our present intellectual/spiritual ethos. "Religion" is often viewed as one among the variety of options that yield an experience or an identity within a larger cultural context.[2]

In the late twentieth and early twenty-first centuries anthropology appeared, for the most part, to have claimed title to the old term, "queen of the sciences." And theology, which long ago claimed that title itself, seemed put upon to describe for itself a new and lesser role. For the most part theology seemed caught up in these anthropological, multicultural trends of the recent past — at least in the United States, where discussions were pressed at times with some fervor. In the most recent past however, especially in the aftermath of the terrorist attack of 9/11, religious fervor, if not theological analysis, has regained increased attention.

In this particular context it is instructive to reexamine a work of another era — a work that addressed, well over fifty years ago, the religion and culture question in terms of the categories "Christ" and "culture." Published in 1951, H. Richard Niebuhr's *Christ and Culture* continues to command interest, especially among theological ethicists, though it is not often a focus of major theological analysis.[3] Niebuhr's book spells

2. An exploration of these themes is found in George A. Lindbeck, *The Nature of Doctrine: Religion and Theology in a Postliberal Age* (Philadelphia: Westminster Press, 1984). As an alternative to an "experiential-expressive" model of religion Lindbeck offered a more theologically, historically attuned "cultural-linguistic" model; see especially pp. 30-35.

3. H. Richard Niebuhr, *Christ and Culture* (New York: Harper & Row, 1951); parenthetical references in the text refer to this edition. In the late 1990s two volumes reviewed and discussed Niebuhr's 1951 analysis of the Christ/culture question: Glen H. Stassen, D. M. Yeager, and John Howard Yoder, *Authentic Transformation: A New Vision of Christ and Culture* (Nashville: Abingdon Press, 1996), and Angus J. L. Menuge, ed., *Christ and Culture in Dialogue* (Saint Louis: Concordia Academic Press, 1999). In the preface to the 2001 printing of Niebuhr's *Christ and Culture* (HarperSanFrancisco), James Gustafson took up criticism of H. Richard Niebuhr's work by John Howard Yoder, who wrote from a Mennonite (Anabaptist) perspective, along with that of a former Notre Dame colleague of Yoder, George Marsden. Gustafson rebutted much of the Yoder/Marsden critique of Niebuhr — to the mind of this reader on fully warranted grounds, not the least of which

out the variety of ways in which the Christian community, in the course of its history, interacted with its broader social/cultural context. Primarily a socio-ethical work, the book's major purpose was to outline the various historical expressions of Christian social interactions. In *Christ and Culture*, Niebuhr identified five types, five patterns, of relationships identifiable, though not realized fully, in the various Christian traditions and/or denominational church groups as they interact with the societies in which they find themselves. Niebuhr described the types under the headings "Christ against Culture," "the Christ of Culture," "Christ above Culture," "Christ and Culture in Paradox," and "Christ the Transformer of Culture." Let us briefly summarize each of the types as a basis for describing the shift in discussion that has taken place in recent times and continues into our present.

With the type "Christ against culture" Niebuhr offered an account of one of the oldest responses of the Christian faith-community to its surrounding social setting. The response is one of antagonism and conflict in which the Christian community sees itself called to be "in the world, but not of the world." The purposes and goals of the larger society are viewed as opposed to those of the faith community and/or "the kingdom of God." The convert, or believer, is called "out of the world" into a tight-knit community of believers, which, in the earliest years of the Christian tradition, even held material possessions "in common." The "world," in this faith perspective, was/is understood to be under the control of the forces of evil and outside the pale of redemption. Withdrawal from the world is the distinctive mark of this sociological response of faith, one in which the saving of individuals out of the world is understood to be the chief Christian task and duty. There are strong features of this "Christ against culture" response to society in the monastic movements of early Christian times and Middle Ages down to the present time. Various Protestant sectarian groups, in contrast to the "mainline churches," have reflected this pattern.

---

was rejection of an inexplicable personal attack by Yoder on Niebuhr himself. Gustafson did not address the criticism of Niebuhr from the confessional Lutheran perspective, criticism found in the 1999 *Christ and Culture in Dialogue,* a work devoted largely to a defense of Luther's "two-kingdoms," or two "realms," teaching, an oft-suggested source of Lutheran social-political quietism. It is of note that Martin Marty wrote a chapter in the latter's defense of Lutheran social ethics as well as paying tribute to Niebuhr in a foreword to Gustafson's 2001 edition of *Christ and Culture.*

3

Niebuhr's second type of Christian response to the world is "the Christ of culture." In this pattern of response no great opposition is seen between Christ and culture: Christ is viewed as the embodiment of all that is best in culture, the fulfillment of its highest aspirations. The ethical teachings of Jesus are extolled as culture's highest achievement and usually there is the expectation that history will move toward an ever-fuller realization of those teachings. Although there are some expressions of this point of view in the early encounter of Christianity and Greco-Roman culture, its most common expression is found in nineteenth-century "Protestant liberalism," with its enthusiastic embrace of the rationalism of the Enlightenment and its corollary belief in Progress, also in the so-called "religion of Jesus" in contrast to assumed distortions of a "religion about Jesus."

Next in Niebuhr's analysis come three types which, in Niebuhr's words, seek to preserve the differences between the two previous types of Christ and culture, yet undertake "to hold them together in some unity" (*Christ and Culture,* p. 41). He identifies at this point "Christ above culture," "Christ and culture in paradox," and "Christ the transformer of culture," types represented most recognizably in Catholicism, Lutheranism, and Calvinism.

With the "Christ above culture" category Niebuhr describes a relationship in which Christ is viewed as the fulfillment of culture, as one who brings into the cultural situation a meaning and possibility that is not inherent in culture itself. Culture has its legitimacy in and of itself; but, distorted by sin, the human condition requires a supra-natural redemption if an eternal bliss is to be gained in the life hereafter. Niebuhr offers the observation: "Christ is, indeed, a Christ of culture, but he is also a Christ above culture. This synthetic type is best represented by Thomas Aquinas and his followers, but it has many other representatives in both early and modern times" (p. 42).

"Christ and culture in paradox," unlike the type just described, sees in culture, in society and its institutions, no evidence of innate openings toward redemption, but rather only an ordering of human life, prescribed by God, allowing for — and needing — the proclamation of an unworldly gospel of redemption. In this tradition the believing Christian has the duty to help maintain a worldly order under the law of God while giving expression to an unworldly charity generated by the grace of forgiveness. Christ and culture live in tension with one another, in an interactive polarity. Christians of this paradoxical type are, Niebuhr writes, "like the 'Christ-against-culture' believers, yet differ from them in the conviction that obedience to God requires obedience to the institutions of society and loyalty to its members as well as obedience to a Christ who sits in judgment on that society. . . . [The believer] is seen as subject to two moralities, and as a citizen of two worlds that are not only discontinuous with each other but largely opposed" (pp. 42-43).

The fifth type, "Christ the transformer of culture," is referred to by Niebuhr as the "conversionist" type. He describes this outlook as consonant with the first and fourth types, which regard culture as pervaded by sin and fundamentally in opposition to the kingdom of Christ. "Yet the antithesis does not lead either to Christian separation from the world as with the first group, or to mere endurance in the expectation of a trans-historical salvation, as with the fourth. Christ is seen as the converter of . . . [people in their] culture and society, not apart from these, for there is no nature without culture and no turning of [people] from self and idols to God save in society" (p. 43). Niebuhr cites Augustine and Calvin, especially the latter, as the chief exemplars of his fifth and final type.

In his "Acknowledgments" at the beginning of *Christ and Culture* (1951), Niebuhr states that he is very much in the debt of the German philosopher-theologian Ernst Troeltsch (1865-1923) for the inspiration of much of his work and of *Christ and Culture* in particular. Influenced by Max Weber and others, Troeltsch, in his 1911 classic study, *The Social Teachings of the Christian Churches*,[4] drew the important, influential distinction between the sociological forms of "church" and "sect." It is important to quote directly from Troeltsch on this matter, not only to understand Niebuhr's assimilation and use of Troeltsch's work, but also to anticipate arguments later in the present work that run counter to what Troeltsch and Niebuhr have argued.

The church, Troeltsch declared,

is that type of organization which is overwhelmingly conservative, which to a certain extent accepts the secular order, and dominates the masses; in principle, therefore, it is universal, i.e. it desires to cover the whole life of humanity. . . . The fully developed church . . .

4. Ernst Troeltsch, *The Social Teaching of the Christian Churches*, 2 vols. (New York: Harper & Brothers, 1960), reprint of a 1931 translation (Allen & Unwin/Macmillan) of *Die Soziallehren der christlichen Kirchen und Gruppen* (1911).

utilizes the state and the ruling classes, and weaves these elements into her own life; she then becomes an integral part of the existing social order; from this standpoint, then, the church both stabilizes and determines the social order; in so doing, however, she becomes dependent upon the upper classes, and upon their development.[5]

By contrast, the sects, again as described by Troeltsch, are

comparatively small groups; they aspire after personal inward perfection, and they aim at a direct personal fellowship between the members of each group. From the very beginning, therefore, they are forced to organize themselves in small groups, and to renounce the idea of dominating the world. Their attitude towards the world, the state, and society may be indifferent, tolerant, or hostile, since they have no desire to control and incorporate these forms of social life. . . . The sects . . . are connected with the lower classes, or at least with those elements in society which are opposed to the state and to society; they work upwards from below, and not downwards from above.[6]

Niebuhr enlarged upon and added to these two major categories described by Troeltsch to provide the five sociological types of *Christ and Culture*. Troeltsch's definition of the sect is incorporated into and best represented by the "Christ against culture" type. Niebuhr then revised the "church" category of Troeltsch, breaking it down into the three "churchly" forms, "Christ above culture," "Christ and culture in paradox," and "Christ the transformer of culture," all three positively related to culture in one way or another. Niebuhr added yet another type, "the Christ of culture," in which Christ essentially collapses into an im-

---

5. Troeltsch, *The Social Teaching*, vol. 1, p. 331.

6. Troeltsch, *The Social Teaching*, vol. 1, p. 331. Apropos of the theme of the current work, Troeltsch observes in a passage following that cited: "*both types vary a good deal in their attitude towards the supernatural and transcendent element in Christianity*, and also in their view of its system of asceticism. The Church relates the whole of the secular order as a means and a preparation to the supernatural aim of life, and it incorporates genuine asceticism into its structure as one element in this preparation, all under the very definite direction of the Church. The sects refer their members directly to the supernatural aim of life, and in them the individualistic, directly religious character of asceticism, as a means of union with God, is developed more strongly and fully" (vol. 1, pp. 331-32; emphasis added).

manent principle of culture and history and serves as an embodiment of the general ethically good.

The point at which Niebuhr moved beyond, or offered emendation of, Troeltsch was in his assimilation of the incisive critique of nineteenth-century liberal Protestant theology by the Swiss theologian Karl Barth (1886-1968). Barth's major contributions to the theology of the twentieth century were a recapture of the biblical sense of divine transcendence and an emphasis on the importance of christology within the faith of the church. Niebuhr picked up on Barth's christocentrism and offered analysis on the basis of a "Christ" and culture dichotomy, an emphasis not found in Troeltsch. Also, in exposition of the term "Christ," Niebuhr accented elements of transcendence in Christ's teaching and person,[7] thereby setting up the dichotomy with culture, a point that Troeltsch seems to have recognized but was inclined to talk about most often in terms of an ethical idealism found, for example, in the Sermon on the Mount.

One can note in Niebuhr's analysis of the Christ and culture issue an appreciation for the significance of divine transcendence in distinguishing alternative standpoints in the debate. Four of the five types that Niebuhr identified are marked by some form of an unworldly, divine intervention in, or disruption of, the continuities of the cultural situation. The term "God" was understood to introduce "polarities," "tensions," and "discontinuities" within the human situation. "Revelation" bore the mark of an "otherworldly" or unworldly intervention in history.

Laying aside a thorough analysis of Niebuhr's theology, which at key points is itself ambiguous on the question of divine transcendence,[8] it is of note for our study that if, in 1951, the weight of the analysis lay with appreciation of the phenomenon of divine transcendence, in subsequent times — in relation to schools of thought such as process, "secular," and feminist theology — discussions of "religion and culture" strongly favored belief in divine immanence, at least in professional, academic circles. This pattern continues into the present, though the most recent

---

7. See especially Niebuhr, *Christ and Culture*, pp. 25-28.

8. See H. Richard Niebuhr, *Radical Monotheism and Western Culture* (New York: Harper & Brothers, 1960), esp. pp. 32-33. Niebuhr writes: "For radical monotheism the value-center is neither closed society nor the principle of such a society but the principle of being itself; its reference is to no one reality among the many but to One beyond all the many, whence all the many derive their being, and by participation in which they exist" (p. 32).

surge of "evangelicalism" has posed new challenges for interpretation and has also had an impact in the political/academic sphere. Prior to this most recent development God was seen primarily as a principle within culture and history rather than as One standing, say, in judgment over history. The reasons for the shift toward immanence after the theological struggles of the first half of the twentieth century have not met with a great deal of scholarly agreement. It is important nonetheless to attempt an account of this shift in order to work toward some judgment about the relevance and continuing viability of Niebuhr's analysis and then to offer a statement of the continuing theological importance of divine transcendence.

Although there have always been close ties between the intellectual history of Europe and that of the United States, there have been important differences as well. In our present situation the United States seems to be the great exporter of popular culture, from blue jeans to rock 'n' roll to Jerry Lewis. But in intellectual and other aspects of "high culture," in philosophy and also in theology, the main currents have, until recent times, flowed primarily from Europe to America. Certainly it is fair to say that in the late nineteenth and at least through most of the twentieth century, American theology was more influenced by the thought of Europe than vice versa. American theology for the most part seemed to lack a dimension of "depth." It seemed always too ready to move on to the next thing. Many will no doubt disagree with this assessment, but American theology seemed inclined to want to fix things, less intent on wanting to plumb the sources and nature of faith. Of course, to this point in time, and with the exception of the Civil War and the historical experiences of racial minority groups in this country, especially the African American and Native American communities, American culture has been less subject than Europe to the tragedies of history. It seems less inclined to "take stock," more inclined to "get on" with things. Pragmatism is an American philosophy, and the American "Social Gospel" of the early decades of the twentieth century illustrates this temper. Nineteenth-century American romanticism and New England "transcendentalism" tended to absent a sense for "tragic" depth.

It is not surprising that in the aftermath of World War II, after a decade of "silence" (the 1950s), a decade that expressed the spiritual exhaustion of World War II and was also marked by the disillusioned, anxious onset of the Cold War, a new generation of younger American theologians should begin to rebel against the sober, probing, "European" theology, commonly referred to as "neo-orthodoxy." The framing of a "new theology" was the task that a new generation assigned itself. The theology of the prison letters of the German theologian Dietrich Bonhoeffer (1906-1945) was an important element in this development.

Bonhoeffer's final letters from a Nazi jail seemed to be written out of a comprehension of Barth's "dialectical" theology, but pointed beyond to a theology of "man's coming of age" and the necessity of living before God "without God." Though Bonhoeffer's *Letters and Papers from Prison* were first published in 1951, it took some time for the mood of the 1950s to lift and for the postwar generation of American theologians to assimilate Bonhoeffer's theological accents and then utter their own constructs, affirm their own *Mündlichkeit,* their coming-of-age. A key sentence found in the prison letters characterizes what was to follow theologically. In an "Outline for a Book" Bonhoeffer wrote: "Karl Barth and the Confessing Church have encouraged us to entrench ourselves persistently behind the 'faith of the church,' and evade the honest question as to what we ourselves really believe."[9] This key text helped provide, as it were, inspiration for an American generation to break free from the perceived classic content of Barth's theology, with the latter's deep involvement in the tragic history of Europe in the first half of the twentieth century.

In 1963 the thrust of Bonhoeffer's criticism, with its claim to authenticity and honest doubt, was taken up and elaborated by a bishop of the Church of England, John A. T. Robinson, in his concise, very popular *Honest to God.* The major thrust of Robinson's book was an attack upon divine transcendence and classical theism. Drawing heavily upon the thought of Paul Tillich (1886-1965), Bonhoeffer, and Rudolf Bultmann (1884-1976), Robinson argued against "supernaturalism" in its popularly understood form and in favor of a divine immanence which Robinson sought to delineate from pantheism. He wrote: "[It] is . . . necessary to rebut rather carefully the suspicion of pantheism, which must doubtless cling to any reconstruction that questions the existence of God as a separate Being."[10] Robinson continued: "[It] is entirely possible to

9. Dietrich Bonhoeffer, *Letters and Papers from Prison,* the Enlarged Edition, ed. Eberhard Bethge (New York: Macmillan, 1972), p. 382.

10. John A. T. Robinson, *Honest to God* (Philadelphia: Westminster Press, 1963), p. 130.

demythologize it without lapsing into pantheism. The essential difference between the Biblical and any immanentist world-view lies in the fact that it grounds all reality ultimately in personal freedom — in Love."[11] Robinson does not explain how the qualifications of personal freedom and "Love" void the problem of pantheism other than to argue, as he apparently believed, that pantheism is synonymous with a sort of impersonal determinism.

Surely, however, a romantic pantheism, which presupposes a nurturing "Nature," is as common as a non-personalistic, deterministic form of pantheism. For example, Tillich's "ground of Being" is put forth by Robinson as an alternative to "a superworld of divine objects," and he concludes with the assertion that "[a]ny alternative language — e.g. of depth — is bound to be equally symbolic. But it may speak more 'profoundly' to the soul of modern man."[12] It should be noted, however, that this "depth" language in Tillich slips rather easily over into a quasi-romantic pantheism, which, in the end, overruled the prophetic, "revolutionary" theme in Tillich's own philosophical theology.[13]

Robinson's "voice" from England had a significant impact on the American generation of the 1960s, lending support and inspiration, along with Bonhoeffer's prison letters, to the American "death of God" theological movement. Harvey Cox's popular work of 1965, *The Secular City*,[14] was associated with this movement. It hailed the secularizing tendencies in some aspects of biblical thought and sought to spell out what Cox thought Bonhoeffer had intended with the sentence, "Before God and with God we live without God."[15] For Cox it meant a religious celebration of the secular — though not in its ideological form of "secular-

---

11. Robinson, *Honest to God*, p. 130.

12. Robinson, *Honest to God*, p. 132.

13. Elsewhere I have discussed Tillich's major reliance on the medieval philosophical principle of the coincidence of opposites, which states that however much two things may stand in contrast a more basic ground of identity is presupposed on the basis of which the contrast is drawn; see my *Tillich: A Theological Portrait* (Philadelphia: Lippincott, 1968), pp. 109-13. See also my article in the Czech journal *Metanoia* 6, no. 3 (Autumn 1996): 104-18, titled "The Presuppositions and Fault Lines of Tillich's System."

14. Harvey Cox, *The Secular City* (New York: Macmillan, 1965).

15. Bonhoeffer, *Letters and Papers*, p. 360. Though Cox makes frequent references to Tillich and Karl Barth in *The Secular City*, he was chiefly inspired by the Bonhoeffer of *Letters and Papers*; see *The Secular City Debate*, ed. Daniel Callahan (New York: Macmillan, 1966), pp. 205-14.

ism." Rather, it meant a celebration of technology with its varied achievements in transportation (ever-increasing mobility) and telecommunications (easy access to information and the accompanying possibilities of anonymity and greater selectivity in personal relationships). In Cox, tragic history and the realities of World War II passed from view, and technology, along with sweeping generalizations on social change and anthropological analyses of "tribe" and "town," were given center place for theological interpretation and assimilation. The city, the urban center, was declared to be the site and source of redemption; the church was presented as the "avant-garde" of God, as "cultural exorcist."

Though one American theologian of note hailed Cox as a young Reinhold Niebuhr,[16] Cox's advocacy of the need "to speak in a secular fashion of God" bore little fruit, though at the time it was received as a noteworthy effort to press forward Bonhoeffer's suggested program of theological revision. What *did* happen, within two years after Cox wrote, was the burning of American cities, first in the Watts section of Los Angeles in 1965 and then in the urban riots of 1968 after the killing of Dr. Martin Luther King. This, and the turmoil of the Vietnam War years, made Cox's book into something of a period piece. Cox himself, during the following troubled years, became, for a time, a theological spokesman for "the counterculture" that arose out of those years.[17]

Although Cox's theological contribution to the 1960s must be viewed within the context of a general climate of opinion, an important offshoot of his work was unanticipated. In developing his argument of *The Secular City*, Cox began his discussion with a strong statement on divine transcendence as the essential factor in modes of biblical thought that made for the "disenchantment of nature," "the desacralization of politics," and — less convincingly — "the deconsecration of values."[18] By the end of his argument, however, Cox had moved a considerable distance from this starting point by incorporating and embracing major immanental themes in a need for "renaming God." He accented the thought of human "partnership" with God, "teamwork," the "Youness" rather than the "Thouness" of God. As Cox put it at the time: "In technopolitan cul-

16. See *The Secular City Debate*, pp. 12, 68.
17. See, for example, Harvey Cox, *The Feast of Fools: A Theological Essay on Festivity and Fantasy* (Cambridge, MA: Harvard University Press, 1969).
18. Cox, *Secular City*, pp. 21-36.

ture, both horizontal kinship and vertical authority patterns are disappearing. What replaces them is a work team. . . . [A] new type of interhuman relationship seems to be emerging in urban society. . . . [I]t is a relationship of alongsidedness."[19] Accompanying this new direction of thought, Cox's initial description of the biblical "disenchantment of nature" — though in no way original with him — caught the attention of a wide audience and created second thoughts among a growing segment of society wearied with the "efficiencies" of a culture dominated by science and technology. An emerging environmental movement — and elements of the counterculture — gave expression to a need and desire for the "re-enchantment" of nature.

This shift of interest and concern is well illustrated in two key articles by the highly respected medieval historian, Lynn White Jr. In 1963 White wrote an informative, speculative-historical article on the rise of technological competence and commitment in Western Europe from the seventh to fourteenth centuries. Titled "What Accelerated Technological Progress in the Western Middle Ages?"[20] the article gave account of the rise of the innovative use of technology in the West and speculated about the spiritual and native-skill factors that lay behind this revolutionary phenomenon. There can be no question that in this 1963 account White's view of technology was wholeheartedly positive, noting in its widespread application an essential distinction between a human work that was dignifying and a work that was bestial, the latter warranting displacement by a machine wherever possible.

Four years later, however — and two years after Cox's book, with its disenchantment theme — White's attitude toward technology and its place in Western culture shifted significantly. In 1967 he published a provocative, widely influential article, "The Historical Roots of Our Ecological Crisis,"[21] in which he charged that the Judeo-Christian rejection of the animistic, quasi-divine character of nature was largely responsible for the subsequent abuse of the environment common in the history of economic development in the West. White came down strongly in sup-

19. Cox, *Secular City,* p. 263.
20. Lynn White Jr., "What Accelerated Technological Progress in the Western Middle Ages?" in *Scientific Change,* ed. A. C. Crombie (New York: Basic Books, 1963).
21. This article first appeared in the March 10, 1967, issue of *Science* magazine. White subsequently included it in a collection of his essays: *Machina Ex Deo: Essays in the Dynamism of Western Culture* (Cambridge, MA: MIT Press, 1968).

port of the need to recover the sort of spirituality marked by St. Francis of Assisi, a spirituality that might correct the "objectification" of nature in what White and others at the time identified as the source of a destructive exploitation and abuse of the natural order. Since 1967 — and White's work — the link-up of ecological concerns with a variety of immanental spiritualities, some traditional and ethnically related, some new, has become a commonplace — though it should be pointed out that a similar concern about the abuse of the environment was heard from representatives of theistic and purely secular quarters as well.

The occasion of the first Earth Day on April 22, 1970, a nationwide anti-technology, anti-pollution observance, marked a kind of takeoff point for the environmental movement in the United States — though growing public awareness of ecological issues must properly also be attributed to the publication in 1962 of Rachel Carson's watershed work, *Silent Spring*,[22] an exposé of the deleterious effects of chemical insecticides on the natural environment. The cumulative effect of the work of Carson, along with White's historical analyses and widespread annual public observance of Earth Day in the United States, gave impetus to a probing reexamination of spiritual resources in the fight to protect the environment. It seems fair to say that for most participants in what became a growing worldwide cause, a doctrine of divine immanence, rather than divine transcendence, seemed to afford a more germane, felt resource for addressing the environmental needs of the time.

Along with an earlier ingrained American nature-romanticism, one that pre-dated by a hundred years and more the emerging environmental concerns of the 1960s and early 1970s, the disposition toward a modern-day, nature-oriented spirituality was furthered by an important philosophical-theological construct known as "process theology." Initiated in part by a post-Darwinian metaphysics set forth by the French philosopher Henri Bergson (1859-1941) but grounded more philosophically in the work of the English mathematician-philosopher Alfred North Whitehead (1861-1947), process theology identified God with an evolving universe in such a way as to affirm a teleological, or purposive, direction in the processes of evolutionary change. Some note of divine transcendence was maintained in the affirmation of a guiding divine purpose. This, in Whitehead's case, stood in sharp contrast to the purely

22. Rachel Carson, *Silent Spring* (Boston: Houghton Mifflin Co., 1962).

naturalistic views of his former colleague and friend, Bertrand Russell (1872-1970). Divine transcendence in Whitehead's thought, however, was/is qualified by the idea that God's agency in the purposive process is essentially only that of "persuasion," never that of radical correction, judgment, or redemption.

This philosophical legacy was taken up and popularized for the American theological community especially in the work of John Cobb (1925-), a philosopher-theologian whose writings not only set forth a "process" interpretation of the nature and activity of God but also sought to assimilate a variety of other religious-theological points of view into the system, elements of Buddhist thought for example, some Christian existential affirmations of selfhood, and later the "liberation theology" of the 1970s and 1980s. In a 1976 popularizing work, *Process Theology: An Introductory Exposition,* Cobb and his co-author, David Griffin, demarcated their own philosophical position from what can best be described as a series of caricatures of traditional theism and divine transcendence. At the start, they rejected representations of God as "Cosmic Moralist," "Unchanging and Passionless Absolute," "Controlling Power," "Sanctioner of the Status Quo," and "Male."[23] Cobb and Griffin, in this work, did not differentiate "common conceptions" from theological ones, and the reader is left with the impression that what is described under these captions is also representative of theologically informed affirmations of divine transcendence. In contrast to such an "other" God, Cobb and Griffin, while still using the term "God," set forth an immanentist deity moving within the whole of creation to an ever fuller realization of "the one intrinsic good, which is the enjoyment of intense experience."[24] They write:

> On the basis of . . . correlation between novelty and increasingly complex order, on the one hand, and increased capacity for enjoyment, on the other, the evolutionary development of our world propounded by modern science can be interpreted in harmony with the character and purpose of God. This creatively and responsively loving God is incarnately active in the present, bringing about immediate good on the basis of activity in the past, and with the pur-

23. John B. Cobb Jr. and David Ray Griffin, *Process Theology: An Introductory Exposition* (Philadelphia: Westminster Press, 1976), pp. 8-10.

24. Cobb and Griffin, *Process Theology,* p. 59.

pose to bring about greater good in the future — a greater good that will involve a fuller incarnation of the divine reality itself.[25]

Major critiques of divine transcendence also emerge in elements of the feminist theological movement, prominent in the 1970s and carrying over into the present time. Although many voices among feminist theologians speak from within traditional creedal and confessional standpoints, one notes among others a forceful, sometimes angry rejection of the idea of divine transcendence in an effort to present a perceived, more-embracing god-image as an alternative to that of an inherited, traditional "male" deity.[26] A common feature of this critique of theism was/is a tendency to associate theological statements of divine transcendence with hierarchical institutional structures and longstanding patterns of social-political patriarchy. While there are certainly valid grounds for establishing connections between some expressions of theism with social, political, and ecclesiastical forms of hierarchy, there certainly is no necessary one-on-one correlation between the two — a point to be made at length in the discussions that follow.[27]

Such debates within the theological community reflected a fairly widespread mindset in the academic community that viewed religion in general, along with the idea of a sovereign deity, as a bulwark, if not a source, of patriarchy and the dominance of paternalism and patronage in the social-political sphere. Illustrative of this point is the work of the highly respected American historian, Gordon Wood. In his award-winning book, *The Radicalism of the American Revolution*,[28] Wood consistently asserts a link between, if not equation of, religion and patriarchal/patronage-reliant patterns of social, economic, political behavior in pre-revolutionary American social history. While in the main, as suggested, there is some warrant for this interpretation, it hardly represents the whole picture and generally lacks a measure of theological-historical discernment.

Throughout his analysis Wood shows only a marginal understanding of the religious/theological ferment that destabilized the traditional social-political order of England in the sixteenth and seventeenth centu-

---

25. Cobb and Griffin, *Process Theology*, p. 68.

26. The feminist theologian Mary Daly is but one exemplar of this point of view.

27. See the discussions in Chapters 3, 4, and 5, below.

28. Gordon S. Wood, *The Radicalism of the American Revolution* (New York: Alfred A. Knopf, 1992).

ries and which carried over, in important measure, to the colonies in America. Nowhere does Wood reveal awareness of, or sensitivity to, the power and actively subversive nature of the theological doctrine of the calling for a traditional, hereditary-ordered society[29] — a doctrine upon which Max Weber laid stress in his 1904-1905 *The Protestant Ethic and the Spirit of Capitalism*.[30] In a recent biography of Benjamin Franklin, Walter Isaacson points out that Franklin's father, Josiah, was especially shaped by a scriptural passage from the book of Proverbs, 22:29: "Seest thou a man diligent in his calling, he shall stand before Kings" — a passage the father often quoted to his son and which Franklin himself reflected upon toward the end of his life in his autobiography.[31] Instead Wood offers an exaggerated emphasis on pre-revolutionary patterns of patriarchy and patronage, which he then uses to accent the revolutionary, democratizing impact of the American Revolution on the general American populace. So great is his commitment to this point that Wood suggests a new periodization of American and European (?) history that describes the years before the revolution as "pre-modern." He writes: "We will never comprehend the distinctiveness of that pre-modern world until we appreciate the extent to which many ordinary people still accepted their own lowliness. Only then can we begin to understand the radical changes in this consciousness of humility, among other things, that the American Revolution brought about."[32]

In much of what follows, the present work will argue against an overdrawn "totalism" of social passivity such as Wood offers, even though Wood expresses in his work appealing egalitarian sympathies that many, including the present writer, are inclined to share.

IN THE light of a more than fifty-year theological shift away from awareness of divine otherness and transcendence, as expressed in H. Richard

29. A point to be more fully elaborated in Chapters 4 and 5, below.

30. Max Weber, *The Protestant Ethic and the Spirit of Capitalism*, trans. Talcott Parsons (New York: Charles Scribner's Sons, 1958).

31. Walter Isaacson, *Benjamin Franklin: An American Life* (New York: Simon & Schuster, 2003), p. 12.

32. Wood, *The Radicalism*, p. 30. To the mind of this interpreter, Wood significantly misreads the revolutionary ferment of the doctrine of the calling, an example of which he cites in the three sentences in the text, which leads into the above-cited quotation.

Niebuhr's *Christ and Culture,* one can speculate on the likely source of many of these immanentist developments in the "idea" of autonomy. Autonomy, self-rule, is something more than a mere concept, since it carries with it heavily laden emotional and psychological commitments. We do not want to disrupt what, at this point, is intended only as a survey account of a decline in the belief in divine transcendence in order to enter upon a discussion of the complex question of autonomy. Suffice it to point out that stress upon human autonomy in the definition of the human self has a major role to play in how one reacts to, and reflects upon, concepts of divine transcendence and, also, immanence. The development of critical rationality in the post-medieval world raised, in an acute way, the question of the interplay between the way in which the human self conceives both itself, the world, and the question of God. It suggests that human projection and fantasy have played, and continue to play, important roles in the conceptualization of the Divine and cannot alone be ascribed to a so-called "primitive mindset." Along with key figures in the eighteenth-century Enlightenment, others, e.g., Feuerbach, Fichte, Darwin, Marx, and Freud, later lent support, if not "authority," to assertions of human rational self-sufficiency and competence. Mythmaking and fanciful projections of the human self persist even into the modern era within a secular frame of reference,[33] a point to be made more fully below in Chapter 5.

When Ernst Troeltsch, in his work *Protestantism and Progress,*[34] identified "autonomy" as one of three distinguishing presuppositions of modernity (along with this-worldliness and progress), he had in mind, on the basis of a science-inspired rationality, the rejection of the medieval notion of knowledge based on authority. This conflict was spelled out in classic form in the Galileo case, when the Italian astronomer, under threat of torture and death, was forced by church authorities in 1633 to recant his belief in a sun-centered solar system. It is clear that Troeltsch meant to accent the contrast between modern, scientific, empirical knowledge and a tradition-bound knowledge based on authority, the former open always to question, continually qualified and revised

33. As suggested below, Francis Bacon in the seventeenth century anticipated the continuation of this problem in the further development of the "modern mind"; see below, pp. 209-16.

34. Ernst Troeltsch, *Protestantism and Progress,* trans. W. Montgomery (Boston: Beacon Press, 1912, 1958), pp. 17-28.

through new knowledge, in contrast to a supposed timeless philosophical truth or heaven-sanctioned dogma.

In the academic world of recent times, autonomy has reached a new height of expression in "postmodern" deconstructionist thought, which has pointed up oppressive bias in inherited systems of thought, especially in the "hegemonic" culture of the West. The wide-ranging deconstructionist critique often carries with it a suggestion of some kind of underlying human innocence, even "goodness," which can be unleashed if set free from oppressive, exploitive modes of thought. Advocates of the postmodern viewpoint have seemed inclined to press for a thoroughgoing liberation and autonomy, perhaps with the expectation of "construction" of new forms of meaning without the dominating, "totalizing" tendencies of the Western past, a multiculturalism without judgment, though perhaps with some lingering concerns about authenticity and the possible end result of mere relativism, filled perhaps by sensory enjoyment.

In 1841, in Copenhagen, Søren Kierkegaard (1813-1855) sketched out some of the lines of this current debate in his university dissertation, *The Concept of Irony*.[35] In the midst of the complexities of his own times, Kierkegaard argued that Socrates' dialectic (a probing questioning), in distinction from that of Plato, was grounded in the recognition of an ultimate ignorance, not a feigned one. He argued that Socrates' ironic stance was not based upon a superior wisdom, but upon the knowledge of his own ignorance.[36] In this alone was Socrates wiser than others. His questioning of the certainties of others only brought to light the emptiness of their claims to "knowledge." In Kierkegaard's reading of Socrates, the dialectical probing of knowledge revealed the crisis situation of the existing individual — which, for Kierkegaard, meant that the individual was addressed, affirmed, and made responsible finally only before God.[37] Hegel's interpretation of Socrates, by contrast, while also rejecting the idea that Socrates affirmed a knowing of "eternal forms," asserted that Socrates' nega-

---

35. Søren Kierkegaard, *The Concept of Irony,* trans. Lee M. Capel (Bloomington: Indiana University Press, 1965).

36. See Kierkegaard, *Concept of Irony,* pp. 72-73, 77, 283-87 for the lines of Kierkegaard's discussion of Socratic irony. It should be pointed out that Kierkegaard looked to J. G. Hamann (1730-1788) as a major source for his view of Socrates; see *Søren Kierkegaard's Journals and Papers,* vol. 2, ed. and trans. Howard V. and Edna H. Hong (Bloomington: Indiana University Press, 1970), pp. 203-4.

37. See Kierkegaard, *Concept of Irony,* pp. 296-98; also pp. 81-83.

tion of assumed knowledge was but a moment in the development of a dynamic truth (Hegel's dialectic of thesis, antithesis, synthesis) within the process of an evolving general consciousness. What deconstructionist thought brings to this discussion is the exposé of all forms of elitist domination of the "other"[38] — in literature, in all modes of rational thought, and in historical social-political relationships and structures, explicated usually on the basis of class, race, and gender. To the degree that individuals and groups that have been the victims of such domination are able to recover and assert their autonomy, some postmodernist interpreters and advocates seem to entertain the thought that a transformed social order will follow — a sort of classless, fully autonomous society. What is less clear in some recent contemporary discussions is how a political process could actually be made to work without the exercise of power — or what would constitute the basis of social cohesion in the context of possible new energized group loyalties. Kierkegaard, in noting one of the features of irony [read "criticism"], observed:

> In order for the acting individual to be able to fulfill his task in realizing actuality, he must feel himself assimilated into a larger context, must feel the seriousness of responsibility, must feel and respect every rational consequence. But irony is free from all this. It knows itself to be in possession of the power to begin from the beginning whenever it pleases, for nothing in the past is binding upon it. . . . Irony is free, to be sure, free from all the cares of actuality, but free from its joys as well, free from its blessings.
>
> As irony contrives to overcome historical actuality by making it hover, so irony itself has in turn become a hovering.[39]

We have, in the abbreviated preceding analysis, attempted to give account of the movement away from divine transcendence in recent American theological thought — in the years since the 1951 publication of H. Richard Niebuhr's *Christ and Culture*. This shift in the climate of opinion has perhaps made Niebuhr's thought less accessible, less applicable to the culture question of our own time. But there is another point

---

38. In Kierkegaard — as in the thought of Martin Buber — the "Other" is distinctively One (God) who stands over against the human self and sets a limit to, as it also helps define, the "otherness" of the human self.

39. Kierkegaard, *Concept of Irony*, p. 296.

to consider in discussion of the continuing relevance of Niebuhr's statement of the Christ and culture problem. This is the matter of Christianity's own ambiguous role in what must be regarded as one of the great cultural transformations in history, the transformation of European culture from a "medieval" to a "modern" understanding and outlook. The question to be asked here is: To what degree did Christianity itself, in its own internal struggle of and for faith, contribute to the displacement of a "religious," church-oriented culture by one that, over time, became dominantly secular, the displacement of a culture oriented to the preservation and imposition of a "divine" order resistant to change by one firmly committed to change? This question is set also against the background of the recent resurgence of religious traditionalism on the world stage.

Niebuhr himself raised this question in relation to two of his proposed typologies, both of which were projected as dynamic and interactive in their relation to the cultural situation. We speak of the fourth and fifth of Niebuhr's categories: "Christ and culture in paradox" and "Christ the transformer of culture." Both, as suggested, are seen as interacting with culture, and yet in tension with the cultural situation; both are freshly reflective of an awareness of divine transcendence. We have previously argued that the "Christ against culture" and the "Christ above culture" categories have also shared a sense of divine transcendence, but the argument that follows qualifies this previous point in the context of the question now being put: To what degree, and on what grounds, was Christianity itself — and elements of the theological tradition — a participant in helping to transform the Western cultural tradition from an essentially static to an essentially dynamic one? To the degree that the "Christ against culture" point-of-view shuns involvement with the broader culture, this social outlook can be viewed as an agent of change only inadvertently. And a similar observation can be made about the "Christ above culture" stance. To the degree that this latter point of view seeks persistently to contain culture within an "eternal order" and maintain a position of command vis-à-vis the general culture — to preside over culture, as it were — it too denies an interactive role with and within culture and history, choosing rather to "monitor" culture.[40]

In describing Christianity's role in helping to transform the Western

40. Much more will be said on this point in the following two chapters.

cultural tradition into a "progressive" mode, the argument that follows does not mean to discount all the established explanations of the forces of change that have also played roles in bringing about the transition from a medieval to a modern "world." The argument that follows seeks only to examine the role of Christian "reformation" — and awareness of divine transcendence — as a factor, a significant factor, in this cultural revision. The argument that follows runs counter to some major assumptions that presently command center stage on the American intellectual scene. We have already suggested an inadequacy, even a futility, in attempts to absolutize the autonomy principle. This point will be developed more fully in the ensuing chapters. Entering into discussion also is the importance of an awareness of discontinuity, in contrast to continuity, for an understanding of the development of the idea of Progress. And we will propose yet another understanding of the relationship of Christian faith to the secular order, one that shuns simple antipathy, but one also that questions the effort to gather faith under the mantle of "religion" and culture as Paul Tillich proposed in his early "theology of culture," and as Harvey Cox, in a lesser way, stated it in *The Secular City*. Throughout, we will raise the question of meaning and the forms of meaning embraced in the past, along with new ones that seem to have emerged in our present time.

It is important as a first step in this discussion to offer a restatement of the nature of the change that took place in the West in the transition from a medieval to a modern world. This is a phenomenon that has been studied and written about at great length over the past two hundred and more years. And there is not a great deal that is new to be said about it. The challenge, of course, is to try to offer a manageable and adequate summary that can be instructive for an understanding of the theological question of divine transcendence. Here treatment must be given to the idea of Progress, an "idea" that, once more, Ernst Troeltsch defined as one of the basic presuppositions of the "modern," post-medieval world, a companion to the already briefly discussed "autonomy" and an also-to-be-treated "this-worldliness."[41] We shall, in the next chapter, re-present the concept of Progress in its historical origins and in its relation

---

41. It should be noted that what follows in Chapter 2 is in part a reformulation of an argument put forth by the author in *Technology, Theology, and the Idea of Progress* (Louisville: Westminster/John Knox Press, 1991).

to what the present writer proposes as a more adequate representation of our present situation, "the culture of change" — a nomenclature that seeks to describe the historical situation in the aftermath of the triumph of technological innovation and its economic exploitation in diminution of a previously prominent social-political understanding.

Chapter 2

The Idea of Progress
and the Culture of Change

The English historian Lewis Namier is quoted as saying, "What matters in history is the great outline and the significant detail: what must be avoided is the deadly mass of irrelevant detail. . . . A searchlight concentrated at the focal point will give more light than rows of candles."[1] Namier's observation is helpful in considering the intricate and complex set of factors that governed the change from the medieval to the modern world — and the nature of that change itself. How one orders an account of the change will surely reflect in part the perspective and presuppositions of the person making the analysis. This is unavoidable and probably true of anyone who would address a pivotal historical event or subject matter. What is at issue in the critique of historical bias is whether or not directions of any sort can be charted for history or whether history and its meaning must be regarded chiefly as a mystery that escapes understanding, something best treated as a source for the telling of human stories, a mine for journalistic enterprise seeking to entertain, to reshape identities, or perhaps to provoke protest of one sort or another.

Writing in the mid-eighteenth century, the French Enlightenment figure Denis Diderot (1713-1784) offered an aphoristic summary of the difference between the medieval and the modern periods of history: "La postérité pour le philosophe, c'est l'autre monde de l'homme religieux" (Posterity is for the Philosopher what the other world is for the reli-

---

1. Quoted by John Kenyon, *The History Men* (London: Weidenfeld & Nicholson, 1983), p. 267.

gious).[2] Diderot was here declaring that the future had become for eighteenth-century "enlightened" people what the other world had been for the Middle Ages, the focus of meaning and commitment. While one can say that otherworldliness certainly persisted as a reality for "religious" persons in Diderot's time, Diderot himself believed that the time of the dominance of religion in Western culture had passed. He was speaking, of course, for an educated elite — and this, before the onset of the Industrial Revolution came to spread a this-worldly, materialist grounding for progress among the working classes. To the minds of growing numbers of informed people in the eighteenth century a major shift in the definition of meaningful human life had taken place, and was continuing to do so. Drawing upon a range of sources, one historian expressed the point as follows: Enlightenment thinkers "called in posterity to exorcise the double illusion of the Christian paradise and the golden age of antiquity. For the love of God they substituted love of humanity; for the vicarious atonement the perfectibility of man through his own efforts; and for the hope of immortality in another world the hope of living in the memory of future generations."[3]

Apparent in this assessment are three principles of modernity identified by Ernst Troeltsch and referred to earlier: this-worldliness, autonomy, and the belief in progress. The Enlightenment rejection of religious otherworldliness was a signal point-of-departure from the Middle Ages, in which the "other world" was widely looked to for definition and sanction of the institutions and social structures of "this world" as well as, most important, providing individuals with the expectation of life after death. The eighteenth-century assumption that modern people had "come of age" and had taken on responsibility for shaping a promising future of their own was integral to the increasingly widespread belief in progress, a belief distinctive of the modern Western cultural tradition — one not found in classical antiquity or in other major cultural-religious traditions.[4]

It is unlikely that the formulation of such a belief would have origi-

2. Carl Becker, *The Heavenly City of the Eighteenth-Century Philosophers* (New Haven: Yale University Press, 1932), pp. 119, 150.

3. Becker, *Heavenly City*, p. 130.

4. For further discussion of this matter, see my *Technology, Theology, and the Idea of Progress* (Louisville: Westminster/John Knox Press, 1991), pp. 33-53. The term "progress" in this sense bears the meaning of "ultimate concern" (Tillich).

nated and spread so rapidly in the West if there had not been some accompanying historical experience and perception of newfound power and competence growing out of an accelerated pace of discovery and invention. In an insightful survey of eighteenth-century European culture, the Swiss theologian Karl Barth offered a description of this new sense of power in its varied manifestations. Against the background of post–World War II events and the horrors of Nazi rule in Germany, Barth sought to counter the absolutism of spirit that he believed had overtaken European culture and set the stage for the catastrophic events of the twentieth century. As a perspective on this development, Barth's cultural commentary on eighteenth-century developments is insightful and provocative. He noted how the gardens of Versailles were fashioned and then replicated throughout Europe, how a human order was imposed on an "imperfect" natural order. Nature, Barth observed, was

> put to rights and formed in accordance with man's sensibility and enjoyment, an idealized, and most preferably a visibly idealized nature, which is meant: the stream as a fountain, the lake as a clean and tidy pond, the wood as a park reduced to visible order, the field and the bushes and flowers as a garden, the tree shaped with the garden-shears, all things reduced to harmony, which inevitably means to geometry, more-or-less; the tamed, . . . and trained animals, . . . a nature which even after the grooming it has had to endure is really beautiful only when there is a Greek temple, a statue or a bust somewhere about which quite unequivocally serves as a reminder of the lords of creation.[5]

Music, Barth suggested, was a part of this assertion of mastery. He proffered that a "sovereign attitude" was present in the eighteenth-century preoccupation with polyphonic instruments and the great new possibilities of sound that could be brought into order and "harmonized."[6] In like spirit, Barth noted, the new cities planned and founded in the eighteenth century reflected the urge to impose a human order. He offered as examples Karlsruhe, Mannheim, Ludwigsburg, cities laid out

5. Karl Barth, *Protestant Thought: From Rousseau to Ritschl* (New York: Harper & Brothers, 1959), p. 33.
6. Barth, *Protestant Thought*, p. 49.

on the basis of grid-and-spoke plans that ignored the natural topography and made clear the hand and mind of human design.

Certainly basic to this development of a growing human consciousness of power was the cumulative impact of the new technologies adapted and developed in Western Europe over the course of the late Middle Ages. In 1963, as noted above,[7] the historian Lynn White Jr. remarked on peculiar features of this phenomenon and speculated about its causes. And much earlier than White, Francis Bacon had taken note of the significance of technological innovation. In 1620 Bacon argued that the impact of technology in the form of the printing press, gunpowder, and the compass had opened a spiritual/intellectual breach between his own times and previous ages, especially those of classical Greece and Rome. In his *Novum Organum* Bacon wrote:

> it is well to observe the force and virtue and consequences of discoveries; and these are to be seen nowhere more conspicuously than in those three which were unknown to the ancients, and of which the origin, though recent, is obscure and inglorious; namely, printing, gunpowder, and the magnet. For these three have changed the whole face and state of things throughout the world; the first in literature, the second in warfare, the third in navigation; whence have followed innumerable changes; insomuch that no empire, no sect, no star seems to have exerted greater power and influence in human affairs than these mechanical discoveries.[8]

Elsewhere in the same work, Bacon declared:

> As for antiquity, the opinion touching it which men entertain is quite a negligent one, and scarcely consonant with the word itself. For the old age of the world is to be accounted the true antiquity; and this is the attribute of our own times, not of that earlier age of the world in which the ancients lived; and which, though in respect of us it was the elder, yet in respect of the world it was the younger. . . . Surely it would be disgraceful if, while the regions of the

---

7. See above, p. 26.

8. James Spedding, Robert L. Ellis, and Douglas D. Heath, eds., *The Works of Francis Bacon* (London: Longmans, Green, Reader & Dyer, 1857-1874), vol. 5, p. 114. Hereafter cited as *WFB*.

material globe, — that is, of the earth, of the sea, and of the stars, — have been in our times laid widely open and revealed, the intellectual globe should remain shut up within the narrow limits of old discoveries.[9]

More will be said later about Bacon's perspective on his world,[10] but it is with good reason that he is looked to by later historians as a key figure in the development of the Enlightenment idea of progress. In the passage just cited, Bacon broke with Renaissance reverence for the learning of Antiquity and sought to project a sense of the superior wisdom of his own day, a confidence inspired, as suggested, by the great strides in technology and in Europe's adventurous exploration of the world. Three centuries later, J. B. Bury, in his pioneering account of the emergence of the idea of progress,[11] a work to be briefly exposited, credits Bacon with the assertion of the utility of knowledge, a key idea in the formulation of the progress concept. Bury wrote:

> Among the great precursors of a new order of thought Francis Bacon occupies a unique position. He drew up a definite program for a "great Renovation" of knowledge; he is more clearly conscious than his contemporaries of the necessity of breaking with the past and making a completely new start. . . . [He] is often regarded . . . as more than a precursor, as the first philosopher of the modern age. . . . [With] Francis Bacon . . . [the] idea of the augmentation of knowledge has an entirely new value. . . . [He] sounded the modern note; for him the end of knowledge is utility. The principle that the proper aim of knowledge is the amelioration of human life; to increase men's happiness and mitigate their sufferings . . . was the guiding star of Bacon in all his intellectual labour. (*The Idea of Progress*, pp. 50-52)

Bury concluded that "in laying down the utilitarian view of knowledge [Bacon] contributed to the creation of a new mental atmosphere in which the theory of Progress was afterwards to develop" (p. 53).

---

9. *WFB*, vol. 4, pp. 81-82.

10. See below, pp. 189-220.

11. J. B. Bury, *The Idea of Progress* (London: Macmillan & Co., 1920; American edition, 1932). Hereafter, page references to this work will be given parenthetically in the text.

The Idea of Progress, the 1920 work of J. B. Bury, has stood for years as not only the first major discussion of the progress idea but also as the standard text and point-of-departure for subsequent efforts to understand and further the history of the idea. Bury's treatment of the subject of progress — a term hereafter occasionally capitalized to indicate its importance as the focus of meaning in the modern era, perhaps the most common shared perspective of post-medieval Western history and culture — requires summary review as an aid to understanding the culture of change which the progress belief has inspired and seemingly left as a heritage not only in the modern Western world, where it had its origin, but in the world at large where it represents a disruptive challenge to tradition-oriented cultures and mindsets.

In a review of Bury's work it is important at the start to fix the purpose of his work, its underlying intent and, one can also say, its special perspective and bias. Bury's intent was not only to trace the steps in the development of the idea of progress but also to define it as a "clear and distinct idea" in the spirit of the French philosopher René Descartes (1596-1650). This underlies Bury's heavy emphasis on progress as an unfolding, logical idea, often to the neglect of peculiar historical circumstances and events that also played roles in the concept's emerging prominence. For Bury it was chiefly, if not exclusively, the Scientific Revolution, growing out of the new Copernican cosmology of the sixteenth and seventeenth centuries, that constituted the chief spur to the idea's provenance and rise to dominance, a view held by almost everyone who shared in the French Enlightenment and a view commonplace today among intellectual historians. Whether or not this is a fully adequate understanding of the emergence of the belief in progress and its widespread embrace in the West is open to some question — as we will maintain in the argument that follows. It represents a major point in Bury's insistence, suggested earlier, that Progress is a modern, post-medieval idea and that it is also a distinctively European idea.

Within this overall frame-of-reference Bury allowed that the Christian and biblical idea of a linear direction for human history, one leading to some ultimate climax or end, played an important role in the displacement of the cyclical view of life and history dominant in Greco-Roman antiquity. Bury insisted, however, that the fully modern idea of progress stood in opposition to any role for Divine Providence. Such a belief in Providence contributed to the decline of the belief in recurring cycles of history and, for a while, was later "held along with a belief in Progress," but, as Bury put it, "the fundamental assumptions were incongruous" (p. 21), since belief in divine agency undercut the sense of human responsibility and initiative in the movement toward a fulfilling human future. The belief in a historical development toward some world-encompassing end, Bury argued, seems to have "prevailed for centuries" — e.g., since Augustine — until people came, in the modern period, to "discard it along with the doctrine of Providence on which it rested" (p. 22).

Bury, in the end, listed Bacon only among the "precursors" to a fully developed belief in progress, because Bacon did not subscribe to human agency alone in consideration of history and the future — and he failed also to embrace the new Copernican cosmology. On this point Bury commented: "For him Copernicus, Kepler, and Galileo worked in vain; he obstinately adhered to the old geocentric system" (p. 51). Whether this is a fully adequate representation of Bacon's views on cosmology is open to question, and it leaves unanswered the very interesting question of why Bacon should have advocated a complete "renovation of knowledge" on grounds other than the cosmological shift from a geocentric to a heliocentric worldview, a renovation of knowledge that went even beyond Bacon's perceptive insights into the influential role of technology in shaping advances in human thought.[12] For Bury, however, "the Scientific Revolution of the sixteenth and seventeenth centuries," the cosmological revolution, was unquestionably the determinative factor in the rise of the belief in progress.

While taking note of the important contributions of Bacon to the idea of progress (pp. 58-59), Bury turned to developments in the French intellectual world to structure his narrative of the unfolding and full delineation of the concept. Along this course he attached special significance to the contention of René Descartes that the laws of nature were immutable, not subject to the arbitrary manipulations of the Deity. In Bury's view, Descartes' immutable laws of nature essentially eliminated the question of divine agency and thus provided a sure base for asserting primacy for human effort alone in setting a course for the future. And after Descartes in Bury's discussion came the figure of Fontenelle (1657-1757), a key early popularizer of modern science. Fontenelle asserted the cumulative nature

---

12. See above, p. 26; and below, pp. 165, 189-220.

of all knowledge and repudiated the idea of human dependence upon an external divine will. He argued that the cumulative nature of knowledge would continue into an indefinite future. Accordingly, "man will have no old age; his intellect will never degenerate; and 'the sound views of intellectual men in successive generations will continually add up'" (p. 109). (This latter point, it should be noted, is found also in Bacon.) Neither was such a development of knowledge to be regarded as a matter of chance: it was to be understood as falling fully within the sphere of human effort and achievement. Bury declared: "Fontenelle . . . was the first to formulate the idea of the progress of knowledge as a complete doctrine" (p. 110), and it was this theory "which was afterwards to expand into a general theory of human Progress" (p. 111) — "afterwards" because Fontenelle had not allowed for moral and social development, that is, "Progress" in its most critical form. This was due to the fact that Fontenelle, in working out Descartes' thesis of the uniformity of the laws of nature, also argued that the resources and powers of nature were constant throughout time and that humanity's destructive passions were similarly distributed. Thus, with Fontenelle, there was little expectation of social and moral betterment.

Yet Bury saw Fontenelle as accomplishing the essential task of broadening the base of scientific knowledge, a step essential to the further development of the idea of progress. In his contention that modern science in the form of the Copernican revolution was primarily responsible for the initiation and rise of the belief in progress, Bury came to lend major significance to Fontenelle's 1686 publication of *Conversations on the Plurality of Worlds,* a work that disseminated the new astronomy among a wide lay audience and, in Bury's view, called forth reappraisals of the human situation and the embrace, subsequently, of a belief in social and moral progress. Bury averred:

> The significance of the Plurality of Worlds is indeed much greater than that of a pioneer work in popularisation and a model in the art of making technical subjects interesting. We must remember that at this time the belief that the sun revolves around the earth still prevailed. Only the few knew better. The cosmic revolution which is associated with the names of Copernicus, Kepler, and Galileo was slow in producing its effects. It was rejected by Bacon; the condemnation of Galileo by the Church made Descartes, who

dreaded nothing so much as a collision with the ecclesiastical authorities, unwilling to insist on it. . . . Fontenelle's book . . . disclosed to the general public a new picture of the universe, to which men would have to accustom their imaginations. (p. 114)

At this point one is called to note Bury's failure to recall his earlier recognition of Bacon's assertion of the utility of knowledge. With Bacon a belief in the indefinite betterment of the human condition had already been clearly stated — independent of the refinement and wider acceptance of the new cosmology. How, in Bury's view, cosmology furthered the doctrine of the utility of knowledge is not explained; for, a new cosmology hardly makes the world at hand more *useful* in practical terms, though in comparison with visions of the afterlife it was now accessible and confirmable with a telescope (newly invented). What Bury seemed intent on asserting was that the new cosmology forced upon thoughtful persons the need to reappraise their view of themselves in relation to the world and thereby to adjust to new responsibilities in that relationship.

It is important to point out in this context that Bury curiously neglected the impact of Isaac Newton's work, over and above that of Fontenelle, in the revision of human perceptions of the world and its workings. In a way that Fontenelle never did, Newton occasioned a celebration of contemporary genius vis-à-vis past "authorities" such as Plato, Aristotle, Ptolemy, et al. Newton occasioned recognition of a new human stature as well as "new" surroundings. The publication of Newton's major work, *Principia Mathematica,* in 1687, one year after Fontenelle's *Plurality of Worlds,* stirred the intellectual world of his day in a manner that Fontenelle's work, on its own, could not have achieved. Newton's work secured widespread acceptance of the new cosmology by spelling out the gravitational mechanics that underlay the entire system, one reaching down to earth itself. One can surmise that Newton's allowance of a role for God in the continuing operation of the great machine of Nature, even if only a corrective one,[13] did not fit with Bury's positivistic philosophical inclinations — nor did it lend much support to Bury's surmise that people in the eighteenth century invented the theory

13. Newton's less-than-precise mathematical computations called for the need of God's periodic corrections in the moon's orbit to prevent its fall into the earth. The French mathematician Laplace later corrected Newton's computations and declared God to be "a useless hypothesis."

of Progress to compensate for their displacement from the center of a geocentric universe.[14] But it was a mindset and perception of a different sort that led Gerard Winstanley, an English political revolutionary in the 1640s, to declare:

> [Priests] lay claim to heaven after they are dead, and yet they require their heaven in this world too, and grumble mightily against the people that will not give them a large temporal maintenance. And yet they tell the poor people that they must be content with their poverty, and they shall have their heaven hereafter. But why may not we have our heaven here (that is, a comfortable livelihood in the earth) and heaven hereafter too, as well as you? . . . While men are gazing up to heaven, imagining after a happiness or fearing a hell after they are dead, their eyes are put out, that they see not what is their birthrights, and what is to be done by them here on earth while they are living.[15]

Such criticism of Bury's work offered here does not intend to diminish the enduring value of his groundbreaking contribution to the study of the idea of progress. His contention that the progress idea was essentially a modern, European one has stood the test of time, despite challenges and subsequent amendments.[16]

Following the discussion of Fontenelle, Bury moved on to attempt to account for the social-political dimension of the belief in progress. Most of what follows in his narrative was an effort to show — primarily through French sources[17] — how the social-political idea of progress grew out of what Bury argued were its roots in Fontenelle's doctrine of the indefinite advance of scientific knowledge. This aspect of Bury's ar-

14. Bury, *The Idea of Progress*, pp. 115-16; cf. pp. 160-61, where Bury identifies Voltaire as also being a proponent of this view.

15. Quoted by Christopher Hill, *The World Turned Upside Down: Radical Ideas during the English Revolution* (Harmondsworth: Penguin Books, 1975), pp. 140-41.

16. See especially the work of Ludwig Edelstein, *The Idea of Progress in Classical Greek Antiquity* (Baltimore: Johns Hopkins University Press, 1967) and Robert Nisbet, *History of the Idea of Progress* (New York: Basic Books, 1980). I offer an assessment and critique of the views of Edelstein and Nisbet in my *Technology, Theology, and the Idea of Progress*, pp. 41-45.

17. Though Bury *does* devote brief discussions to English and German developments in the idea of progress, along with the contribution of Charles Darwin's theory of evolution.

gument hangs chiefly on the assertion that in the early decades of the eighteenth century "the contrast between [humanity's] mental enlightenment and the dark background — the social evils and miseries of the kingdom, the gross misgovernment and oppression — began to insinuate itself into men's minds" (p. 127). Bury contended that the gap between what was being accomplished in the sciences and technology ("improvement of the arts of life") and the sorry conditions of the social-political situation determined that the latter should be radically reordered on the basis of the former. But here again, it must be pointed out that Francis Bacon, a hundred years earlier, had made social betterment the chief goal of all knowledge, though Bacon hesitated at a major reshaping of the political order. Gerard Winstanley felt less restricted at this point. With Winstanley, radical social-political overhaul derived its inspiration from a source other than Bury's simple contrast between scientific enlightenment and the "dark background" of social evils.[18]

In support of his argument of growing rational concern about the contrast between cumulative, new scientific knowledge and social-political conditions, Bury accented the role of the Abbé de Saint-Pierre (1737-1814), who proposed innumerable schemes to reform government, eliminate war, and improve finances and education. Saint-Pierre was a veritable fount of reform proposals, the mere reasonableness of which he believed would be sufficient for their adoption by the king and other persons in power. But Bury also observed that Saint-Pierre maintained as well that the factors of "wars, superstition, and the jealousy of rulers who feared . . . [for their own power]" stood in the way of general human progress (p. 137). Bury pointed out that though Saint-Pierre was convinced that advances in physical science were important to progress in "universal human reason," he also held that "two other sciences . . . [were] much more important for the promotion of happiness — Ethics and Politics" (p. 139). Bury concluded that if Saint-Pierre's basic beliefs had not been obscured in the welter of projects that came from his fertile mind and pen, he would have been recognized as the true precursor of the French Encyclopaedists, the standard-bearers of the Enlighten-

---

18. Michael Walzer's study, *The Revolution of the Saints: A Study in the Origins of Radical Politics* (Cambridge, MA: Harvard University Press, 1965; Atheneum, 1968), has put to rest this particular argument of Bury, at least as it may have applied to English history and, of course, to the history of the development of the idea of Progress.

ment. As Bury put it: "His principles are theirs. The omnipotence of government and laws to mould the morals of peoples; the subordination of all knowledge to the goddess of utility; the deification of human reason; and the doctrine of Progress" (p. 141) — the latter defined by Bury as "the new creed of . . . indefinite social progress"[19] grounded in the belief of human perfectibility. (p. 143) Anticipating the great historical event that was to follow, Bury offered comment on the spirit and outlook of those who compiled the French *Encyclopaedia* in the years 1751-1765:

> Beneath all philosophical speculation there is an undercurrent of emotion, and in the French philosophers of the eighteenth century this emotional force was strong and even violent. They aimed at practical results. Their work was a calculated campaign to transform the principles and the spirit of governments and to destroy sacerdotalism. The problem for the human race being to reach a state of felicity by its own powers, these thinkers believed that it was soluble by the gradual triumph of reason over prejudice and knowledge over ignorance. Violent revolution was far from their thoughts. (p. 162)

From the tumult of the ensuing French Revolution, Bury salvaged the vision of Antoine-Nicolas de Condorcet (1743-1794), a victim of the revolution's Reign of Terror. In prison, awaiting execution, Condorcet penned a *Sketch of a Historical Picture of the Progress of the Human Mind*. In this work Condorcet set forth an encompassing view of human history through ten stages, a history culminating in the tenth stage, which was to see the "cessation of war and the realisation . . . of the equality of the sexes" (p. 212). Bury saw the vision of human advance through history coming to culmination in Auguste Comte's (1798-1857) formulation of a three-stage process of linked cultural and personal individual advance. In Comte's scheme, the first, the theological stage, the human mind invented and then subscribed to imaginary deities. In the second stage, the metaphysical, the mind abstracted and identified "essences." In the final stage, the positivist-scientific, the human mind simply submitted "to positive facts" (the scientific method, observation, ex-

19. Bury, *The Idea of Progress*, p. 162. Bury's positivistic proclivities led him to discount the utopian tendencies and implications in "the creed of human perfectibility."

perimentation). These stages and outlooks, for Comte, became socially embedded, and elements of the previous stages persisted into the present. It thus became the task of the new, climactic science of "sociology," a stage initiated by Comte's own work, to interpret and guide civilization's future course. Bury summarized Comte:

> The movement of history is due to the deeply rooted though complex instinct which pushes man to ameliorate his condition incessantly, to develop in all ways the sum of his physical, moral, and intellectual life. And all the phenomena of his social life are closely cohesive. . . . By virtue of this cohesion, political, moral, and intellectual progress are inseparable from material progress, and so we find the phases of his material development correspond to intellectual changes. (p. 293)

Bury added: "The massive system wrought out by Comte's speculative genius — his organic scheme of human knowledge, his elaborate analysis of history, his new science of sociology — was a great fact with which European thought was forced to reckon. The soul of this system was Progress" (p. 290).

In 1859, two years after Comte's death, Charles Darwin published his *Origin of Species*. Bury argues that with the publication of Darwin's work another major piece was put in place to undergird the belief in progress. Darwin swept aside the notion of the fixity of the species and gave scientific credibility to the ideas of developmentalism and transformism. The concept of evolution, as a scientific theory, did not of itself confirm the belief that human society was advancing toward a fixed, positive goal. In the aftermath of Darwin there were those who despaired of the social implications of natural selection and its law of "tooth and claw." Yet, in the main, Darwin's theory was able to evoke expectations of movement toward a desirable, humane future. Darwin himself concluded his epic work with the words: "And as natural selection works solely by and for the good of each being, all corporeal and mental environments will tend to progress towards perfection" (p. 336). In this more positive reading of Darwin, Bury cited the work of the English philosopher Herbert Spencer (1820-1903), who gave utterance to optimistic expectations of "indefinite variability" and thus also to perfectibility and the inevitability of society's betterment. Toward the end of the nineteenth century, Thomas Huxley (1825-1895), Darwin's chief defender against his religious critics, expressed the widely accepted view that humanity's "long progress through the past, . . . [provided] a reasonable ground of faith in [its] attainment of a nobler future."[20]

In an Epilogue, Bury offered his own personal word on the matter of Progress. Turning once more to the field of science as the origination point of his thought, Bury argued that no end to progress can be set, that the continuing advance of scientific knowledge bore with it also an indefinite progressive advance for humanity in its social-political existence. Science, Bury contended, shattered "the illusion of finality" (pp. 351-52), a point that Comte, like Hegel before him, failed adequately to perceive in assuming that a climax had been reached in his own philosophical work. Bury suggested that even progress as an idea, just as the concept of Providence before it, would likely be displaced by another idea. At the end he put the question:

> Will not that process of change, for which Progress is the optimistic name, compel "Progress" too to fall from the commanding position in which it is now, with apparent security, enthroned? . . . A day will come, in the revolution of the centuries, when a new idea will usurp its place as the directing idea of humanity. Another star, unnoticed now or invisible, will climb up the intellectual heaven, and human emotions will react to its influence, human plans respond to its guidance. It will be the criterion by which Progress and all other ideas will be judged. And it too will have its successor. (p. 352)

As has been noted, the main lines of Bury's 1920 account of the history of the idea of progress stood up well over the years. The "main lines" as described earlier are the origins of that idea in sixteenth- and seventeenth-century scientific thought, the rejection of "otherworldly" preoccupations, and the conviction that humanity had become responsible for its own historical destiny. For Bury it was essential that the belief in Progress be seen to supersede the belief in Providence and that agency in history be consigned solely to the human actor. For Bury, as for most

---

20. Quoted by Bury, *The Idea of Progress*, p. 342. Toward the end of his life, Huxley, however, entertained less optimistic views of human destiny. Bury noted this change of view in Huxley (pp. 344-45), but made no point of it.

of the Enlightenment figures, expanding modern scientific thought and the empirically grounded rationality instilled by it were the bedrock of the belief in progress — again, a point to be reexamined in subsequent discussion.

Criticism around the edges of Bury's overall argument has been common over the years. In an early, 1920 review of Bury's book, Carl Becker, an American intellectual historian, offered a very positive estimate of what the author had at that point accomplished. Becker praised Bury for his "penetrating analysis," for his having outlined steps in the development of the progress idea with "fine precision," and for having made key points "with succinct perfection." But Becker suggested that Bury had not adequately treated the tendency of important nineteenth-century advocates to speak of progress more in terms of "an impersonal historic process . . . than . . . [as] the deliberate effort of man to shape his own destiny."[21]

In 1932 an American edition of Bury's book was published in connection with the 1933 "Century of Progress Exposition" in Chicago. In the introduction to this American edition of Bury, the historian Charles Beard offered two points of criticism and addition. These he set forth after first addressing Bury's view on the role of ideas in defining the human future. On this point Beard quoted from an early 1903 lecture by Bury:

"It may be said that, so far as concerns the actions and movements of men which are the subject of recorded history, physical environment has ceased to act mechanically, and in order to affect their actions must affect their wills first; and that this psychical character of the causal relations substantially alters the problem. The development of human societies, it may be argued, derives a completely new character from the dominance of the conscious psychical element, creating as it does new conditions (inventions,

---

21. See the review of Bury's book by Becker in *The American Historical Review* 26 (October 1920). This point is also made by John Baillie in *The Belief in Progress* (New York: Charles Scribner's Sons, 1951) when he faults Bury for neglecting the thought of Karl Marx. A similar point is later made by Joel Colton in his preface to the published papers of a 1979 conference on the theme of "Progress and Its Discontents": Gabriel A. Almond, Marvin Chodrow, and Roy Harvey Pearce, eds., *Progress and Its Discontents* (Berkeley: University of California Press, 1982), pp. ix-x.

social institutions, etc.) which limit and counteract the operation of natural selection, and control and modify the influence of physical environment."[22]

Beard suggested that it was this line of thought in Bury that led to his involvement with the idea of progress and also to the contention that "if the idea of progress is not a stubborn outcome of true history, it may, as a faith in possibilities, actually *make* history."[23]

Beard went on to propose two additions to the Bury treatment of progress — or better, two aspects of the subject on which he believed greater stress should have been placed. One was the increasing importance of technology. Beard offered his own perspective: "Though historically associated with the type of economy generally known as Western capitalism, technology by its intrinsic nature transcends all social forms, the whole heritage of acquired institutions and habits. . . . In catholicity it surpasses all religions."[24] Beard's 1932 concern on this point has become ever more critical with the passage of time, though, to be fair to Bury, the latter *did* underline the importance of the great 1851 Exhibition of London, a celebration of material advance in Europe and America, made possible by new technologies and "the growing power of man over the physical world."[25] Albert, the Prince Consort of Queen Victoria, marked the Exhibition as "a new starting-point from which all nations will be able to direct their further exertions."[26]

Along with his contention that Bury underplayed the universal scope and force of technology, Beard expressed disappointment at a second point. He charged that Bury had failed to treat adequately the question of the ethics of progress and to carry through on his own earlier statement that "Progress involves a judgment of value, which is not involved in the conception of history as a genetic process. It is also an idea distinct from evolution."[27] Beard observed that Bury did not make enough of this early point in his later larger study. Beard's words here are instructive because the two factors of technology and the need for a supra-

22. Bury, *The Idea of Progress*, p. xix.
23. Bury, *The Idea of Progress*, p. xxviii.
24. Bury, *The Idea of Progress*, p. xxiii.
25. Bury, *The Idea of Progress*, p. 329.
26. Bury, *The Idea of Progress*, p. 330.
27. Bury, *The Idea of Progress*, p. xxix.

historical point of reference play important roles in the present author's discussion of the historical interconnections of divine transcendence, the history of the idea of progress, and the present realities of technological change. Beard wrote:

> In the idea of progress, . . . there is inevitably an ethical element. It implies that the stream of history flows in a desirable direction, on the whole; and at once we are plunged in the middle of ethics. Immediately a fixed point of reference, benchmark, must be set up from which to determine whether the movement of history is in a desirable direction and, in the living present, what choices are to be made to accelerate the march toward the good. In other words some standard must be planted in the universal flux to furnish a guide for determining directions. A man on a steamer cannot tell by looking at the deck whether he is going east or west.[28]

Beard stated unease with Bury's dependence upon the indefinite expansion of scientific knowledge as the controlling source and paradigm for the idea of Progress. He suggested the need for an ethical benchmark outside of, or above, history in order to fix goals and establish a basis for critical assessment. Though he failed to note it at the time, Beard, with this point, indirectly but perhaps also unknowingly, posed the problem of possible loss of confidence if the human sacrifice demanded for pursuit of future goals failed to provide satisfying realization.

In the same year that Beard introduced the American publication of Bury's book, another book was published that offered critical interaction with Bury's perspective on progress. In 1931 Carl Becker, the American intellectual historian and Bury reviewer previously cited,[29] was invited to give some lectures on history at the Yale Law School. The four lectures were published the following year by Yale University Press under the title *The Heavenly City of the Eighteenth-Century Philosophers*. This little book has represented an insightful, puzzling presence ever since its publication. In 1956, on the twenty-fifth anniversary of Becker's Yale lectures, a conference of American intellectual historians was convened to probe the validity of its distinctive arguments and to exchange

28. Bury, *The Idea of Progress*, pp. xxix-xxx.
29. See above, p. 37, n. 21.

views on the book's significance and continuing appeal.[30] The book has continued in print for over seven decades.

As noted, Becker offered an early review of Bury's book on progress and in 1920 praised the book for its "penetrating analysis" and the "precision" with which Bury had recounted the development of the idea. Becker pursued his own inquiries into the idea of progress over the years after Bury wrote and developed a distinctive perspective on the subject. What is especially provocative in Becker's argument in *The Heavenly City* is his assertion that the Enlightenment spokesmen were closer in spirit to the Middle Ages than they were to the outlook and temper of Becker's own times, a curious fractionalizing of the modern age that runs counter to the common assumption that the "philosophers" of the eighteenth century were the chief spokesmen of modernity. Becker, with scholarly wit and literary charm, attacked this assumption and argued the parallels between the "heavenly city" of the eighteenth-century philosophers and the program of medieval salvation.[31] He also called attention to their "spiritual" similarities as well: their superstitions, their dogmas, their propensity to "enthusiasm," their unwarranted self-assurance.

Becker charged that the Enlightenment *philosophes* invoked a beneficent and rational "Nature" as sanction for all their best beliefs about themselves, a nature that for the most part acquiesced in human design, though when the Lisbon earthquake struck in 1755, a few, Voltaire among them, came to question nature's universal benignity. For the most part, however, nature yielded to eighteenth-century optimism; so too did history. Becker called attention to the "new history" which the *philosophes* wrote in order once again to reinforce their self-images, a new history which touted the fundamental nobility of humanity and justified the new task of setting society right. He quoted Hume on the point: "'A man has but a bad grace who delivers a theory, however true, which . . . leads to a practice dangerous and pernicious. Why rake into those corners of nature, which spread a nuisance all around? . . . Truths which are pernicious to society, if any such there be, will yield to errors, which are

30. The papers delivered at this conference were edited by Raymond O. Rockwood under the title *Carl Becker's Heavenly City Revisited* (Ithaca, NY: Cornell University Press, 1958).

31. Becker, *Heavenly City*, pp. 31, 149-50. Hereafter, page references to this work will be given parenthetically in the text.

salutary and advantageous'" (p. 38). Becker observed: "[In] midcareer Hume abandoned philosophical speculations [and skepticism] for other subjects, such as history and ethics, . . . from which useful lessons could be drawn" (pp. 38-39).

Becker contended that the history which the eighteenth-century *philosophes* narrated passed over the question of how society had come to its then-current state, because their object was to define the principles by which society could be corrected and improved (p. 98). He suggested that the Enlightenment visionaries were at this point giving voice in a new way to the old Christian call to service (p. 39), though they sought to do this by denigrating the Christian past. History, they felt, "would confirm the verdict of reason, that Christian philosophy and the infamous things that supported it were inimical to the welfare of mankind" (p. 108). The eighteenth-century savants were convinced that the present had broken with the past and was superior to it. They reasoned that the future would be better, a future they looked to "as to a promised land, a new millennium" (p. 118), a this-worldly "heavenly city."

It is from this point that Becker launched into his main point and his altered addition to the story told by Bury. Throughout his account of the development of the idea of progress, Bury had been intent to describe the rise in the awareness and importance of human agency in history and, correlatively, to put down belief in divine providence. In making his argument Bury moved from the idea of the cumulative nature of knowledge, especially scientific knowledge, to the assumption of a recognized need to improve society. Becker, by contrast, underlined the similarities between Enlightenment and medieval Christian thought at the point of a shared affirmation of the need for social correction and service. In a key passage Becker opined:

> The directing impulse of . . . [Enlightenment thinkers] was that mankind had been corrupted and betrayed by false doctrines. Their essential task was to destroy these false doctrines; and in order to do so they had of course to meet the doctrines of Christian philosophy with opposed doctrines, contrary ideas. But not with radically different ideas, not with ideas of a different order altogether, since it is true of ideas, as of men, that they cannot fight unless they occupy the same ground: ideas that rush toward each other on differ-

41

ent levels of apprehension will pass without conflict or mutual in-
jury because they never establish contact, never collide. In order to
defeat Christian philosophy the Philosophers had therefore to meet
it on the level of certain common preconceptions. They could never
rout the enemy by denying that human life is a significant
drama . . . ; their best hope of displacing the [pernicious] Christian
. . . [drama] lay in recasting it, and in bringing it up to date. In
short, the task of the Philosophers was to present another interpretation of the past, the present, and the future state of mankind. (pp.
122-23)

Within this interpretive scheme Becker fit his earlier discussion of
Enlightenment concern for "Nature" and the "new history," adding
then an account of the *philosophes'* adoption and revision of the Christian theme of hope, the theme that in Becker's view allowed for the triumph of the Christian drama over the fundamental pessimism of the
classical Greek view of recurring cycles. On this earlier displacement of
worldview, Becker remarked: "The Christian version put an end to the
helpless, hopeless world by substituting for the eternal 'nothing new' another world altogether new, a golden age to come in place of a golden
age past and done with . . ." (p. 126). Entrance into the medieval heavenly world required only the cultivation — in Becker's phrasing — of the
"negative virtues" common to common people: resignation and obedience. In light of theological discussions to follow, it is important to note
Becker's ensuing comment on the Christian story: "No interpretation of
the life of mankind ever more exactly reflected the experience, or more
effectively responded to the hopes of average men" (p. 126).

The source of Christian success, the hope in an otherworldly future
over against the metaphysical pessimism of the Greco-Roman world,
could not simply be negated by Enlightenment critics. It had to be transformed and then enlisted by the philosophers in their struggle against
the ecclesiastical culture of the Middle Ages. Becker put it this way:

No "return," no "rebirth" [Renaissance] of classical philosophy,
however idealized and humanized, no worship of ancestors long
since dead, or pale imitations of Greek pessimism would suffice for
a society that had been so long and so well taught to look forward
to another and better world to come. Without a new heaven to re-
place the old, a new way of salvation, of attaining perfection, the

religion of humanity would appeal in vain to the common run of men. (p. 129)[32]

Thus the "enlightened" ones, who were themselves also "believers," relocated the new heaven within the bounds of earthly life, setting it in the future as an achievable, beckoning perfection. They eliminated the agency of a supernatural God, even that of a philosopher-king, and made humankind itself, in its cumulative sacrificial labors, the agent of its own redemption. Posterity would complete and fully enjoy the unfulfilled, imperfect labors of the present. Becker, as previously quoted, summarized his account of the revised Enlightenment "gospel" in these words: "Thus the Philosophers called in posterity to exorcise the double illusion of the Christian paradise and the golden age of antiquity. For the love of God they substituted love of humanity; for the vicarious atonement the perfectibility of man through his own efforts; and for the hope of immortality in another world the hope of living in the memory of future generations" (p. 130).

It is clear that Becker, as a positive critic, embraced the main lines of Bury's work. For Becker, too, the idea of progress was/is a modern and distinctively Western idea, related closely to the rise of scientific thought in the sixteenth and seventeenth centuries. But, unlike Bury, Becker noted closer ties of the eighteenth-century idea of progress to the medieval religious world than Bury and most "moderns" were led to perceive or allow. Becker thus came up with the distinctive argument that affinity between the eighteenth-century Enlightenment and the medieval world of meaning was greater than that which existed between his own post–World War I point-of-viewing and that of the eighteenth century. Whereas Bury was concerned to chart the rise of the idea of progress as such — largely in terms of a contrast between the "medieval" and the commonly delineated "modern" era — Becker was intent on treating the idea of progress in the context of a disaffected, cynical, twentieth-century climate of opinion that cast doubt on the Enlightenment projection of hope.

In 1933, one year after he wrote the introduction to the American edition of Bury, Charles Beard wrote a review of Becker's book in which he

---

32. Becker here seems to overlook Bury's point that the common people were broadly enlisted in the belief in Progress primarily through the onset of material progress in the Industrial Revolution.

seemed unsure what to make of Becker's argument. However, he noted — perceptively — that Becker was dealing with a comparison and contrast of three, not two periods of history — the medieval, the eighteenth century, and the twentieth century.[33] Beard did not offer elaboration on this point, but it is important and needs exploration. More than once in the course of his lectures, Becker charged the *philosophes* with being "over-credulous" and "naive" (pp. 31, 39-40, 45). He suggested that twentieth-century "moderns" agreed with the eighteenth-century enlightened "more readily when they are witty and cynical than when they are wholly serious." Becker continued:

> They . . . put off the fear of God, but maintained a respectful attitude toward the Deity. . . . The Garden of Eden was for them a myth, no doubt, but they looked enviously back to the golden age of Roman virtue, or across the waters to the unspoiled innocence of an Arcadian civilization. . . . They renounced the authority of church and Bible, but exhibited a naive faith in nature and reason. . . . They denied that miracles ever happened, but believed in the perfectibility of the human race. (pp. 30-31)

Defining the breach between his own time and the eighteenth century, Becker declared: "These skeptics who eagerly assent to so much strike our sophisticated minds as over-credulous. We feel that they are too easily persuaded, that they are naive souls after all, duped by their humane sympathies, on every occasion hastening to the gate to meet and welcome platitudes and thin panaceas" (pp. 45-46).

Three observations need to be made about this aspect of Becker's critique of the Enlightenment belief in Progress. The first has to do with the perspective from which Becker himself wrote. Becker very much mirrored, in major part, the post–World War I climate of opinion in America and Europe. His perspective on history was governed by two factors: his philosophical commitment to positivism and the disillusioning impact of World War I, with its far-reaching political and socio-economic after-effects. The first of these factors, his positivism, was somewhat limited in the fact that he claimed too much for it. At one point, early in his discussion, when describing the distance between the twentieth-century world and that of the eighteenth century, Becker declared:

33. *The American Historical Review* 38 (April 1933): 590-91.

"[The] essential quality of the modern climate of opinion is factual rather than rational. . . . [We] can easily do with a minimum of the theoretical" (p. 27). Becker made this assertion almost a decade after Einstein broke with Ernst Mach and highlighted a growing defection from philosophical positivism in continental European scientific circles.[34] For Becker it was not Einstein but Bertrand Russell who spoke for the intellectual community and helped define Becker's own intellectual outlook. Early in *The Heavenly City* Russell is quoted at length by Becker — with Becker's clear approbation — on the ultimate meaninglessness of human existence, understood best as "the outcome of accidental collocations of atoms" (pp. 13-14).

It was, however, not so much late nineteenth-century scientific, philosophical positivism, but the disheartening experience of shattered historical hope in the aftermath of World War I that seems chiefly to have triggered Becker's historical cynicism. There are not many direct references to World War I in *The Heavenly City*, but Becker's rejection of "enthusiasm" for the 1918 Russian Revolution dominated the closing pages of the book. For a number of postwar intellectuals it was the Russian Revolution, rather than liberal humanism, that offered a possibility to believe again in progress and a future-fulfilling social goal. Becker's repudiation of Marxist utopianism was rooted not so much in Bertrand Russell's depiction of humanity as "accidental collocations of atoms," but rather in his own sober assessment of historical experience, an assessment that undercut much of the optimism in the promise of "posterity." The historical experience of World War I and its aftermath led Becker to call attention to the dictum of Marcus Aurelius: "The man of forty years, if he have a grain of sense, in view of this sameness has seen all that has been and shall be" (p. 168).

In *Progress and Power*, a book he wrote four years after *The Heavenly City*, Becker made clear the critical nature of World War I for his own thought in ending "naive" optimism in the belief in Progress. He cited Bury's view that "The hope of an ultimate happy state on this planet to be enjoyed by future generations . . . has replaced, as a social power, the hope of felicity in another world." Then Becker added his own troubled view: "Since 1918 this hope has perceptibly faded. Stand-

---

34. See Gerald Holton, *Thematic Origins of Scientific Thought: Kepler to Einstein* (Cambridge, MA: Harvard University Press, 1973), pp. 219-59.

ing within the deep shadow of the Great War, it is difficult to recover the nineteenth-century faith either in the fact or the doctrine of progress."[35]

An observation should be made at this point about Becker's reappraisal and amendment of Bury's work. This pertains to the problem of "disillusion," which Becker himself manifested but did not directly address. Throughout *The Heavenly City*, Becker, as noted above, makes frequent attacks on Enlightenment naiveté and credulity, attacks that veil the deeper problem of disillusion, a seemingly inevitable concomitant of the incongruence between the hopes and outcomes of a progress-oriented history. In his charges of naiveté against the *philosophes* it must be asked if Becker did not demand of them a historical understanding that, at their point in history, they could hardly have been expected to share. His charge of naiveté seems to imply that Enlightenment spokesmen should have anticipated the sobering historical experiences of the French Revolution and the later World War — events that fostered deep doubts about the possibilities of social-political progress. The question arises whether the historical experience of the Enlightenment philosophers was conducive to the nature of critical questioning that Becker arrived at on the basis of 150 years of subsequent history.

Also at issue is a historical judgment about the cumulative impact of the devastating religious wars, the wars fought between Catholics and Protestants throughout France, the Low Countries, and Central Europe during the sixteenth and much of the seventeenth centuries, wars that certainly helped to shape the outlook of the Enlightenment era. Rather than serving as a source of stability and comfort in the midst of chaos and change as it once had done for the early Middle Ages, the church and questions about Christian belief became sources of instability and chaos in the early modern period. That the population of Germany fell from sixteen million to less than six million over the course of the religiously inspired Thirty Years War (1618-1648) has to be reckoned as a major spiritual-intellectual trauma with long-term historical aftereffects.[36] Numbers of informed and thoughtful people were led, on the

---

35. Carl Becker, *Progress and Power* (New York: Vintage Books, 1965), p. 7.

36. Williston Walker, *A History of the Christian Church*, rev. ed. (New York: Charles Scribner's Sons, 1959), p. 396, offers a brief picture of seventeenth-century religious conflict and turbulence.

basis of historical experience, to identify religion as a source of earthly suffering and destruction and then, on that basis, to envision a different sort of earthly future. On the face of it this cannot be characterized simply as "naiveté."[37] Post-Enlightenment historical experience and understandings fostered more guarded expectations, but to summon the *philosophes* to the dock on the charge of simple credulity and naiveté is almost to charge them with a lack of prescience and does not allow them the parameters of their own world.

The problem of disillusion has a persistent, troubling meaning, especially for those who would chart a human future without a heaven. In the interests of clarifying the idea of Progress, Bury was intent to define it exclusive of any agency and motivation beyond the human. To this end, in the spirit of the Enlightenment, he presented an understanding of progress devoid of ambiguity, yet vulnerable to disappointment, especially in its social-political hopes and expectations. It is of note that Bury published his progress study two years after the end of World War I. Yet, in his work he failed to take cognizance of the event through which he himself and his generation had so recently lived — and which raised such serious questions for the subject matter of his study. By contrast, Becker, a little more than a decade later, fully absorbed the crisis into which the belief in progress had fallen. And it is chiefly from the World War I event that Becker came to his charges against the *philosophes*. It was in this context that he also proposed his startling linkage of the "enlightened" with the religious age that had preceded their own and charged them with "enthusiasm" and the fanaticism of "true belief." Becker exemplifies the cynicism and the thinly veiled *angst* of meaninglessness that followed upon the historical disillusion occasioned by World War I.

For this interpreter, such cynicism led Becker — not without weight — to his view that Enlightenment affinity with the Middle Ages is found in a shared belief in "service." Remarking on this phenomenon, Becker wrote of the eighteenth century: "Its characteristic note is not a disillusioned indifference, but the eager didactic impulse to set things right.

---

37. Becker's cited example of David Hume's effort to salvage a historical optimism from the seeming dead end of his philosophical skepticism is not, I think, chargeable to naiveté, intellectual "cowardice" perhaps, but not naiveté; see Becker's discussion of Hume, *Heavenly City*, pp. 37-39.

Bienfaisance and *humanité* — the very words, we are told, are new, coined by the Philosophers to express in secular terms the Christian ideal of service."[38] Yet Becker does not mention — if he was aware — that the word "disillusion," in his use of the phrase "disillusioned indifference," was also a new word,[39] one that gained usage in the nineteenth century, not the eighteenth. He thus seems unfairly to rebuke the *philosophes* for not knowing, in the mid-eighteenth century, what they lacked the later historical experience of the nineteenth and early twentieth centuries to understand: the phenomenon of historical disillusion. The philosophers laid claim to an earthly bliss in a historical future. In their context they were hardly in a position to conjure with future disillusion. Becker failed to note, in contrast with the *philosophes,* that "the religious" did not face such a problem since an otherworldly heaven does not, even to this day, breed disillusion — fanaticisms often, but not disillusion. No one returns to tell believers that sacrifice in the hope of a heavenly reward is not worth the effort.

All of this does not say that Becker was himself a victim of "disillusioned indifference." It was something he fought in himself — and from which he sought a way out. He admits to a large measure of cynicism but finally does not entirely yield to it. What he maintained was a committed realism, a naturalistic outlook, leavened by a chastened, very modest hope. He found this chastened hope in technology and its long, cumulative history. For Becker, in the mid-1930s, technology's benign bequest of power and rational discipline offered a sober promise of only a reasonable future: In 1935, in the less well-known lectures at Stanford University, lectures published under the title *Progress and Power,* Becker declared, baldly, that "man has emerged without credentials or instructions from a universe that is as unaware of him as of itself."[40] He maintained, nonetheless, that by pursuing "facts that speak for themselves" it was possible to descry a progressive human history arising out of the ages-old history of civilization. Anthropological studies made clear, Becker averred, that humankind had been able, incrementally, to extend command over natural sources of power and, over thousands of years,

38. Becker, *Heavenly City,* p. 39.

39. *The Oxford English Dictionary,* 1933 edition, s.v. "disillusion."

40. *Progress and Power,* p. 9. Hereafter, page references to this work will be given parenthetically in the text.

to improve its techniques for exploiting such sources of power. He offered a list of the natural sources of power exploited over the years: gravitation, fire, domestic animals, planted seeds, water, air, magnetic force, artificial explosives, steam, gas, electricity, radiation. (By "radiation" Becker, in 1935, had in mind X-ray technology, not the subsequent development of atomic energy.) He observed that "the instruments for exerting power are far more numerous than the sources of power" (p. 28). With increased control of the sources of power, the human community had shown expanded mastery of the external world and had come in the process to increased self-awareness. Becker wrote: "From the beginning . . . man has increasingly implemented himself with power. Had he not done so, he would have had no history, nor even the consciousness of not having any. . . . Without power no progress" (p. 24). And he quoted Francis Bacon to this effect: "Neither the naked hand nor the understanding left to itself can effect much. It is by instruments and helps that the work is done. . . . Human knowledge and human power meet in one."[41]

Despite this growing mastery of the physical world, human efforts to advance or reorder social life in Europe and America, the chief centers of determinative technological advance,[42] had yielded — in Becker's view — considerable "confusion and despair." In the aftermath of the Great War and in the midst of a worldwide economic depression, Becker anguished over the prospects for the future. He determined that a major source of the problem lay in the fact that the new wealth made possible by the scientists and engineers was placed in the hands of the few and was poorly distributed throughout the rest of society. The situation pointed up a troubling incapacity "to subdue . . . social relations to rational direction" (pp. 101-3). At this point Becker in fact contrasted two forms of progress, the social-political and the technological. It was the historical failure of the belief in progress "to subdue . . . social relations to rational direction" that concerned Becker most and induced his cynicism. His despair at the economic situation after the Great War prompted him to note: "The exceptional few have little in common with

41. Becker, *Progress and Power*, p. 25. Becker offers the quote from Bacon as the overall theme of his Stanford lectures; see p. vii.

42. Becker ascribes the dominant role in the development of modern technology to Europe and America; Becker, *Progress and Power*, pp. 73-75.

the undistinguished many, except the implements of power and the symbols of wealth with which to obtain them; so that while the outward activities of both are conditioned by the same material needs and appliances, their respective views of the world in which they both perforce live are too discordant to be easily woven into a harmonious pattern of psychological responses" (p. 107).

Becker blamed this situation not alone on the privileged wealthy and those with greatest access to technological power, but also on untutored common people who persisted in viewing the world in traditional modes of thought and belief. In Becker's view, the inability of the mass of unsophisticated people to live by "matter-of-fact" knowledge, to break with habit, and simultaneously to adjust to the dictates of technological and economic change were perhaps the root cause of the problem. He remarked that the vast majority of people, unable to grasp the realities of empirical scientific knowledge and an ever more complex society, "wander aimless and distrait in a shadowy realm of understanding, alternately enticed by venerable faiths that are suspect but not wholly renounced and by the novel implications of factual knowledge accepted on rumor but not understood. . . . Truth emerges from an agreement of minds." And, looking at the developments in the Europe of his time, Becker expressed the view: "[For] common men minds agree most effectively when bodies act in unison. Myriad hands lifted in salute are more convincing than facts or syllogisms, whether the object be to worship or to fight, to suffer martyrdom or to mete out vengeance" (pp. 108-9).

Having fashioned a ground for belief in progress on the basis of a sweeping overview of the history of technology, Becker could not but look to the same source for escape from disillusion and nihilism in the sphere of social relations and politics. Like many before him, and even more after him, Becker contemplated a "technological fix."[43] He looked to a continued adjustment of the human community to technology as a means to instill, over the long term, a rational discipline that would diminish traditional and fanciful popular mindsets. He proposed that matter-of-fact knowledge would continue to accrue and would extend increasingly not only to control over the outer world of nature but also

43. The term "technological fix" is used to describe the effort to solve a social-political problem, or problems, by technological applications or innovation.

to "the world of human relations." In the midst of the Great Depression, he believed that economic duress would teach the unsophisticated masses that "realities are less dangerous than fancies" and that machines would increasingly breed awareness that "a matter-of-fact apprehension of their problems brings the most salutary if not the most inspiring solutions" (p. 111). To this observation Becker added: "Time, slow-moving, indifferent to men's purposes, in the long-run gives its validation to matter-of-fact knowledge while dismissing value judgments as useless or insufficiently discriminated" (p. 111). A final hope expressed by Becker was that over time the rate of discovery and the introduction of new technologies would gradually slow, thus allowing society greater time to adjust more adequately in "ideas and habits" to the changes that science and technology invariably introduce (p. 112).

If one were to bring the perspective of another seventy-five years, the perspective of the first decade of the twenty-first century, to Becker's hopes for reformation and social renewal through technology, it would be difficult to avoid the assessment that Becker in his turn shared at least much of the naiveté and credulity with which he charged his Enlightenment predecessors. Nevertheless, with his two lecture series of the 1930s, Becker brought development and depth to the original narrative of Bury. His lectures underlined the sense of disaffection and growing doubts about the belief in Progress, especially in the form of Enlightenment utopianism — or, in Becker's descriptive phrase, in the form of a this-worldly "heavenly city." Though he maintained a diminished belief in a future "society of equal, and equally rational and humane individuals" (p. 99), Becker guarded himself against final disillusion with the thought that a modern person, disciplined by matter-of-fact knowledge, ought also entertain the idea that "[a]part from man, the cosmos merely is; it does not ask or answer questions. The significance of man is that he is that part of the universe that asks the question, What is the significance of man? . . . The significance of man is that he is insignificant and is aware of it" (p. 115).

It should be observed that whereas Bury sought to sever most ties between the belief in progress and the Christian tradition and to establish the turn to social betterment on the dual basis of belief in human malleability/perfectibility and growing sensitivity to the gap between cumulative scientific knowledge and social-political realities, Becker, by contrast, argued that the crisis in the post–World War I belief in progress was due in part to an uncritical adoption by Enlightenment spokesmen of Christian ideals of compassion and service. Becker, without discussing the problem of disillusion, attempted to skirt its full significance by rejecting ethical determinations. He rejected "value judgments as useless or insufficiently discriminated." Charles Beard, on the other hand, in his introduction to the 1932 American edition of Bury, argued that Bury had inadequately defined an ethical viewpoint on the basis of which Progress itself could be measured, a point at variance from Becker. Despite disagreement on this point of ethics, Beard and Becker shared common ground on the crucial significance of technology in assessing a belief in progress. In fact, both seemed to imply that technology, in its links with science, had become the chief bearer of the belief in progress, especially in the face of the defeats and uncertainties attending social-political hopes and expectations. Bury had pointed to the great London Exhibition of 1851, with its celebration of technology and the material benefits of industrialization, as a mark of the spread of the progress belief beyond intellectual elites to the broad masses of the people. Becker and Beard saw technology as having become the essential bearer of the belief. With Becker, it is clear, technology afforded hope of advance even in the face of social-political disillusion, in its capacity — long-term — to inculcate rational thought.[44]

In the decades that followed the Bury/Becker/Beard perspectives on progress, the Second World War and subsequent historical developments further underlined the dominant role of technology both in warfare and in shaping human hopes and expectations about the future. But new technological achievements brought with them new uncertainties and anxieties unknown to Becker and Beard. The development and use of atomic energy in World War II — the dropping of the bombs on Hiroshima and Nagasaki — confronted humanity with the possibility of its own self-destruction. In the context of the Cold War that followed World War II, doubts about an assured technological future became more widespread, doubts significantly deepened by increased knowledge and awareness of the cumulative impact of technological advances upon

---

44. In 1980, with the development of computer technology, Seymour Papert, in a book widely circulated among school educators, argued that the great promise of the computer would be its likely impact of "mathematizing" and rationalizing young minds; see Seymour Papert, *Mindstorms: Children, Computers, and Powerful Ideas* (New York: Basic Books, 1980), an idea in line with Becker's hope of the 1930s.

the natural environment. Thoughts about the future have more and more registered concern about human survival. Technological innovation has been directed increasingly to resolving problems spawned by technology's own unforeseen consequences.

Whereas Becker had modestly fashioned a hope on the basis of "progress" and "power," developments into the twenty-first century have raised more and more questions about the technological pursuit of power beyond social-political purpose, a pursuit insufficiently questioned within the political process itself, except most recently in the matter of climate change and the varied threats of global warming. Apart from the search for a "technological fix," this uncertainty is due in no small part to the phenomenon that the purposes and motivations of technological innovation are very diverse and do not offer as much focus on future social-political goals as commonly supposed. To be sure, a justifying claim of some sort of human betterment accompanies almost all technological innovations, but responsibility for the possible negative side-effects of such innovations are usually consigned to highly lobbied political processes or simply to the economic workings of the market. At this point concerns persist that long-term future outcomes are captive too frequently to short-term considerations — even in the face of growing environmental concerns.

The problem of linking belief in progress to technology as its major driving force, even though the latter may continually be accompanied by promises of future human benefits, was presciently anticipated in a work, contemporary with that of Becker and Beard (but unnoted by them), Aldous Huxley's 1932 *Brave New World*.[45] In this futuristic novel Huxley raised many concerns about the possibility of a technocratic-managerial elite in command and control of society for the primary, if not sole, purpose of maintaining order. A major instrument of control, along with population restriction and other manipulative techniques, was the mental conditioning of children and its adult citizenry. Especially noteworthy was Huxley's portrayal of the use of sensory satiation as a means of diverting the citizenry from social and political criticism. As an advance beyond mere motion pictures Huxley's futuristic conformist society was offered "feelies" designed to indulge the full range of human sensory sensations. He projected, as well, the widespread distri-

45. Aldous Huxley, *Brave New World* (New York: Harper & Row, 1932, 1946).

bution of tranquilizers, especially a perfected "soma," as a means of allaying individual and social anxieties.

In this projection of a dystopian future Huxley was suggesting that technology could be directed to sensory satiation in the present in the stead of political sacrifice and struggle for long-term goals of human well-being, personal worth, and equity. Thus, along with the powerful appeal and utilization of technology as a means to near-term goals of power and wealth, Huxley suggested that technology afforded the seductive allure of maximizing sensory satisfaction as a social opiate. The ability to enhance sight and sound, to enlarge everyone's "experience of life" through expedited global transportation and communication, the stimulation of consumptive appetites — at least for those able to afford it, would make technology an ambiguous, uncertain partner in the furtherance of the original humanizing goals of progress. This problem is nicely expressed in one of the social-conditioning maxims Huxley offered in his "brave new world": "Never put off to tomorrow the fun you can have today."[46] The maxim is expressed again in the novel's Director Mustapha Mond's rhetorical question to an indoctrinated audience: "Have any of you been compelled to live through a long-time interval between the consciousness of a desire and its fulfilment?"[47] As Huxley suggested in the introduction of the book's reprint edition, technology affords the possibility of ever more effectively addressing the problem of having "people love their servitude."[48]

In the 1946 edition of *Brave New World,* Huxley confessed to some limitations in the arguments of his original work but rejected thought of a revision. Overall he saw the work continuing to speak to "Western" social-political conditions in the aftermath of the Second World War. And, in 1958, in *Brave New World Revisited,* he pointed to the emergence of the new mass medium of television as means for exploitation by marketers and politicians in pursuit of economic and political power. In this later 1958 work he wrote: "In the world we live in, . . . vast impersonal forces are making for the centralization of power and a regimented society. The genetic standardization of individuals is still impossible; but Big Government and Big Business already possess, or will very

46. Huxley, *Brave New World,* p. 62.
47. Huxley, *Brave New World,* p. 30.
48. Huxley, *Brave New World,* p. xii.

soon possess, all the techniques for mind-manipulation described in *Brave New World,* along with others of which I was too unimaginative to dream."[49] In a conclusion he predicted:

> Under the relentless thrust of accelerating over-population and in-creasing over-organization, and by means of ever more effective methods of mind-manipulation, the democracies will change their nature; the quaint old forms — elections, parliaments, Supreme Courts and all the rest — will remain. The underlying substance will be a new kind of non-violent totalitarianism. All the traditional names, all the hallowed slogans will remain exactly what they were in the good old days. Democracy and freedom will be the theme of every broadcast and editorial — but democracy and freedom in a strictly Pickwickian sense. Meanwhile the ruling oligarchy and its highly trained elite of soldiers, policemen, thought-manufacturers and mind manipulators will quietly run the show as they see fit.[50]

In 1977, in the aftermath of the onset of the civil rights, student-power, and feminist movements, along with the protests against the Vietnam War, Langdon Winner addressed the issue of "autonomous technology,"[51] suggesting that far from facilitating the political move-ment toward an equitable, humane future, technology had come to bear the character of an autonomous force, by which he meant a force be-yond any definable political direction. Increasing note was taken of what was termed "the technological imperative," an adaptation of a precept of the German philosopher Immanuel Kant. At the end of the nineteenth century, Kant made an argument for the reality of human freedom on the basis of the experience of moral obligation and duty, what Kant identified as the experience of "ought." Kant argued that the sense of "ought," or duty, a moral imperative, pointed beyond itself to the certainty of freedom, since the latter was the necessary condition of the former. Awareness of the growing autonomous power of technology subsequently led many to observe that Kant's maxim of " 'ought' implies

49. Aldous Huxley, *Brave New World Revisited* (New York: Harper & Row, 1958), pp. 125-26.

50. Huxley, *Brave New World Revisited,* p. 134.

51. See Langdon Winner, *Autonomous Technology: Technics-out-of-Control as a Theme of Political Thought* (Cambridge, MA: MIT Press, 1977).

'can'" had been virtually replaced, through the increased dominance and fascination with technology, by its ethical opposite: "If I can, I ought!" Such analyses, at least during the latter decades of the twentieth century, suggested that rather than serving as a support for the original social-political conception of progress, technology, with its diverse, often conflicting, motivations, had become the driving force of a mere culture of change. Whatever poured forth from the cornucopia of technological innovation and its capitalist exploitation laid demand upon society for adaptation and adjustment without any vision of social goal. In line with Huxley's analysis, technology was seen by many to require acceptance, acceptance by the citizenry of a subtly induced servitude under the mantle of free-market economics.

Unease with the state and condition of the belief in progress in 1979 prompted a call for a major conference on the theme "Progress and Its Discontents." The conference was hosted by the Western Center of the American Academy of Arts and Sciences at the University of California at Berkeley. Papers were solicited from leading representatives of most major academic disciplines. They were subsequently published in 1982 under the conference theme: *Progress and Its Discontents*.[52] As might be expected, a variety of views and perspectives were expressed in the papers presented; but, in the main, the broad outline of Bury's view on the origins of the idea of progress was reaffirmed, along with recognition of the essential political-social nature of the idea. A summary view was stated by the historian Georg Iggers:

> The shortcomings of the idea of progress are apparent: the failure to appreciate the resistance to rationality, the very ambiguities of reason, and the powerful needs for domination, which turn science and technology into powerful instruments of control and destruction. Growth for the sake of growth has proven to be not only a dubious value from the view of human needs but a threat to human existence; but then growth for its own sake was never what the idea of progress in its classical form was about. Progress was always conceived in broad social terms. A basic assumption of the theorists of progress has been that "man is not merely a natural be-

---

52. Gabriel Almond, Marvin Chodorow, and Roy Harvey Pearce, eds., *Progress and Its Discontents* (Berkeley: University of California Press, 1982).

ing; he is a human natural being"; that he cannot be submerged fully into the order of nature; that civilization is the setting in which he expresses and develops his humanity.[53]

And Harvey Brooks, a Harvard Professor of Technology and Public Policy, concluded:

[G]iven continued scientific and technological progress and the capacity to embody such progress in new capital investments and new institutions, and given the continuation of a relatively free world trading system in which both materials and knowledge can move freely across national boundaries from where they are produced to where they can be used, there do not appear to be any fundamental physical or technical obstacles to continued material progress in the world. The question is whether these two "givens" can be assumed to continue into the indefinite future and whether the worldwide social cohesion necessary for them is compatible with the diversity of individual and group aspirations or, indeed, even with an equitable distribution of power and influence in the world. In other words, the obstacles to continued material progress in the world are social, political, and institutional; they are determined not by the relations of humans and nature but by the relations of humans to one another. This is more than just the perversity of human nature; it may well be that what we regard in most of the world as desirable goals for the relations among humans cannot be reconciled with the necessities of interdependence and technological progress. We do not know. One thing is clear; the rate of change may be the most important negative factor in trying to reconcile material and social goals.[54]

The onrush of technology, for many observers, is as much a threat to the essential belief in progress as a support for it, a point that Carl Becker implied in the mid-1930s when he hoped for a slowing in the rate of technological innovation in order to allow time for society to assimilate its varied impacts and implications.[55] Currently the contemporary

---

53. *Progress and Its Discontents*, pp. 65-66.
54. *Progress and Its Discontents*, pp. 299-300.
55. See above, pp. 50-51.

writer Bill McKibben, among many others, offers an example of continuing concern with technological developments over recent years, even in the light of some positive political, informational, and organizational developments made possible by the revolution in computer technology.[56]

It is of special note that the problem of historical disillusion was also forthrightly addressed at the 1979 conference on "Progress and Its Discontents." In spite of the conference consensus that the classic idea of progress ("European and modern," as Bury presented it) remained central, the conference leadership confronted forthrightly the negative impact of historical events upon continuing commitment to the original idea. Citing the great impact of the First World War, the Great Depression, the rise of fascism in Europe, the Nazi horror of the Holocaust, and the subsequent Cold War, with its threat of nuclear destruction, the editors observed in the preface that "the idea of continuing progress received staggering blows in the twentieth century."[57] With the later collapse of the Soviet Union and its dependent Soviet bloc of nations in the years 1989-1991, the Marxist concept of historically determined social progress was vitiated, if not destroyed, by disillusion. In the aftermath of that event, the field seemed left open to the continuing surge of scientific-technological advance in league with liberal market economics, a dominant orientation of the decade that followed, and which was presented by one interpreter as "the end of history."[58]

Yet the extraordinary event of September 11, 2001, and the complications of the Iraq War that followed, have posed new challenges to the idea of progress. The unresolved issue after 9/11 is the degree to which the Islamic world may choose to embrace modernity and the idea of social-political progress, or whether instead it will choose to sharpen its opposition to that idea, while perhaps continuing to affirm scientific-technological innovation and the culture of change it inevitably brings with it.[59] Most recently, the severe economic crisis that has swept the

---

56. See especially Bill McKibben, *Enough: Staying Human in an Engineered Age* (New York: Henry Holt & Co., 2003).

57. *Progress and Its Discontents*, p. x; see also pp. ix-xi.

58. Francis Fukuyama, *The End of History and the Last Man* (New York: Free Press, 1992).

59. In the immediate aftermath of the September 11 attack, a number of books offered interpretations of the sources of this radical assault upon the United States and the West from within the Islamic tradition. In June and July 2003, under the title "Which Way to

global economy from the year 2007 to the present has raised serious new questions about the sustainability and the equity of the world economic system.[60]

It has still to be asked at what cost the Western, post-medieval world itself accedes to the decline of the belief in progress, at least in the form of acquiescence to domination by scientific-technological change, along with its economic exploitation. This is a question also for theology, since it may yet appear that theological understandings and faith commitments have had a greater involvement in the rise of the idea of progress than either Bury or Becker, along with many others, have perceived. It must be asked whether Christian theology, in this matter, does not have a greater stake in its actualization and survival than many have assumed.

Mecca?" Clifford Geertz authored a two-part review and assessment of thirteen books (out of many more) that sought to probe an understanding of Islam and the phenomenon of "jihadism." Geertz's article appeared in the June 12 (50, no. 10) and July 3 (50, no. 11) issues of *The New York Review of Books*. Along with offering a brief four-category typology of the responses to questions about Islam, Geertz expressed special concern about a premature "construction" of a comprehensive image of the religio-political phenomenon of contemporary Islam. Some four years later a second assessment of later analyses of Islam appeared in the same journal (November 8, 2007; 54, no. 17) under the title "How to Understand Islam," by the Scottish historian of religion Malise Ruthven. Ruthven offered critical description of five subsequent works and pointed up the continuing uncertainties within the Muslim tradition about its own theological/philosophical struggle with the question of its relation to modernity, not the least of which is the meaning of "jihad" within that tradition and the conflicting interpretations of that term, especially those that go beyond those of personal, internal struggle or simple "resistance" to external threat.

60. It goes virtually without saying that a perspective on and assimilation of the current world economic crisis, viewed by many as the worst since the Great Depression of the 1930s, will require years to assess.

Chapter 3

Divine Transcendence and the Critique of Otherworldliness: Luther

The thesis probed in this third chapter is that Christianity reached its peak of "religious" development in the Middle Ages. When Diderot proclaimed that "posterity is for the *philosophe* . . . what the other world is for the religious [person]," he gave expression to the common assumption that otherworldliness and "religion" were/are virtually synonymous. The historical-theological argument that follows suggests there is validity to this assumption, but also that it is false to conclude that divine transcendence and "otherworldliness" are essentially synonymous. The argument to be pursued in this third chapter is that Martin Luther (1483-1546), in reasserting a sense of biblical, divine transcendence, initiated an early modern theological-sociological critique of "religion" and its generic concept of otherworldliness centered in concern for life after death. After setting a context for a discussion of Luther, the latter's dawning awareness of God's transcendent judgment and grace will be interpreted in its interactions with his situation in life and not alone as an elucidation and interpretation of Scripture, decisive and formative as that was in his life. This is to argue that Luther's reading of Scripture was itself informed by the events in which he became engaged and through which he lived out faith. This helps to underline, as others have observed, that Luther was no "systematic theologian."

As preface to the discussion of Luther, it is helpful to consider some aspects of contemporary thought about the relationship of "religion" and society or "religion" and culture. By placing the term "religion" in quotation marks at this juncture, the present writer seeks to make room for the theological point that much of what is construed as religion in our present historical context can be understood as a human construct addressing the problem of death, the puzzling phenomenon of human consciousness and its accompanying "ontological anxiety" rooted in the individual's sense of his/her unique existence in a world.[1] As otherworldliness cannot be equated with divine transcendence, neither can "religion" as an answer to death, as hope for "life after death," be understood as the substantive ground for understanding God's transcendence.

Writing in 1973 the anthropologist Clifford Geertz offered a revised definition of religion, "revised" in the sense that Geertz felt that anthropologists, at the time of his writing, had become doctrinaire in their too easy acceptance of the established definitions and critiques of religion offered by the pioneering figures of Emil Durkheim, Max Weber, Sigmund Freud, and Bronislaw Malinowski. He suggested that just as those figures had tapped into the available pool of ideas in their time for framing their theoretical definitions of the nature of religion, so it was time, in 1973, to do the same and offer a reformulation and reappraisal of the religious phenomenon.

In a chapter titled "Religion as a Cultural System" in *The Interpretation of Cultures*,[2] Geertz offered an updating of the definition of religion. "Religion," Geertz proposed, "is (1) a system of symbols which acts to (2) establish powerful, pervasive, and long-lasting moods and motivations in men by (3) formulating conceptions of a general order of existence, and (4) clothing these conceptions with such an aura of factuality that (5) the moods and motivations seem uniquely realistic" (p. 90). Geertz then proceeded to offer systematic exposition of these enumerated points.

In the main, Geertz provides a heightened appreciation of the role of

---

1. This view of "religion" is/was a consistent and distinctive theme in the theological work of Karl Barth, a point made early in his career in 1916; see *The Word of God and the Word of Man* (New York: Harper Torchbooks, 1957), pp. 28-50; and later in 1963, see *A Karl Barth Reader*, ed. Rolf J. Erler and Reiner Marquard, trans. Geoffrey W. Bromiley (Grand Rapids: Eerdmans, 1986), pp. 28-31. Cf. also Karl Barth, *Church Dogmatics* I/2, trans. G. T. Thompson and H. Knight (Edinburgh: T. & T. Clark, 1956), pp. 297-303. The phrase "ontological anxiety" represents a borrowing from the thought of Paul Tillich; see Paul Tillich, *The Courage to Be* (London: Nisbet & Co., 1952), pp. 38-43; Tillich, *Systematic Theology*, vol. 2 (Chicago: University of Chicago Press, 1957), p. 67.

2. Clifford Geertz, *The Interpretation of Cultures* (New York: Basic Books, 1973). Hereafter, page references to this book will be given parenthetically in the text.

religion within culture, suggesting that religion, like some other perspectives within a culture, functions to provide a mental and motivational outlook upon the world that moderates undue or debilitating fear or rage (p. 75), a characteristic that can also be ascribed to culture generally. Yet religion is viewed as a particular development within culture, any culture. And, as one might expect, Geertz, as an anthropologist, gives culture precedence over religion, the latter operating within the framework of culture.

In developing his encompassing concept of culture, Geertz quotes the British philosopher Suzanne Langer on a critical point:

"[It is] mental activity . . . [that] chiefly determines the way a person meets his surrounding world. Pure sensation — now pain, now pleasure — would have no unity, and would change the receptivity of the body for future pains and pleasures in only rudimentary ways. It is sensation, remembered and anticipated, feared or sought, or even imagined and eschewed that is important in human life. It is perception molded by imagination that gives us the outward world that we know. And it is the continuity of thought that systematizes our emotional reactions into attitudes with distinct feeling tones, and sets a certain scope for the individual's passions. In other words by virtue of our thought and imagination we have not only feelings, but a *life of feeling*." (pp. 80-81)

From this point of departure in Langer, Geertz develops his working definition of culture. He writes: "[The] culture concept to which I adhere has neither multiple referents nor, so far as I can see, any unusual ambiguity: it denotes an historically transmitted pattern of meanings embodied in symbols, a system of inherited conceptions expressed in symbolic forms by means of which men communicate, perpetuate, and develop their knowledge about and attitudes toward life" (p. 89). Geertz's positive view of religion derives from the fact that religion bears many of the characteristics of a culture but is set within the frame-of-reference of, and is limited by, the "reality" defined by culture itself. For Geertz culture, as suggested, is a broader term than religion and is also the bearer of a measure of critical rationality that helps to set certain limits to the imaginative propensities of religion. While religion works in the first instance in shaping human moods and motivations, its sacred symbols often prove deficient in representing adequately — or convincingly — a "model of reality" (pp. 92-94). Religion's implied metaphysic frequently fails to convince.

This point was made somewhat later in a thoughtful theological study by George Lindbeck, who concurs in Geertz's "anthropological" judgment by insisting on the need for "categorial adequacy" in any and every particular religious tradition.[3] From Geertz's anthropological standpoint the descriptive-theoretical function of anthropology as a science is not to be surrendered to religion. Religion, in its various manifestations, remains an object of study, subject at critical points to the encompassing cultural perceptions of "reality" and the "commonsense" needs of human survival. Although Geertz does not deny the possibility of religion's potential to grasp the "really real," he maintains also the necessity of critical distance vis-à-vis religion's imaginative constructs.

Geertz's dynamic, dialectical view of the relation of religion and culture[4] is spelled out in the following quotations:

> For an anthropologist, the importance of religion lies in its capacity to serve, for an individual or for a group, as a source of general, yet distinctive, conceptions of the world, the self, and the relation between them, on the one hand — its model *of* aspect — and of rooted, no less distinctive "mental" dispositions — its model *for* aspect — on the other. From these cultural functions flow, in turn, its social and psychological ones.
>
> Religious concepts spread beyond their specifically metaphysical contexts to provide a framework of general ideas in terms of which a wide range of experience — intellectual, emotional, moral — can be given meaningful form.[5]

3. George Lindbeck, *The Nature of Doctrine* (Philadelphia: Westminster Press, 1983), pp. 47-49.

4. In terms of H. Richard Niebuhr's Christ/culture categories, Geertz's views of religion and culture are very close to Niebuhr's categories of Christ and culture in paradox ("dialectical" relationship) and Christ the transformer of culture.

5. Geertz, *Interpretation*, p. 123. Geertz's discussion here is instructive and suggests parallels with the thought of Paul Tillich. Especially interesting are Geertz's categories of "model of" and "model for" in analyzing religion. These categories in Geertz are very close in meaning to Tillich's conception of the "grasping" (in the sense of the German *verstehen*) and "shaping" functions of "ontological" reason. Compare also Geertz's description of the importance of historical change for religion with Tillich's theology of history (the *kairos* concept); see Geertz, *Interpretation*, pp. 216-20, esp. pp. 218-19.

However its role may differ at various times, for various individuals, and in various cultures, religion, by fusing ethos and world
view, gives to a set of social values what they perhaps most need to
be coercive: an appearance of objectivity. In sacred rituals and
myths values are portrayed not as subjective human preferences
but as the imposed conditions for life implicit in a world with a
particular structure.[6]

Subsequent major criticism of Geertz's definition of religion was undertaken by Talal Asad, a researcher at the New School of Social Research in New York. Two points in Asad's criticism of Geertz are of interest for what follows. The first is Asad's charge that Geertz, by
insisting that religious symbols and rituals bear an implicit metaphysic
and are bound by claims to truth about an overarching cosmic order,
manifests an elitist, Enlightenment point of view that subordinates practice to theory. Asad contends that a specific history underlies Geertz's
definition of religion and that that definition represents a surrender to
the "authorizing powers" of Western, secular culture, powers imbued
with an innate tendency to domination. Asad claims that as a result of
developments since the Middle Ages, religious theory developed in the
West was/is held to be "necessary for a correct reading of the mute ritual
hieroglyphics of others, for reducing their practices to texts," and that
such theory is an essential condition "for judging the validity of their
cosmological utterances."[7] Asad asserts that "Geertz is . . . right to make
a connection between religious theory and practice, but wrong to see it
as essentially cognitive, as a means by which a disembodied mind can
identify religion from an Archimedean point" (p. 44).

In defense of Geertz, it is important to point out that he in no way
denies a historical rootage for his definition of religion, though he offers
it in the historical context of the names of Weber, Durkheim, et al.,
whereas Asad is intent on a longer history that "explains" the secularization of Western thought. Asad's claim that Geertz puts forth his defi-

---

6. Geertz, *Interpretation*, p. 131. It is important to note that Geertz does not deny the
possible ultimate validity of religious truth claims, only that such ultimate validation lies
beyond the scientific limits of anthropological analysis; see *Interpretation*, p. 123.

7. Talal Asad, *Genealogies of Religion* (Baltimore: Johns Hopkins University Press,
1993), p. 43; see pp. 40-43 for the lead-up to Asad's argument. Hereafter, page references to
this book will be given parenthetically in the text.

nition "as a means by which a disembodied mind can identify religion from an Archimedean point" does an injustice to the stated purpose of Geertz's definition. Rather than closing down discussion, Geertz intends to enrich and enliven thought about religion. What he offers is not an "essentialist" definition of religion, but rather a broadened functional definition designed to provoke discussion of the relationship between religion and culture. By contrast Asad's reductionist definition of knowledge as power leaves little room for curiosity and understanding as motivational factors in the pursuit of knowledge. While Asad's critique of "power" may stimulate critical thought in the short term, its capacity to sustain such thought over the long term is dubious at best. This is so because critical thought must also bear the potential of self-criticism, and there is little in Asad's discussion of Geertz that shows appreciation for this latter condition of the inquiring, critical mind. If there is a line to be drawn between postmodernism and simple anti-modernism, that line is not discernible in Asad's discussion of Geertz.

But there is a second point in Asad's critique of Geertz that bears upon the question of Luther, upon Luther's "understanding" of divine transcendence and his theological criticism of medieval religion — an argument to be developed below. This is Asad's effort to offer a critique of "Enlightenment rationality" by juxtaposing the earlier cultural dominance of medieval Christianity to its commonly perceived, more restricted, social valuation in the aftermath of the Reformation and the sixteenth- and seventeenth-century Scientific Revolution. In Asad's reading of Western religious and intellectual history this decline of a once-dominant ecclesiastically ordered society and system of belief was the result of a shift in power by never fully defined "authorizing processes," which undercut traditional religious authority, knowledge, and morality.

In commenting upon what appears to him to be a shift in Geertz's understanding of one role of religion in society to a second, lesser one, Asad declares: "This [second,] modest view of religion (which would have horrified the early Christian Fathers or medieval churchmen) is a product of the only legitimate space allowed to Christianity by post-Enlightenment society, the right to individual belief. . . . [The] suggestion that religion has a universal function in belief is one indication of how marginal religion has become in modern industrial society as the site for producing disciplined knowledge and personal discipline" (pp. 45-46). He follows this point shortly after with the statement: "The medieval valorization of pain as the mode of participating in Christ's suffering contrasts sharply with the modern Catholic perception of pain as an evil to be fought against and overcome as Christ the Healer did. That difference is clearly related to the post-Enlightenment secularization of Western society and to the moral language which that society now authorizes" (pp. 46-47).

One could add numerous other such medieval/modern contrasts of religion that Asad introduces into his proposed critique of Geertz. The most important of these is the suggestion that in the medieval world belief was viewed in large part as a conclusion from knowledge, whereas "in modern society . . . knowledge is rooted either in an a-Christian everyday life or in an a-religious science . . ." (p. 47). It is worthwhile quoting Asad on this matter, because the theologies of Luther and Calvin are very much at odds with what Asad is trying to argue. In contrast to what Asad describes as a post-Enlightenment restriction of "religion" to belief, he suggests that for the

> pious learned Christians of the twelfth century, . . . knowledge and belief were not so clearly at odds. On the contrary, Christian belief would then have been built on knowledge — knowledge of theological doctrine, of canon law and Church courts, of the details of clerical liberties, of the powers of ecclesiastical office (over souls, bodies, properties), of the preconditions and effects of confession, of the rules of religious orders, of the locations and virtues of shrines, of the lives of the saints, and so forth. Familiarity with all such (religious) knowledge was a precondition for normal social life, and belief (embodied in practice and discourse), an orientation for effective activity in it — whether on the part of the religious clergy, the secular clergy, or the laity. (p. 47)

It is difficult to lay hold on what Asad believes he accomplishes with this line of reasoning. If he is saying that the Middle Ages was a church-dominated cultural period fixated on the "other world," few would argue with such a proposition. But he seems to suggest that a description of this pattern of social order in this particular period of history somehow carries an implicit critique of the complex relationship of religion and secular society in the modern West. It would appear that Asad feels an inner sympathy with the relation of religion to culture in the medieval

West because, one may surmise, that particular relation at that particular time is closest in spirit and in form to what Asad's own cultural tradition claims for itself. Rather than the dialectical, interactive patterns suggested in our previous discussion of H. Richard Niebuhr's typology ("Christ and culture in paradox" [Luther] and "Christ the transformer of culture" [Calvin]),[8] Asad argues for a "religion-above-culture" typology. Here, however, it is unfortunate that Asad did not familiarize himself with the thought of the Reformation so that he might have entertained the possibility that the critique of the medieval religious-cultural system had roots, deep roots, within the religious-theological tradition itself. It is to that story that we now turn.

IN ANTICIPATION of the observance in 1983 of the 500th anniversary of Martin Luther's birth, the noted Reformation historian Heiko Oberman published a noteworthy intellectual biography titled *Luther: Mensch zwischen Gott und Teufel*.[9] Oberman opened his discussion of Luther in a striking and unexpected way with a description of Luther's death and the wide interest that it commanded. Oberman suggests that the viability and acceptance of Luther's reforming work hung in the balance right up to the very end of his life. The question uppermost in the minds of friends and foes alike was whether Luther's death would be a sudden and abrupt one, a seizure of some sort, an apoplectic stroke for example, which would be interpreted as a sign that the Devil had taken him and that also God had passed a negative judgment upon the entirety of his work. Alternately it was believed that if Luther died a relatively peaceful death, one more or less anticipated, that would be regarded as a sign of approval by God.

When in fact Luther died on February 18, 1546, at the respectable age of sixty-four, those who were in his company — Luther had been away from Wittenberg on a political, peacemaking mission — sent word first to the leading political figures of the time, assuring them that Luther's death had been a peaceful one and that he remained firm in his faith to the very end. Oberman explains:

8. Geertz, *Interpretation*, p. 75.
9. Heiko Oberman, *Luther: Mensch zwischen Gott und Teufel* (Berlin: Severin und Siedler, 1982); Eng. trans. Eileen Walliser-Schwarzbart, *Luther: Man between God and the Devil* (New Haven/London: Yale University Press, 1989).

While simple believers imagined the Devil literally seizing prey, the enlightened academic world was convinced that a descent into Hell could be diagnosed medically — as apoplexy and sudden cardiac arrest. Abruptly and without warning, the Devil would snip the thread of a life that had fallen to him, leaving the Church unable to render last assistance. Thus, in their first reports, Luther's friends, especially Melanchthon, stressed that the cause of death had not been sudden, . . . but a gradual flagging of strength: Luther had taken leave of the world and commended his spirit into God's hands. . . . Justus Jonas carefully recorded Luther's last twenty-four hours, addressing his report not to Luther's widow, as one might expect, but to his sovereign, Elector John Frederick, with a copy for his university colleagues in Wittenberg.[10]

From this original and provocative introduction to a study of Luther and his work, Oberman leads on to accent Luther's struggle with the on-slaughts of the Devil as a major motif in Luther's effort to maintain faith in God and God's grace over much of the turbulent course of his adult life. Oberman argues that this very un-modern feature of Luther's life story is much neglected and played down by his post-Enlightenment in-terpreters but that to do this distorts the picture of the historical Luther. At the same time, however, it is important to deal with Luther's, at times, explicit, though perhaps more implicit, assault on the canons of otherworldliness that so dominated the Christianity of his day, even while acknowledging Oberman's point about Luther's long-term con-cerns with the Devil's persistent challenge to Christian faith, a faith to be lived out amid the concrete realities of this world. Søren Kierkegaard, in the nineteenth century, provided insight on this question in *Fear and Trembling,* when he proposed that Abraham, the father of faith, "be-lieved precisely for this life,"[11] and not primarily for the "life to come."

It is unquestionably the case that Luther was very much a part of the medieval world against which he rebelled. The question is: To what de-gree and by what agency did he break free — or begin to break free — from that dominantly otherworldly religious ethos of his times? The an-swer offered in the argument that follows is that the break with obses-

---

10. Oberman, *Between God and the Devil,* pp. 3-5.
11. Søren Kierkegaard, *Fear and Trembling and The Sickness unto Death,* trans. Wal-ter Lowrie (Princeton: Princeton University Press [paperback edition], 1968), p. 35.

sive otherworldliness in Luther lies in his (re)discovery of the unnatural grace of a transcendent God revealed in the cross of Christ as testified to in the Christian Scriptures and in interaction as well with events of his time, interactions that lent weight in turn to his interpretation of Scripture.

Oberman's accent upon popular concern with Luther's death should properly be yoked with the account of Luther's own uniquely personal, near-fatal encounter with a lightning bolt, an experience that set him on the course of his early monastic vocation. The story is retold in virtually all accounts of Luther's life: At the age of twenty-one Luther was returning to the University of Erfurt in the eastern German province of Saxony when he was knocked from his horse by a lightning bolt during a sudden thunderstorm. Picking himself up from the ground on that July day in 1505, Luther pledged to St. Anne that he would enter a cloister and devote his life to the pursuit of a holy life. At the time, even as a young man, he fully subscribed to the common medieval belief that the surest path to eternal salvation lay in entering a monastic order. Thus, two weeks after the lightning bolt experience Luther gave up his studies in the law to enter the Augustinian monastery in Erfurt. As Roland Bainton observed in his 1950 award-winning biography of Luther: "Luther knew perfectly well why youths should make themselves old and nobles should make themselves abased. This life is only a brief period of training for the life to come, where the saved will enjoy an eternity of bliss and the damned will suffer everlasting torment."[12]

AT THE beginning, Luther shared fully in the medieval ethos and outlook on sin, penance, death, and eternal life that is so evident in the descriptions of Oberman and Bainton. But, for Luther there developed a rather unexpected shift in outlook on these questions of death, guilt, and salvation over the course of the decade and a half that passed after his assumption of the monk's cowl and leading up to his protest against the sale of indulgences in October 1517. Intent at the start on pursuing the prescribed and customary course of confession and satisfaction for sin, a rigorous observance of obedience and penance, Luther began to ques-

12. Roland Bainton, *Here I Stand: A Life of Martin Luther* (Nashville: Abingdon Press, 1950), p. 33.

tion this whole system of salvation. Then, by 1519, in the aftermath of the Leipzig debate with John Eck, the latter a defender of the traditional ecclesiastical system of salvation, he came to recognize the grave possibility of his condemnation for heresy and the supposed loss of eternal salvation that such condemnation was believed to entail. With his excommunication by the papacy in Rome and then his hearing and condemnation at the imperial Diet of Worms in April and May of 1521, Luther faced not only exclusion from the sacraments and the apparent forfeiture of salvation but the threat of imminent death for heresy.

In light of this story the question should be asked: From such early beginnings in a common piety, with its concomitant fear of death and judgment, the concern for sin, and the quest for assurance of salvation, how did Luther, prior to the onset of Enlightenment "objectifying thought," come to break with this medieval Christian system of salvation — a break that was seen to have subsequent wide-ranging ramifications?

This matter, of course, has been a major theme in the long history of Luther scholarship, especially over the course of the last one hundred and more years.[13] The present study assumes much of this previous work, but proposes to view it in the special light of Luther's insufficiently noted critique, not always explicit, of medieval religious otherworldliness. This theological feature of Luther's work is, I believe, often overridden and obscured by the two counterbalancing, otherworldly motifs in his thought: apocalyptic expectation and the related concern, highlighted by Oberman, of Luther's struggle with the Devil. Whereas Oberman introduces his study of Luther with an account of widespread concerns over the nature and possible meaning of Luther's death, it is important to keep in mind his own second confrontation with death that came as a result of his public condemnation at the Diet of Worms — an existential point of no return that may have inspired Luther's later observation that as everyone must do his, or her, own dying so everyone at some point must do his, or her, own believing, a matter of faith and not simple "assent."

The point to be made in regard to this very existential question is that it is not enough to try to determine the step-by-step logical develop-

13. Gordon Rupp offers a helpful summary of Luther research up to the year 1951; see Gordon Rupp, *The Righteousness of God: Luther Studies* (London: Hodder & Stoughton, 1953), pp. 3-36.

ment, or progression, to his liberating understanding of justification by faith, his "reformation breakthrough," as it is often termed. Rather, it is important also to consider the progression to the Diet of Worms as an interactive faith/life progression and Worms as a point from which one may look back to a series of life/thought developments that made for a climactic moment at Worms. Rather than try to fix sequentially all the possible rational, logical steps — based almost exclusively on biblical insights — that led Luther to the Worms moment on the model of an unfolding idea that leads seemingly inevitably to his "Here I stand . . . ," one can argue that it was Luther's interactions with, and sense of responsibility before, the transcendent God revealed in the Scriptures and active in events around him and in his own life, that decisively defined his experience, helped to define and refine his theological perceptions, and led to his conclusive stand at Worms.

In relation to the Worms event a particular feature of Luther's experience at that point stands out and puzzles some scholars: the apparent moment of self-doubt, or uncertainty, which seems to have marked his request for a day's delay to consider/reconsider the ecclesiastical demand put to him at the end of the first day of the hearing, the demand in the presence and with the approbation of the emperor that he immediately recant his "heretical" views, this on the 17th of April, 1521. The historical theologian Martin Brecht describes this moment as follows: "[T]he request for time for thought provoked surprise even at that time, and it has continued to do so down to the present day. It has been surmised that what was behind it was either a sudden lack of Luther's nerve or a shrewd move of Electoral Saxon strategy."[14] Brecht himself reasons that the request for a day's delay is not so puzzling, that Luther had been prepared for a detailed questioning about his many writings and thus was not expecting the demand for a simple recantation of his views, a repudiation of all his "little books." (Luther previously had admitted to verbal excesses in responses to theological opponents.) But one must consider as well the weight of the emperor's presence and Luther's own regard for governmental rule along with his hope for reform by that means. Be that as it may, on the following day no hesitation or doubt was apparent in Luther. He refused to recant, insisting that he could not yield if he could

---

14. Martin Brecht, *Martin Luther: His Road to Reformation, 1483-1521*, trans. James Schaaf (Philadelphia: Fortress Press, 1985), p. 455.

not be proven in error on the basis of Scripture and a reasoned argument from Scripture — that his conscience was "captive to the Word of God."[15] One must note nonetheless that a few months later Luther seemed to have harbored some regrets that, on the advice of friends, he had held back in some of his early responses to questions at Worms, that he had not confronted, like Elijah, the idols he encountered there.[16]

Shortly after his departure from Worms on the 28th of April, Luther authored a letter to the emperor, Charles V. A copy of the letter was sent to the Imperial Estates, represented at the Diet by delegates from the imperial cities, three archbishops (from Mainz, Cologne, and Trier), and four elector-princes from the provinces of Saxony, Brandenburg, Bohemia, and the Palatinate. The Imperial Estates were part of the governance structure of the declining Holy Roman Empire. Luther's letter to the emperor was probably never passed on by Spalatin, court chaplain and advisor to Frederick the Wise of Saxony. The copies to the Imperial Estates, written in German, *were* however dispatched by Spalatin — and then the essentially same version to the emperor was published in both Latin and German and widely distributed. In the letter Luther recounted his position at Worms and expressed his understanding of the theological issues involved. Of special note was Luther's accent upon the freedom and sovereignty of God's Word in relation to the question of human salvation. But then too, Luther affirmed the need for obedience to established authority in all earthly political affairs and professed his willing obedience to the emperor in such things. He duly thanked the emperor for fulfilling the promise of safe conduct at Worms. A key paragraph in the letter reads:

> God, who searches the heart, will be my witness that I am definitely ready to comply with and obey Your Sacred Majesty, whether it bring me life or death, glory or shame, gain or loss. For I have often offered myself in this way, and now do so again. I make no exceptions save the Word of God, by which not only man lives, as Christ teaches in Matthew 4[:4], but which also the angels long to see, according to 1 Peter 1[:12]. Since [the Word of God] is *above everything, it has to be held absolutely free and unbound in all things, as*

---

15. Brecht, *Martin Luther,* p. 460.
16. Brecht, *Martin Luther,* p. 472.

Paul teaches. . . . [It] is never subject to any man's whim to lower its importance or challenge it, no matter how great, how numerous, how learned, and how holy the men are. This is true to such an extent that St. Paul in Galatians 1[:8] dares to exclaim and reiterate, "If we or an angel from heaven should preach to you a gospel [contrary to that which we preached to you] let him be accursed." And David says, "Put not your trust in princes, in children of men, in whom there is no help." Nor is anyone able to depend on himself, as Solomon says, "He who trusts in his own mind is a fool." And Jeremiah says, 17[:5], "Cursed is he who trusts in man."[17]

What is of note in this portion of Luther's letter to the emperor and the Imperial Estates is not only the reaffirmation of the need for the unrestricted proclamation of the gospel (Luther's understanding of God's gracious forgiveness, "justification by faith") in his evolving controversy with the medieval church, but, after Worms, the declaration that the secular powers and authorities also were confronted with a defining limit and responsibility in relation to the freedom of God's Word. A clear meaning of Luther's words at this point is that political authority is itself responsible before God in its exercise of power vis-à-vis the role and place of the Word of God in society. As Luther put it: the Word "has to be held absolutely free and unbounded in all things." Luther was saying at this point that the sovereign Word of God has no earthly overseer, that both the ecclesiastical institution and the political institution need to see themselves as servants of the Word, or at least agents for its free proclamation and preaching. What Luther does in this letter is subject traditional understandings of the relationship of church and state to necessary reconsideration of the greater sovereignty of a transcendent Word of God. The various levels of social, political, and ecclesiastical life were to be opened to a reality greater than human conventions, interpretations, and structures of power. Clearly, people who bear the responsibility of political office are confronted in Luther's "letter to the emperor" with an understanding of political loyalties and duties different from that prescribed under the medieval system of salvation.

Luther's steadfastness at Worms stemmed from his further discovery,

---

17. *Luther's Works* (Philadelphia: Fortress Press, 1955-1986), vol. 48, p. 206; emphasis added. *Luther's Works* hereafter cited as *LW*.

a developing matter with him, of the freedom of the Word of God — in this case, an awareness heightened by his immediate experience of the realities and forms of political power represented in the person of the emperor. Perhaps sobered, even awed at first, by regal presence and power, Luther could well have seen that his own, original personal struggle with guilt, along with his earlier 1517 critique of the ecclesiastical exploitation of indulgences, had developed in unexpected ways into an Old Testament prophetic-like confrontation, calling even kings and princes to account before God's Word. In this letter, Luther provided those in positions of political power an alternative understanding of responsibilities vis-à-vis ecclesiastical authorities, an alternative to the call to submission characteristic of the medieval church tradition, a tradition long carried through also in the church's judgment against heretics and the threat of death for those who failed to recant.[18]

A little more than a year earlier, Luther, in his treatise on the ban (excommunication),[19] had argued that the chief purpose of ecclesiastical power was that of admonition and correction, not punishment. Its purpose, as Luther put it, should be to seek only "the improvement of our neighbor, . . . [it] should stop short of his ruin or death."[20] In this earlier 1520 discussion of the ban, Luther placed accent upon a proper understanding of the ban's use not only by church authorities but also for those over whom it might be exercised. Then, in his later letter to the emperor and the Estates General, Luther inferred that an even greater responsibility of secular authority was to assure the preaching of free grace via God's Word. One can trace here some of the lines of upheaval that attached to the perception of a transcendent, sovereign God and a freely proclaimed Word — confined, even as it still was for Luther, within the scriptural parameters of obedience to governmental authority as expressed in the key passage of Romans 13:1-7.

The event that was Worms points ahead to the development of a later theory of resistance to imperial power by the princes and lesser magistrates of the various estates that shared the power of rule within the empire. The Middle Ages had before this produced theories of lim-

---

18. Cf. Thomas Aquinas, *Summa Theologica*, vol. 2 (New York: Benziger, 1947-1948), pp. 1226-27.

19. "A Sermon on the Ban," in *LW*, vol. 39 (1970), pp. 7-22.

20. *LW*, vol. 39, p. 9.

ited monarchy, but the period following the Diet of Worms gave rise to new thought and arguments on this question for those persuaded by the theological understandings and insights of Luther. Although resort was made earlier to the theories of the natural law and the views of the conciliarists,[21] a dimension of post-Worms legal and theological thought asserted the responsibilities of all who exercise political authority to make judgment to protect, make room for, a transcendent Word of God and also for a private religious sphere of life not subject to imperial dictate or control. While not espousing fully democratic political views which later grounded sovereignty in the will of the people (citizens still owed a religious duty to obey the authorities in all political matters), the Saxon jurists and theologians who were persuaded by Luther's understanding of the gospel argued increasingly, as did Luther, for an independent sphere of conscience and faith.[22] They saw in the elective, non-hereditary office of the emperor an institution of inherently limited power, one restricted by contractual obligations. For those princes and imperial cities drawn to Luther's views, the good of the general populace, their spiritual well-being, was bound up with assured access to the preaching and exposition of the Word of God. To be sure, emerging economic and political forces played a major role in the politics of this time. But, also at work and standing in contrast to the medieval sacramental system, a system that encompassed the whole course of human life from birth through marriage to death and then delivered the believer to the "life beyond," was Luther's call to faith in a salvation at hand, one efficacious in this life. At different levels, sometimes explicitly, sometimes more implicitly, "justification by faith" pried earthly life loose from the inherited, sacramentally ordered goal of salvation in the next life.[23]

21. The "conciliarists" were those who favored the authority of church councils over that of the papal office.

22. This definition of two realms, two "kingdoms," the outward political, social, and economic sphere and an inward personal, spiritual sphere, underlies much of Luther's and later Lutheran social ethics and is at the root of Niebuhr's characterization of the "Christ and culture in paradox" form of social thought. Critics of this line of theological-ethical thought have seen in it a problem of "political quietism," which, it is often argued, contributed to significant German Lutheran acquiescence in the Nazi years. See also p. 128, n. 22, below.

23. For example, in his treatise on "The Blessed Sacrament of the Holy and True Body of Christ, and the Brotherhoods" (1519) Luther declared that baptism "leads us into a new life on earth." *LW*, vol. 35 (1960), p. 67.

While in no way rejecting the hope of eternal life, Luther's understanding of faith involved an interplay of freedom and obedience that took on new, this-worldly meanings, some of them with inevitable political implications. Luther himself, with his expectations of an imminent end-time and his frequent embrace of suffering as a Christian response to oppressive political rule, only hesitantly accepted the idea of resistance to the "higher magistrates" by the "lesser magistrates," a view put forward ever more often by people around him.[24] Unlike the medieval rationales for tyrannicide, which generally allowed the removal of the tyrant by any means, then a return to the old order, the status quo ante, the theories of the Saxon jurists and those of theologians such as Johannes Bugenhagen and Martin Bucer pointed up the need for further discussion in these matters, for a reconceptualization of the nature and responsibilities of political power in the context of religious/theological developments. It was in Zurich, however, in the person of Ulrich Zwingli, and especially later in Geneva, with John Calvin, that these lines of thought were more fully pursued.[25] Luther himself, after Worms, devoted his thought and energies chiefly to the necessities of structuring an evangelical church body — a project not without its own political implications since it suggested that an assumedly sacred, divinely ordained ecclesial structure was open to change and refiguration on the basis of evangelical principles. In this light the question could also be asked: Why not also inherited political institutions? What is notable about Luther's later reflections on Worms was that, beyond his subsequent regret that he had not been forceful enough in the first day of the hearing, he did not also reconsider, or reinterpret, beyond Romans 13, some of the wider political ramifications of that event. His final words at Worms

---

24. Cynthia Schoenberger suggests that the anonymity of the friends of Luther favoring this view at the time "may be attributed to the fact that Luther was not himself convinced" on this point. See Cynthia Grant Schoenberger, "The Development of the Lutheran Theory of Resistance: 1523-1530," *Sixteenth Century Journal* 8 (1977): 71.

25. Schoenberger, "Lutheran Theory of Resistance," pp. 75-76. Schoenberger's 1977 discussion of a Lutheran "theory of resistance" points out that subsequent Reformed discussions around this resistance theme (the "lesser" vs. the "higher magistrates") in Calvin, the Huguenots, et al., were not the point of origin for this idea as many in the Reformed tradition have assumed. Not discussed in Schoenberger's otherwise careful analysis is Luther's own contagious articulation of "the freedom of the Word of God" in the face of imperial power, its implicit critique of political power even as Luther continued to accent the enjoinments of Romans 13:1-6 and prohibitions against the use of force by the general citizenry in political protest.

were, in the end, a signal affirmation of his earlier insights into, and discovery of, the nature of faith in God's grace. And this sustained and directed his future course.

In this context it is important to note also that patterns of reappraisal of previous experiences were evident in later reflections and assessments by Luther. The interaction between faith and events describes a dialectical development in Luther and not simply a linear one. An obvious example of retrospective revision was, of course, Luther's later perspective on his original decision to enter the monastery in quest of salvation. He came to regard that purpose as having been wrong. The historian Martin Brecht recounts Luther's subsequent reflections on this earlier decision: Luther, Brecht says, originally committed to the monastery with the intent "to become truly pious, to serve and obey God, something that could occur in a special way in the monastery. The reason for this service . . . was the concern for the salvation of one's soul. [Brecht quotes Luther:] 'I took the vow for the sake of my salvation.'"[26] Brecht notes that Luther later came to understand his decision to become a monk "not as a turning to, but as a turning away from, a demanding God."[27]

Another such event that underwent reappraisal was Luther's 1510 visit to Rome. Undertaken in its primary purpose as a political assignment on behalf of the Erfurt Augustinian chapter, Luther also embraced the journey to Rome as a spiritual pilgrimage. Over the course of his four-week stay in Rome Luther was able to visit all the major holy sites and undertake the spiritual exercises associated with those sites. He visited the seven major churches in the city — a one-day event prescribed for pilgrims. He visited the catacombs. Wherever possible he said masses at the holy sites. Some of these exercises were supposed to assure the release from purgatory of pre-deceased loved ones. "On his knees in the Lateran palace, Luther . . . climbed the stairs from Pilate's palace which were located there, saying the Our Father on each step."[28] Luther shared many of these common beliefs, though he expressed doubt at the time that the exercise of climbing the supposed steps of Pilate's palace was truly efficacious. During the visit Luther noted the great number of ill-

26. Brecht, *Martin Luther,* p. 49.
27. Brecht, *Martin Luther,* p. 50.
28. Brecht, *Martin Luther,* p. 103. Cf. Oberman, *Between God and the Devil,* pp. 146-47.

informed and virtually illiterate priests. He witnessed the luxury and extravagances of monasteries and cardinals' palaces and heard much about clerical immorality. For Luther these original negative reactions did not override the positive ones. He seems to have borne with some equanimity the manifest abuses, believing that one had to remain loyal to the church in order to accomplish reform within the church.[29] Again, the historian Martin Brecht says of Luther's visit to Rome: "The . . . [political] mission was a failure, the general confession was a disappointment, and the religious abuses could not be overlooked. However, there were the riches of grace in which he participated in Rome, and because of them the positive impression predominated. Only later did the critical and completely negative evaluation of the Roman experiences occur."[30]

The later, negative reappraisal is manifest in Luther's 1520 pamphlet *Address to the Christian Nobility of the German Nation.*[31] Beyond much question, Luther's increasing appreciation of the saving gift of righteousness through faith played the major role in his call for the nobility to take the lead in reforming the church. Luther scholarship has long viewed "justification by faith" as fundamental to the understanding of his reforming work. But also, there is the powerful influence on Luther of the scriptural passage in 1 Corinthians 1 that speaks of "the foolishness of God [that] is wiser than men, and the weakness of God [that] is stronger than men." The passage warrants quotation in full, for it plays an often neglected presence in Luther's theological perceptions, one that offers a distinctive statement of God's transcendence and one that colors as well the key Romans verse (1:17) which declares that "the righteous shall live by faith." The 1 Corinthians 1:18-25 passage reads as follows:

> For the word of the cross is folly to those who are perishing, but to us who are being saved it is the power of God. For it is written, "I will destroy the wisdom of the wise, and the cleverness of the clever I will thwart." Where is the wise man? Where is the scribe? Where is the debater of this age? Has not God made foolish the wisdom of the world? For since, in the wisdom of God, the world did not know God through wisdom, it pleased God through the folly of

29. Brecht, *Martin Luther,* p. 102.

30. Brecht, *Martin Luther,* p. 104. Cf. Oberman, *Between God and the Devil,* pp. 149-50.

31. *LW,* vol. 44 (1966), pp. 123-217.

what we preach to save those who believe. For Jews demand signs and Greeks seek wisdom, a stumbling block to Jews and folly to Gentiles, but to those who are called, both Jews and Greeks, Christ the power of God and the wisdom of God. For the foolishness of God is wiser than men, and the weakness of God is stronger than men.

This passage is a forceful statement of the transcendence of God as revealed in the cross. It draws upon key passages in the Hebrew Scriptures, such as that quoted in the text itself (Isa. 29:14), and applies them to Jesus' death on the cross as the expression of God's "foolish" wisdom. Heiko Oberman cites a portion of this passage in *Luther: Man between God and the Devil* and notes: "This passage was fundamental to Luther. Already a shaping factor in the exegetical work of his first Psalm lectures [in 1513], it was frequently referred to later on, and, in the form of theses presented with all its implications before his own order at the disputation in Heidelberg in 1518."[32] One could wish that Oberman had developed this important insight more fully. It is the case that this passage, as Oberman observes, informs a number of points in Luther's Heidelberg Disputation, points in which he associated the wisdom of the world with the works of the law (everyone's effort to secure his/her salvation through good works).[33] But it also informs Luther's attack upon the scholastic tradition — and upon Aristotle — in his 1517 *Disputation against Scholastic Theology*. There he writes: "It is a wrong thing to say that a man cannot become a theologian without Aristotle. . . . The truth is that a man cannot become a theologian unless he becomes one without Aristotle."[34]

Certainly the 1 Corinthians passage inspired Luther's criticism of the church at Rome in *Address to the Christian Nobility of the German Nation* — along with the passage in 1 Peter 2:9 which declares the whole of the believing community to be a royal priesthood. Much of the introductory theological section of the *Address* draws upon the Corinthians passage, and in the salutation to the German nobility Luther embraced the characterization of himself as a "fool" for the sake of Christ and the gospel. He writes:

32. Oberman, *Between God and the Devil*, pp. 257-58.
33. This is of note in Articles 18-25 of the Heidelberg Disputation; see *LW*, vol. 31 (1957), pp. 40-41.
34. *LW*, vol. 31, p. 12.

I am acting, I confess, as if there were no other in the world than Doctor Luther to play the part of a Christian, and give advice to people of culture and education. But I shall not apologize, no matter who demands it. Perhaps I owe God and the world another act of folly. For what it is worth, this pamphlet is an attempt to pay the debt as well as I can, even if I become for once a Court-fool. . . . A fool often says wise things and frequently sages speak very foolishly. St. Paul said: "If any wishes to be wise, he must become a fool" [1 Cor. 3:18].[35]

What informs much of the argument in the *Address* is Luther's conviction that the church at Rome had taken on most of the world's trappings of power. And, by making the claim of possessing Peter's keys (Matt. 16:19) the hierarchy of the church, in Luther's view, had come to exercise an unwarranted spiritual lordship over believers. By contrast, Luther argued that the keys of forgiveness are a possession common to the church as a whole — a gift to, and responsibility of, every Christian.[36]

A factor closely related to this reappraisal of the earlier Rome experience — and one that provided impetus to Luther's critique of the extravagances of the church at Rome — was a re-publication and translation into German, by Ulrich von Hutten, of Lorenzo Valla's 1440 exposé of the fraudulent "Donation of Constantine." The latter was an eighth- or ninth-century forged document, framed within the chancellery of the Vatican, which purported to be the bequest of the western half of the Roman Empire to Pope Sylvester I by the Emperor Constantine (280?-337). Luther read Hutten's translation of Valla's exposé in February of 1520, shortly after the debate with Eck. In the light of the 1 Corinthians 1 passage, this fixed in Luther's mind the sense of a betrayal in Rome of the crucified Christ. Oberman comments on this point:

Not until early 1520 did . . . [Luther] receive a copy of the newly published Hutten edition of . . . Valla's proof [of the forgery]. . . . The Donation of Constantine a fraud! This was more than the exposure of a brazen lie. It not only exacerbated the resentment the

35. The quote is from the Bertram Woolf 1953 translation of Luther's writings cited by John Dillenberger, Martin Luther, *Selections from his Writings* (Garden City, NY: Doubleday, Anchor Books, 1961), p. 404; cf. *LW*, vol. 44, pp. 123-24.

36. *LW*, vol. 44, pp. 133-35.

German nation already bore against Rome; it destroyed trust as well. By excluding emperors and kings, whole empires and countries from its communion through excommunication and interdict, the Church, hiding behind the cloak of law, had been leading man away from salvation in the name of God.[37]

Brecht observes on this same point, that after reading von Hutten's edition of Valla's exposé, Luther "was incensed about the centuries-long darkness and evil which had been enshrined in canon law as well, and he had virtually no more doubts that the pope was the expected antichrist."[38] In the *Address to the Christian Nobility of the German Nation* Luther wrote:

> An ordinary bishop's mitre ought to be good enough for the pope. It is in wisdom and holiness that he should be above his fellows. He ought to leave the crown of pride to Antichrist, as his predecessors did centuries ago. The Romanists say he [the pope] is a lord of the earth. That is a lie! For Christ, whose vicar and vicegerent he claims to be, said to Pilate, "My kingdom is not of this world" [John 18:36]. No vicar's rule can go beyond that of his lord. Moreover, he is not the vicar of Christ glorified but of Christ crucified. As Paul says, "I was determined to know nothing among you save Christ and him only as the crucified" [1 Cor. 2:2] and in Philippians 2[:5-7], "This is how you should regard yourselves, as you see in Christ, who emptied himself and took upon himself the form of a servant." Or again in I Corinthians 1[:23], "We preach Christ, the crucified."[39]

Apparent in Luther's critique of the structure and ethos of the medieval church is the sense of the transcendent revaluation of values that is conveyed in the 1 Corinthians 1 passage of Scripture. It is an ambiguous affirmation of otherworldliness — Christ's kingdom is "not of this world," but at the same time it confronts this world with the judgment of the cross. While Luther's oft-characterized "theology of the cross" most often enjoined the quietism of suffering in the face of injustice and abuse, it also, at the same time, inspired resistance to abusive pride in its

---

37. Oberman, *Between God and the Devil*, p. 261.
38. Brecht, *Martin Luther*, p. 346.
39. *LW*, vol. 44, p. 140.

many earthly manifestations. In the *Address* Luther focused the criticism engendered by the foolishness of the cross upon the excesses of ecclesiastical power and appealed to Christian princes to become agents of reform in the church. Later, among Luther's Saxon jurists and especially among the later partners in faith of the Geneva reformers, the lines of judgment, addressed to the social-political order, were gradually more sharply drawn, more fully explored.[40]

If Luther's view of his earlier 1510 experiences in Rome underwent significant revision in his later discernments of faith, this movement can be traced as well in another event and critical decision in Luther's life: his 1512 assignment by his abbot, von Staupitz, to study for the doctor of theology degree in preparation to become a professor of Bible at the University of Wittenberg. Luther had proven to be an able student while at the monastery in Erfurt; and, shortly after his ordination as a priest in April 1507, he began more formal theological studies, receiving the bachelor's degree in Bible in March 1509. Not long after that he took examinations for the bachelor's degree in theology, a step that involved giving expository lectures on Peter Lombard's *Sentences,* the basic theological textbook of the medieval church. These lectures were presented at the Erfurt Augustinian monastery over the course of the following year, interrupted by his November 1510 mission to Rome. It was after his return from Rome and a temporary assignment to teach at the university in Wittenberg that von Staupitz moved to have Luther prepare for the doctoral degree in order to qualify as professor of Bible at Wittenberg, an assignment Luther at first resisted.

During his earlier years at the monastery Luther had shown deep interest in the Bible as he sought answers to his many doubts and anguished spiritual struggles *(Anfechtungen)*. He found in the Psalms not only many answers to his personal struggles but also, at times, an intensification of others. Overall, however, Luther came to see that the Bible offered the clearest answers to his *Anfechtungen*. He described "this process as the coming of Christ who opened the Bible for the troubled one and bestowed comfort and counsel with his Word."[41] From von Staupitz Luther learned that comfort could come only through a sense of humility and openness to the word of Scripture. Martin Brecht com-

40. This point will be discussed more fully in Chapter 4, below.
41. Brecht, *Martin Luther,* p. 88.

ments on this development: "Here was an impetus [in Luther's monastic years] which lay outside a theoretical study of the Bible and one that was nourished from a deeper source than the reading of learned commentaries. . . . Here significant perspectives were already arising, ones which later emerged as a Reformation."[42] The yield came in Luther's recognition — a question remains whether in stages or in a more signal "breakthrough" — of a transcendent message of grace and healing, one that did not arise from an inner human intuition but came as a Word from God, spoken and heard, one that was fixed in the heart.

In Luther one notes a distinctive recognition of the authority of Scripture in an unresolved tension between certainty and openness, akin to the previously mentioned interplay in Luther between freedom and obedience.[43] His insistence that the message of the gospel, the word of forgiveness and justification, constituted the very basis of faith and was conjoined with recognition that the hearing and understanding of that same message was always an event, a happening, a hearing by formerly deaf ears, through the agency of the Holy Spirit. In remarking on Luther's openness to advice in his projects of translating Scripture, Oberman writes of this self-critical feature in Luther:

> The open-ended and thus necessarily common search for the right translation [did] not preclude certainty of faith, nor [did] trust in the Word of God make critical study of the text superfluous. The Scriptures do not reveal themselves to everyone in the same way, and many a [person] gets lost in them, as Luther explains in the vivid words of Pope Gregory: "An elephant drowns in this sea [of Scripture]; a lamb that is looking for Christ and perseveres, stands on firm ground and reaches the other side." It is not he who knows everything but he who allows himself to be guided that finds solid footing in the Bible.[44]

The way to Luther's final testimony before the Diet and the emperor at Worms followed from this course of encounter with Scripture, from

---

42. Brecht, *Martin Luther,* p. 88. Brecht does not generally integrate correlation of Luther's internal spiritual struggles with the concreteness of past and present historical experiences (e.g., the Rome visit) as here proposed.

43. See above, pp. 98-100.

44. Oberman, *Between God and the Devil,* pp. 308-9.

the 1512 decision by von Staupitz — and Luther — that he prepare for a Bible professorship. For Luther instruction and profession became inseparable: "Unless I am convinced by the testimony of the Scriptures or by clear reason (for I do not trust either in the pope or in councils alone, since it is well known that they have often erred and contradicted themselves), I am bound by the Scriptures I have quoted and my conscience is captive to the Word of God. I cannot and I will not retract anything, since it is neither safe nor right to go against conscience. May God help me. Amen."[45]

These words by Luther at Worms in April 1521 point to a personal reality for Luther, the reality that in treating the Scriptures one is confronted with a transcendent God who, as in the cross, challenges the wisdom of the world and simultaneously offers grace and forgiveness. Luther understood his own salvation and the promise of the gospel to be fixed in the message of Scripture — a message that is not innate in humankind or known "by nature."[46] Gerhard Ebeling, in a 1964 study of Luther's thought, offered assessment of this Scripture-based theology:

> [Here] a theology came into being which was not merely new by normal standards, but overwhelmed the force of . . . [hundreds of] years of tradition. Luther's . . . [fresh] understanding of the word of God, the sacraments, the Church, moral action and secular authority left no part of life untouched. An upheaval of this nature cannot be the product of uncommitted theoretical speculation; nor can it be the product of revolutionary activity. . . . Rather, it is the putting into effect of a theological thinking so involved in its subject that to carry it out means the endurance of struggles of conscience, the risking and accepting of unavoidable decisions, and the total commitment of one's personal existence in the form of a theology which is lived existentially.[47]

Ebeling might well have added: all made understandable and concrete only in the awareness of a transcendent God.

A final example of the vital interplay of events and faith perception

45. *LW*, vol. 32 (1958), pp. 112-13; cf. Brecht, *Martin Luther*, p. 460 and p. 537, n. 24.
46. On this point, compare Brecht, *Martin Luther*, pp. 460-61.
47. Gerhard Ebeling, *Luther: An Introduction to His Thought*, trans. R. A. Wilson (Philadelphia: Fortress Press, 1970), pp. 32-33.

in Luther is the debate between Luther and John Eck at Leipzig, June 27
to July 16, 1519. It is the occasion that led up to Luther's aforementioned
reading of Lorenzo Valla's exposé of the "Donation of Constantine." As
a further example of Luther's theology in motion and its grounding in
life situations, the debate with Eck warrants fuller elaboration as a theological lead-up to the later "hearing" at Worms.

Luther was joined in the debate by his Wittenberg colleague Andreas
Carlstadt, but the debate fell out chiefly between Luther and Eck. The
originating event, of course, was Luther's earlier posting of the ninety-
five theses. The Leipzig debate, however, brought Luther even greater
public attention and elicited further church concerns about his further
criticisms of other traditional practices and beliefs, questions about penance, purgatory, and the power of the papal office to remit the sins of
people in purgatory. It is certain that the church authorities in Rome
came to see Luther's growing criticism as a basic assault upon the
church's "spiritual powers." For Luther, however, at least through 1518
and probably up to the debate with Eck, his effort was that of "a faithful
son of the church," seeking chiefly reform of some of its practices, a reform inspired by Luther's Bible-centered understanding of faith. He regarded the pope with respect and still held him in honor as a lead authority in the church. But he had also come more and more to see the
Scriptures as the nurturing source of faith in the context of an expanding
life situation and not only as a personal spiritual guide. Prior to the debate and leading up to Worms, Luther seems to have seen developments
as an outgrowth of his own spiritual quest, as they no doubt were. But
he also increasingly saw his questions as an occasion and call for discussion of a broadening array of issues within the church — in debate not
only with his own growing list of critics but also calling for fuller discussion, even by a church council if need be. Over the course of an escalating exchange of written views, Luther entertained appeal as well to political authorities for the calling of a council, a view that came to the fore
as his own condemnation by papal authorities seemed ever more likely.

In a letter to von Staupitz, on May 18, 1518, only seven months after
posting the ninety-five theses and a month after the Heidelberg disputation, Luther gave account of how he came to his controversial stand,
offering elaboration on key points. With this letter to von Staupitz he
enclosed a copy of *Explanations of the Theses Concerning the Value of
Indulgences,* an explication and expansion of the indulgence theses

and a work that Luther addressed to the pope. He asked von Staupitz to forward the *Explanations*[48] to the pope in the hope of gaining wider discussion and also as a counter to the attacks made against him after the original indulgence theses were printed and widely distributed. Von Staupitz, in attendance at the Heidelberg disputation a few weeks earlier, had pressed Luther to offer an elaboration and explanation of the theses, something he had already begun but had set aside to prepare for the Heidelberg discussion.

The May 18th letter to von Staupitz is important because it spells out Luther's spiritual indebtedness to his former prior and the crucial guidance provided by von Staupitz in helping to fix direction for Luther's spiritual/theological journey. In the letter Luther attributed to von Staupitz the formative insight that trust in the love and forgiveness of God must precede the act of penance, otherwise all atoning acts would tend to be done either grudgingly or fearfully. Luther wrote:

> Reverend Father: I remember that during your most delightful and helpful talks, through which the Lord Jesus wonderfully consoled me, you sometimes mentioned the term *"poenitentia."* I was then distressed by my conscience and by the tortures of those who through endless and insupportable precepts teach the so-called method of confession. Therefore I accepted you as a messenger from heaven when you said that *poenitentia* is genuine only if it begins with love for justice and for God and that what they [most teachers in the church] consider to be the final state and completion is in reality rather the very beginning of *poenitentia*.[49]

In the *Explanations* Luther stated the point as follows: "The people must first be taught faith in Christ, the gracious bestower of remission. Then they must be persuaded to despair of their own contrition and satisfaction so that, when they have been strengthened by confidence and joy of heart over the compassion of Christ, they finally may despise sin cheerfully, become contrite, and make satisfaction."[50] Luther made the point in the following phrasing: "Without doubt good works are the outward fruits of penance and of the Spirit, although the Spirit makes no

48. This work of Luther is also referred to as the "Resolutions."
49. *LW,* vol. 48, p. 65.
50. *LW,* vol. 31, p. 103.

sound except that of the turtle-dove, that is, the groaning of the heart which is the root of good works."[51]

The *Ninety-Five Theses,* and especially the *Explanations,* introduced issues broaching questions of spiritual power and authority within the church. It is apparent that von Staupitz at a later time was unable to follow Luther along other avenues which he himself had helped open up to Luther.[52] This was the case especially in matters having to do with the demarcation of those spheres of spiritual power and authority belonging to the church in distinction from those belonging to God — and also with Luther's refusal to accede to ecclesiastical, institutional command of the nature, means, and extent of God's grace. In the situation in which official dogma on purgatory had yet to be defined — a step taken by Rome only over the course of the dispute with Luther and pronounced in November 1518,[53] it seemed untenable to Luther that persons in ecclesiastical office should claim power to determine satisfactions for sins, satisfactions extended previously by canon law beyond death.

In the original theses and in the *Explanations,* Luther maintained that for the papacy and its supporters to claim the right to forgive the sins of the dead and to fix penalties beyond death was a usurpation of God's own powers. It represented an abridgment of divine transcendence — a projection of this-worldly powers and authority beyond this world, into the realm of God's final, graceful, and just determinations. Luther wrote in the *Explanations:* "Surely the church would act wickedly if by its inferior jurisdiction it should retain one whom God [at death] already calls before his highest tribunal. When does the pope allow a defendant to be bound by the laws and rules of the inferior jurisdiction of a bishop or prelate after he has been summoned to appear before his own jurisdiction? Or does he require something from his subordinates which he himself, being a man, does not concede to God who is his superior?"[54]

In early May 1518, Luther still affirmed a doctrine of purgatory and

51. *LW,* vol. 31, p. 87.

52. See *LW,* vol. 48, p. 64, n. 1 for a brief description of von Staupitz's relationship with Luther; cf. also Brecht, *Martin Luther,* pp. 251-58 for the circumstances attending von Staupitz's release of Luther from his monastic vows following the latter's October 1518 audience with Cardinal Cajetan.

53. Brecht, *Martin Luther,* p. 261.

54. *LW,* vol. 31, p. 115.

accepted the practice of granting indulgences, but only on the condition of faith by the recipient and only for penance and punishments applied in this life.[55] In the *Explanations* Luther attacked the papacy's long-standing claim to spiritual power and authority associated with the concept of "the keys," a reference to the scriptural passage in Matthew 16:19 in which Jesus said to Peter: " 'I will give you the keys of the kingdom of heaven, and whatever you bind on earth shall be bound in heaven, and whatever you loose on earth shall be loosed in heaven.' " Luther leveled at least four scriptural and "reasonable" arguments against what had become the understanding and common practice of "the keys" in the church. First, he reasoned exegetically that the meaning of the passage is not "whatever you shall have loosed either in heaven or on earth, shall be loosed" because the meaning of the passage, as suggested above, is that only temporal remission and punishment of sin are confirmed in heaven (forgiveness is an earthly human responsibility and gift). God's own special judgments still obtain in this life and especially beyond the grave.[56] For example, *God's* chastisement in this life is still a means of correction and instruction for the people of God, as evidenced by much of the Old Testament record, especially in the work of the prophets. Also, Christ's teaching about the "unforgivable sin" against the Holy Spirit (Matt. 12:31) is unaltered by any gift of the keys. Luther writes that the meaning of the keys passage is that "whatever you loose, shall be loosed, although you shall not loose everything that is bound, but only that which is bound by you, not that which is bound by me. . . . Christ purposely added the words 'on earth' to restrict the power of the keys to earth, for he knew that otherwise they would perforate heaven itself."[57]

A second delimitation of the power of the keys, as Luther saw it, was that true penance is dependent upon faith in God's grace, the atoning power of Christ's death on the cross. Since no one knows the full extent of one's own sin, penance and the fixing of punishments has its limits in God's own knowledge of each human heart, a knowledge that escapes the full command even of the penitent one. Never knowing the full extent of sin in the heart, a person is unable fully to confess the depth of

---

55. Even in March 1521 Luther remained open to a belief in purgatory, though not as an established doctrine of the church and necessary for salvation; see *LW*, vol. 32, pp. 95-96.

56. *LW*, vol. 31, p. 93.

57. *LW*, vol. 31, p. 93.

alienation from God. Thus each soul is ultimately brought to rely on the sufficiency of Christ's atoning work. Faith, for Luther, is the only possible response to the transcendent love of God revealed in the cross and revelatory of the depth of human sin. Something of the scope of the gospel message was expressed in the first of Luther's ninety-five theses of 1517: "When our Lord and Master Jesus Christ said, 'Repent' [Matt. 4:17], he willed the entire life of believers to be one of repentance."[58] This point was developed further in the twenty-eighth thesis of the Heidelberg Disputation in April 1518: "The love of God does not find, but creates, that which is pleasing to it. [By contrast] the love of man comes into being through that which is pleasing to it."[59] What Luther was saying in this Heidelberg formulation is that God loves humankind in spite of the lack of each individual's understanding of the depth of his/her own sin. In loving the sinner, one incapable of fully "confessing" sin in ecclesiastical, confessional terms (with all attendant penalties), God creates a distinctive and unique loveliness in the sinner, something alien by nature to humankind. In this twenty-eighth thesis of the Heidelberg Disputation Luther argued against the philosophical (Aristotelian) part of the thesis that would equate human love, a love inspired by the value of the thing loved, with God's love for the sinner. As Luther put it: "[S]inners are attractive because they are loved; they are not loved because they are attractive."[60] As described above, such a godly, transcendent love qualifies the individual's capacity for penance and calls for a faith relationship that moves beyond the indexing of particular trespasses, a practice basic to the traditional confessional and associated with the evolved, ecclesiastical practice of the keys.

This second critique of the keys led on to a third, stated most clearly by Luther in a later 1519 "Sermon on the Sacrament of Penance," a sermon delivered at the time of the Leipzig debate with Eck. The keys of forgiveness, Luther declared, are a gift by Christ and God to the whole church, laity and ecclesiastics alike. They are not restricted to high office within the church. Beyond what the church allows for baptism by the laity under special conditions, the forgiveness afforded by the gift of the keys is a possibility and possession of the entire body of believers. As

58. *LW,* vol. 31, p. 25.
59. *LW,* vol. 31. p. 57.
60. *LW,* vol. 31, p. 57.

Luther put it in 1520: "[T]he keys are given only for the sake of the sacrament of penance, which is the common property of all Christians. No one has a greater or smaller part in it, save in proportion to his faith,"[61] a point made more tentatively earlier in the *Explanations*.[62]

Luther's fourth departure from, and criticism of, then-current church practice and belief in the keys was the suggestion — not the assertion — that despair and the fear of death in this life have virtual equivalency to hell and purgatory in the next life. While this point repeats Luther's understanding of the this-worldly limits of the power of the keys, it goes beyond that point by suggesting that rather than the keys "perforating," or breaching, heaven, it is the reality of a transcendent God that accents confrontation with the actualities of the present life. Without absolutizing this life as the measure of God, Luther felt compelled to raise questions about a fearful fantasizing of purgatory and hell as distortions of the human situation in the present. The sixteenth of the ninety-five theses reads as follows: "Hell, purgatory, and heaven seem to differ the same as despair, fear, and assurance of salvation." The fourteenth and fifteenth theses which precede this thesis read: "Imperfect piety or love on the part of the dying person necessarily brings with it great fear; and the smaller the love, the greater the fear," and "This fear or horror is sufficient in itself, to say nothing of other things, to constitute the penalty of purgatory, since it is very near the horror of despair."[63]

To use a contemporary term, what Luther suggested here was a "demythologizing" of the imagined punishments of the "other world" in order to address realistically the human condition in this world. Existential clarity about the human situation vis-à-vis God was set against humanly projected terrors of the next life, terrors used to enhance the ec-

---

61. *LW,* vol. 32, p. 51. It is of note that in response to the situation posed by the recent scandal of sexual abuse of children within the Catholic Church — also the concealment of that abuse by members of the hierarchy, Pope Benedict XVI, on a visit to the United States in 2008, apologized to representative victims of the abuse (see *New York Times,* April 18, 2008, sect. A, p. 1). In line with Luther's point that forgiveness is a gift to and for the whole church, one could ask whether the pope might better have sought forgiveness for complicit hierarchy and priesthood *from* the abused, rather than simply apologizing *to* them. The same apology *to* victims, rather than asking forgiveness *from* the victims, seems to have been repeated on Pope Benedict's later visit to Australia.

62. *LW,* vol. 31, pp. 156-57.

63. *LW,* vol. 31, pp. 26-27.

clesiastical power of the keys at the expense of the proclamation of the gospel of free grace. It was these issues that Luther had begun to explore in one form or another and brought to the Leipzig debate with Eck in June/July of 1519. Again, Luther still regarded himself a faithful son of the church and still held the pope in high regard.[64] He believed that many of the issues he was raising lay in still un- or ill-defined areas and were at a distance from those essential to faith and salvation in New Testament terms. For the most part he believed his accent upon scriptural authority was in no way alien to the essential tradition and the views of major figures among the church fathers. He went to the Leipzig debate with an increasingly articulate criticism of then-current understandings of the power of the keys, a critique founded upon his own growing conviction about the core message of the New Testament. In the course of the Leipzig debate with the tactician Eck, Luther was effectively linked by Eck to the views of previously condemned heretics, John Hus (1374-1415) and John Wyclif (1320-1384). The former was convicted of heresy by the Council of Constance in 1415 and burned at the stake in spite of the assurance of safe conduct. Wyclif, who had died thirty years earlier, was also condemned at Constance, excommunicated, and his bones ordered exhumed and burned.

Eck's persuasive effort at aligning Luther with previously condemned heretics was the accepted theological means of cornering and suppressing views regarded as erroneous and as threat to the church's spiritual authority. Oberman, in a 1966 work, *Forerunners of the Reformation,* described this established procedure as the "search for the tail of . . . [heresy's] many-headed Hydra." He writes: "The medieval method of doctrinal investigation, whether executed by a papal or academic committee or at a later date by means of the Inquisition, can be characterized as 'the search for the tail,' that is, the effort to reduce the particularity of any given teaching or teacher to one of the known or previously condemned types of heresy."[65] This was a central purpose of Eck in the debate. He was able in debate to link Luther with Hus's "heresy." Along with the latter's emphasis on biblical authority in criticism of church teaching, Hus was condemned for teaching that the laity should be full

---

64. See Oberman, *Between God and the Devil,* pp. 246-47.

65. Heiko Oberman, *Forerunners of the Reformation: The Shape of Late Medieval Thought Illustrated by Key Documents* (Philadelphia: Fortress Press, 1966, 1981), p. 26.

participants in the eucharist and receive both elements of bread and wine, a matter that Luther had not, to that point, addressed. Hus was condemned as well for criticizing then-current beliefs about purgatory.

Obviously there were points of affinity between the views of Hus and Luther, an observation made earlier by Tetzel, the purveyor of indulgences, and also by Sylvester Prierias,[66] a papal court theologian. But Luther seems not fully to have noted the many commonalities he shared with Hus until these were underlined by Eck and later critics. Luther actually diverged from the views of Hus at important points, especially from Hus's emphasis upon a Christian life grounded in strict moral discipline, a rigorous works-righteousness that fell short of Luther's accent upon grace and faith. All this became clearer to Luther after the Eck debate, when he was sent a copy of Hus's treatise *De ecclesia* (On the church) by a member of the Bohemian Hussite community. Upon reading it, he wrote to Georg Spalatin in February 1520: "I have taught and held all the teachings of John Hus, but thus far did not know it. John Staupitz has taught it in the same unintentional way. In short we all are Hussites and did not know it. . . . I am so shocked that I do not know what to think when I see such terrible judgments of God over mankind, namely, that the most evident evangelical truth was burned in public and was already considered condemned more than one hundred years ago."[67] From this point on Luther stressed, in principle, that the church had no power of the keys to punish heresy beyond an exclusion from the earthly fellowship of the church: he argued that the church had no right to compel belief by means of the threat of death. Luther moved, in encounter and debate, from the earlier questions posed in the indulgence controversy, to questions about the church's extension of its spiritual powers beyond this life to purgatory and God's sovereign rule. After Leipzig he denied that the church had any justifiable power to coerce faith: faith was this life's only viable response to the transcendent message of the grace of God.

Further fallout from the Leipzig debate was manifested in an ever more heated resort to polemics on the part of both Luther and his ecclesiastical critics. This reflected growing awareness on Luther's part that doctrinal reform within the church was increasingly unlikely as his own

66. Brecht, *Martin Luther*, pp. 208-9.
67. *LW*, vol. 48, p. 153.

condemnation for heresy became more likely. Certainly a factor in the polemical extremes of these exchanges was the public nature of the debates made possible by the development of the printing press some sixty or seventy years before the outbreak of the indulgence controversy. The reserve of civility and forbearance was difficult to maintain in dispute of issues perceived to be so theologically pressing and crucial. The line between public matters and private belief was not well drawn at a time when religion was viewed as an essential source of social stability and cohesion. Luther was prone to excoriate his opponents, even those of more moderate inclination — one example: the court cleric and humanist Jerome Emser. But from the start the issues were such that the people at large were caught up in the controversy and were in turn publicly addressed. They were drawn into the discussions often via illustrated pamphlets when literacy was still quite limited among the general populace.[68]

The three-week debate with Eck at Leipzig, in June and July of 1519, forced Luther to recognize that even appeal to a church council might not resolve the issues that had grown out of the indulgence dispute, though he continued to entertain that hope. The fate of John Hus at the Council of Constance — and Luther's post-Leipzig realization of his own shared views with an "evangelical" Hus — heightened his sense of a destructive, demonic distortion of the church's proper focus and duties. Earlier Luther had thought that the church needed simply to proclaim a message of forgiveness and refrain from imposing and extending beyond death penalties and "satisfactions" for earthly sins. With his January 1520 reading of von Hutten's republication of Lorenzo Valla's exposé of the forged "Donation of Constantine," Luther came to regard the papal church's claim to secular power as a betrayal of its gospel-preaching mission. The hundred-year suppression of Hus's evangelical preaching, Luther's puzzlement that God should have allowed it, was now compounded by a seven- to eight-hundred year deceit in the church's claim to oversee and even exercise secular rule. In the light of the critical passage in 1 Corinthians 1, which spoke of the weakness and foolishness of God, the offense of the cross which is "stronger and wiser

---

68. See John W. Cook's 1984 Paine Lecture, "Picturing Theology: Martin Luther and Lucas Cranach," on the role of art in Luther's reform: *Art and Religion: Faith, Form and Reform*, ed. Osmund Overby (Columbia: University of Missouri-Columbia, 1986), pp. 22-39, esp. p. 39.

than men," Luther became convinced that there existed within the church a destructive counter-agency, the work of the Devil.[69] Thereafter, his characterization of the excesses of papal power as the work of the Antichrist found growing expression in his writings, even while he allowed that the pope himself was largely a victim of the destructive counsel of curial advisors and "flatterers."

In the context of the Leipzig debate and its subsequent fallout, the key writings of 1520, *Address to the Christian Nobility of the German Nation* [70] and *The Babylonian Captivity of the Church,* marked the widening of the breach between Luther's movement of reform and the opposition to that reform on the part of the church establishment and hierarchy. What had begun as a criticism of current practice within the church, the indulgences issue, had broadened into the second, very large issue of the nature and source of power and authority within the church. In *The Babylonian Captivity,* published October 6, 1520, Luther utilized the historical, biblical image of Israel's captivity at the hands of a pagan invading power to suggest that the church's overreaching pursuit of power was an expression of its bondage to an alien spiritual power and a simultaneous betrayal of the message of the cross. In elaborating his critique of the medieval church's sacramental system, Luther pointed to the encroachments, often through popular religious practice and superstition, that had been condoned and exploited by the institutional church and then incorporated into its beliefs and practices. The growth of ceremony and ritual was a special vehicle of accommodation to popular religious inclinations and was frequently also the source of economic gain by the church. The sale of indulgences was certainly one such example, but the increasingly widespread medieval and profitable use of private

69. Although Oberman's assertion of the importance of the Devil in Luther's theology provides light in understanding the historical Luther, it is argued here that Luther's reading of Valla's exposé of the "Donation of Constantine" inspired new insight and a hermeneutical shift from a largely personal, subjective perception of the Devil and the Devil's work to a critique of, and interaction with, a perceived extra-subjective social-ecclesial world. This involved a shift also in an understanding of 1 Corinthians 1 primarily from an enjoinment to humility in the sense of Philippians 2:1-11 (the self-emptying "kenosis" passage) in the direction of prophet-like, social-ecclesial engagement. It represents, in Luther, the rejection of the medieval spiritual injunction that obedience should be viewed as the highest form of humility. Cf. Heiko Oberman, *The Reformation: Roots and Ramifications,* trans. Andrew C. Gow (Edinburgh: T. & T. Clark, 1994), pp. 53-75, esp. pp. 66-68.

70. Discussed above, see pp. 80-83.

masses for the dead was also singled out by Luther as an abuse and distortion of the New Testament message. In *The Babylonian Captivity,* Luther underlined the argument that the growth of "tradition," frequently a response to popular beliefs and motivations, along with ceremonies that cultivated the sense of mystery and anxiety about the other world, served as a means for the domestication of divine transcendence and the subversion of the message of grace. In criticizing aspects of the church's practice of the eucharist, Luther wrote:

> [W]e must be particularly careful to put aside whatever has been added to its original simple institution by the zeal and devotion of men: such things as vestments, ornaments, chants, prayers, organs, candles, and the whole pageantry of outward things. We must turn our eyes and hearts simply to the institution of Christ and this alone, and set nothing before us but the very word of Christ by which he instituted the sacrament, made it perfect, and committed it to us. For in that word, and in that word alone, reside the power, the nature, and the whole substance of the mass.[71]

Luther reiterated this concern for cultural accretions at other points in *The Babylonian Captivity.*[72] But most notably, toward the end of his life in 1545, he observed in his famous "Preface to the Latin Writings" that "[h]ere, in my case, you may also see how hard it is to struggle out of and emerge from errors which have been confirmed by the example of the whole world and have by long habit become a part of nature, as it were. How true is the proverb, 'It is hard to give up the accustomed,' and, 'Custom is second nature.' How truly Augustine says, 'If one does not resist custom, it becomes a necessity.'"[73] And then Luther added a word that identifies the source of his critical perspective: "I had then already read and taught the sacred Scriptures for seven years, so that I knew them nearly all by memory. I had also acquired the beginning of the knowledge of Christ and faith in him, i.e., not by works but by faith in Christ are we made righteous and saved."[74] And he concluded his re-

71. *LW,* vol. 36 (1959), p. 36.

72. *LW,* vol. 36, pp. 41, 49, 50; cf. also Luther's rejection of the allegorical method of biblical interpretation in favor of the text's literal meaning, pp. 30-31.

73. *LW,* vol. 34 (1960), p. 334.

74. *LW,* vol. 34, p. 334.

marks with an observation about the papacy, enjoining the need to distinguish between God and the Devil. (Here, it is necessary again, to underline the suggestion, made above, that the criterion crucial to Luther's distinction between God and the works of the Devil was provided by the cross and its this-worldly transvaluation of the world's values in the I Corinthians I passage, the contrast of God's foolishness and weakness with the assumed wisdom and power of the world. God's Word stood in judgment upon the world's canons of power and wisdom.)

In his October 1520 treatise on the "Babylonian" ("pagan") captivity, Luther made three further points in the course of his challenge to medieval ritual/ceremonial developments. He argued against the observance of seven sacraments in favor of two: Baptism and the Lord's Supper. These he viewed as alone instituted and enacted by Jesus. In a discussion of the nature of a sacrament, Luther offered what he regarded as the two essential characteristics of "sign and promise," an action and a defining word, the latter not an incantation but always an invitation to a response of faith — without which the sacrament was a mere spectacle, however mysterious and awe-inspiring. Second, he strongly affirmed Baptism and the Lord's Supper as expressions of the gospel message of promise, signs of assurance of the forgiveness of sins. In affirming infant baptism — and the baptism of adults as well — Luther underlined the theological point that the individual brings nothing of merit to the rite but is essentially a passive recipient of God's acceptance, God's free grace, the acceptance/possibility of a second birth and a life of faith lived in God's presence.

A third point comes in Luther's discussion of the Last Supper. Here he strongly asserted a basic egalitarian motif by insisting that the laity is in no way inferior to the clergy and should share in the full sacrament of both bread and wine, very like the Hussite understanding condemned at the Council of Constance but tolerated by the Council of Basel (1431-1449). In discussion of the eucharist, Luther rejected the conception of the mass as a sacrifice offered by the priesthood on behalf of the people, even when viewed as a gifted ritual for the forgiveness of sin. For Luther this development in the practice/belief of the church represented a reversal of the scriptural representation of the believer as the recipient of an abiding, personal grace, received in faith, rather than as a liturgical, institutionalized good work offered from the human side to God. Such a practice meant, for Luther, abandonment of the sufficiency of the one act of God in Christ on the cross, an act received and apprehended in faith and determinative for the life of the believer. The medieval practice of the eucharist was, for Luther, a repetitive form of penance, a good work aimed at securing the next life, the substitution of a priestly function for the proclamation of a gospel message made effective through faith and the work of the Holy Spirit. As previously noted, while in no way denying the promise of eternal life for the believer, Luther insisted that the gospel message was, in the first instance, affirmative of every individual's life in this world. The affirmation of spiritual equality and Christian freedom in this life were, for Luther, the outgrowth of a rediscovery of divine transcendence and divine love, realities that could not be contained by an ecclesiastical structure and sacramental system dominated by concern for the next life, a system increasingly reflective of accretions over the years of "spiritual" anxieties arising out of the fragility of human life as such.

In November 1520, about a month after publishing *The Babylonian Captivity of the Church,* Luther added another "little book" to his publications of the year 1520. In this third treatise, *The Freedom of a Christian,* Luther offered a summary statement of his understanding of the Christian life and sent it on to Rome with an accompanying open letter to Pope Leo X. Dedicated to the pope, this work was Luther's last effort to work out conciliation with Rome. It is by far Luther's most electric work, likely his most influential. In it he developed and stressed his understanding of Christian liberty, a theme already broached in *The Babylonian Captivity.* He also treated further the theme of the priesthood of all believers. In relation to its primary subject the work is especially significant for decoupling Christian ethics from its traditional medieval, otherworldly goal. Luther startled his sixteenth-century readers with the view that Christian ethics is essentially a believer's joyful response to the message of a graceful God, not the means — via obedience to a hierarchically structured church — of securing a blessed place in the next life. The substance of Christian freedom, as described by Luther, is the spontaneous and creative response of the believer to the neighbor in need, a response without thought of reward. In a notable passage in *The Freedom of a Christian* Luther wrote:

> Therefore, if we recognize the great and precious things which are
> given us, as Paul says [Rom. 5:5], our hearts will be filled by the

Holy Spirit with the love which makes us free, joyful, almighty workers and conquerors over all tribulations, servants of our neighbors, and yet lords of all. For those who do not recognize the gifts bestowed upon them through Christ, Christ has been born in vain; they go their way with their works and will never come to taste or feel those things. Just as our neighbor is in need and lacks that in which we abound, so we were in need before God and lacked his mercy. Hence, as our heavenly Father has in Christ freely come to our aid, we also ought freely to help our neighbor through our body and its works, and each one should become as it were a Christ to the other that we may be Christs to one another and Christ may be the same in all, that is, that we may be truly Christians.[75]

In this work Luther enunciated what he had long struggled with in his monastic career, and he enlarged upon the partial answer which he had garnered from von Staupitz: Trust in the love and forgiveness of God must precede penance.[76] This had now come to resolution in the discovery of Christian freedom and the believer's active involvement in creative love. From anguished doubt and pursuit of a moral rectitude deserving God's acceptance and salvation, Luther turned to acceptance, in faith, of God's acceptance. The embrace of "an ethics of gratitude"[77] was, for Luther, the free response of the graceful, joyful believer. Such a response entailed a measure of discernment and critical judgment, but the stirring motive was a reflected love — in the words of 1 John 4:19: "We love, because he first loved us." This "first love" was the creative love of God anticipated initially by Luther in his exposition of the last proposition of the Heidelberg Disputation, where he averred: "[S]inners are attractive because they are loved; they are not loved because they are attractive."[78]

Luther saw this response as one of a different order from that which

<hr>

75. *LW,* vol. 31, pp. 367-68.

76. See above, p. 87.

77. I am personally indebted to 1954 lectures by the German theologian Helmut Gollwitzer (1908-1993) for this characterization of Luther's ethics. Gollwitzer was a rare survivor of a Soviet prisoner-of-war camp in World War II. See also Helmut Gollwitzer, *Forderungen der Umkehr: Beiträge zur Theologie der Gesellschaft* (München: Kaiser Verlag, 1976), pp. 75-94, esp. pp. 82-83, 83-85.

78. See above, pp. 86-87, 90; see also pp. 120-21.

had earlier contained the thirteenth-century Franciscan reform effort — the call to "a piety of obedience," the idea that the highest form of humility was obedience.[79] For Luther Christian love demanded not simply self-abnegation, but insight into, and awareness of, the need and condition of the neighbor. Adjustment to the need and weakness of the fellow believer, although a possibility of loving response, by no means foreclosed the need of the neighbor to confront his/her own condition. In rendering commentary on the Christian life — and the spontaneity of Christian love, Luther framed a dialectic of the Christian as "perfectly free lord of all, subject to none" and simultaneously, "perfectly dutiful servant of all, subject to all."[80] Two paragraphs following the key passage quoted above on "hearts made free by the Holy Spirit," Luther cited the historical response of Paul to two different demands for the circumcision of Paul's missionary companions, Timothy and later Titus. With regard to Timothy, in the Acts 16:1-3 account, Paul agreed to circumcision because he did not want, in Luther's words, "to offend or despise the Jews [Jewish Christians] who were weak in the faith and could not yet grasp the liberty of faith." But in Galatia, in response to a later demand to circumcise Titus, Paul refused that course because those making the demand "despised the liberty of faith and insisted that circumcision was necessary for righteousness (Gal. 2:3)."[81]

Here Luther commented: "Just as . . . [Paul] was unwilling to offend or despise any man's weak faith and yielded to their will for a time, so he was also unwilling that the liberty of faith should be offended against or despised by stubborn, works-righteous men. He chose a middle way, sparing the weak for a time, but always withstanding the stubborn, that he might convert all to the liberty of faith." Luther concluded: "What we do should be done with the same zeal to sustain the weak in faith, as in Rom. 14[:1]; but we should firmly resist the stubborn teachers of works."[82]

It is not too much to say that here a line was crossed. With Luther the goal of ethics could no longer be the quest of reward in another

79. See Steven Ozment, *The Age of Reform: 1250-1550* (New Haven: Yale University Press, 1980), pp. 113-14; cf. also pp. 414-16 for the later Jesuit rendering of this obedience theme. See below, pp. 241-44. For the latest statement of it in the 1998 encyclical *Ratio et Fidei*. Cf. Calvin on this question; see below, pp. 146-47, with n. 46.

80. *LW,* vol. 31, p. 344.

81. *LW,* vol. 31, p. 368.

82. *LW,* vol. 31, p. 369.

world, life after death. Rather, the thrust and purpose of ethics became distinctly this-worldly. Again, there was still the hope and expectation of an eternal life, but the message of God's sovereign grace was understood to be a motivating, here-now reality. It defined love of neighbor not only in terms of a creative response to the physical need of the neighbor, but also a response to the fellow believer's need for growth in maturity of faith, a vital condition for the broadening realization of Christian liberty. Heiko Oberman put it well when he observed: "Good works [in Luther] are not repudiated, but their aim and direction have been radically 'horizontalized': they have moved from Heaven to earth."[83]

One is at a signal remove at this point from an earlier perspective of Luther in which he stressed the cultivation of humility as the precondition of faith. Martin Brecht describes this earlier stage of Luther's theological development during the years 1514-1516 as the period of Luther's "theology of humility."[84] An echo of this earlier theology of humility is evident as late as August 1518, with the delayed and revised publication of the *Explanations*. There Luther wrote — in the passage above: "Without doubt good works are the outward fruits of penance and of the Spirit, although the Spirit makes no sound except that of the turtle-dove, that is, the groaning of the heart which is the root of good works."[85] This passage can be dated earlier than its publication date in August,[86] perhaps back into February 1518; but, certainly the statement equating the work of the Spirit with a penitential groaning of the heart as the wellspring of good works strikes a very different note from the joy and spontaneity of Luther's November 1520 essay on Christian freedom. Underlining this point is one of the most pivotal passages in all of Luther. The paragraph needs quotation in full. It is the final paragraph of Luther's *The Freedom of a Christian*. He writes there:

> Since human nature and natural reason, as it is called, are by nature superstitious and ready to imagine, when laws and works are prescribed, that righteousness must be obtained through laws and works; and further, since they are trained and confirmed in this opinion by the practice of all earthly lawgivers, it is impossible that

83. Oberman, *Between God and the Devil*, p. 192; cf. also p. 206.
84. Brecht, *Martin Luther*, pp. 128-37.
85. LW, vol. 31, p. 87. See above, pp. 87-88.
86. See LW, vol. 31, pp. 79-80.

they should of themselves escape from the slavery of works and come to a knowledge of the freedom of faith. Therefore there is need of the prayer that the Lord may give us and make us *theodidacti*, that is, those taught by God [John 6:45], and himself, as he has promised, write his law in our hearts: otherwise there is no hope for us. If he himself does not teach our hearts this wisdom hidden in mystery [1 Cor. 2:7], nature can only condemn it and judge it to be heretical because nature is offended by it and regards it as foolishness. So we see that it happened in the old days in the case of the apostles and prophets, and so godless and blind popes and their flatterers do to me and to those who are like me. May God at last be merciful to them and to us and cause his face to shine upon us that we may know his way upon earth [Ps. 67:1-2], his salvation among all nations, God, who is blessed forever [2 Cor. 11:31]. Amen.[87]

This passage is a summary rejection of the centuries-old theological tradition of natural theology by which the church sought to winnow and then claim the world's wisdom — in order to preside over it. This was a companion doctrine to that of the keys whereby the church projected its power and its "domain" beyond the grave and sought, in Luther's words, to "perforate heaven." Luther distinctively linked this natural-law theological tradition with the whole ethos of works-righteousness and regarded it as a presumption on the part of the church. In the quoted passage, Luther describes the works-righteousness mindset as "superstition" and characterizes it as a bondage, distorting and subverting the prime message of justification and Christian freedom in grace.

In this concluding paragraph of *The Freedom of a Christian* there are two further points of note. Here Luther has fixed upon a perceived fulfillment of a prophecy of Jeremiah as ground for his theology of Christian freedom, something not apparent earlier. In chapter 31, verses 31 to 34, the words of Jeremiah read:

Behold, the days are coming, says the Lord, when I will make a new covenant with the house of Israel and the house of Judah, not like the covenant which I made with their fathers when I took them by the hand to bring them out of the land of Egypt, my cov-

87. *LW*, vol. 31, pp. 376-77.

enant which they broke, though I was their husband, says the Lord. But this is the covenant which I will make with the house of Israel after those days, says the Lord: I will put my law within them, and I will write it upon their hearts; and I will be their God, and they shall be my people. And no longer shall each man teach his neighbor and each his brother, saying, "Know the Lord," for they shall all know me, from the least of them to the greatest, says the Lord; for I will forgive their iniquity, and I will remember their sin no more.

Luther saw this prophecy — as does also the author of the Epistle to the Hebrews (8:8-13) — as fulfilled in the preaching of the Christian gospel. It is through the preaching and hearing of the gospel that the Holy Spirit imprints on the faithful believer's heart the law of love embodied in the crucified Christ's redemptive act. When the law gets written on the heart ethics becomes spontaneous, the overflow of a grateful heart. This, for Luther, was the ethical reality of the new covenant conveyed in the proclaimed message of the forgiveness of sins. This in essence is Christian freedom: the recognition in faith that one can live simultaneously as "free lord of all, subject to none," and "dutiful servant of all, subject to all." Gone is bondage to the law, to works-righteousness, which labors under guilt and looks to the end of life, to extreme unction and the far side of death, for resolution, an outlook bound by the thought of punishment and reward. Luther writes: "So . . . our works should be done, not that we may be justified by them, since, being justified beforehand by faith, we ought to do all things freely and joyfully for the sake of others."[88] And, "Our faith in Christ does not free us from works but from false opinions concerning works, that is, from the foolish presumption that justification is acquired by works."[89] It is not the "other world" that is determinative for Luther's ethics but God's transforming and transcendent grace in and for this world, the grace afforded by the gospel of cross and resurrection. It is this affirmation of the freedom and spontaneity of righteousness found in the Jeremiah and Hebrews passages that lies at the base of Luther's subsequent, sharp distinction between the law and the gospel. Illustrative of the point is the

88. *LW,* vol. 31, p. 368.
89. *LW,* vol. 31, pp. 372-73.

suggestion that for Luther it is possible for the faithful believer to be sometimes surprised by his, or her, own goodness.

A second point that needs underlining in the summary paragraph of *The Freedom of a Christian* is the continuing, formative role of the previously emphasized 1 Corinthians 1 passage. Apparent in this paragraph is the coming together of the foolishness-and-weakness-of-God passage with the *locus classicus* of justification by faith, the verse in Romans 1:17: "For in . . . [the gospel] the righteousness of God is revealed through faith for faith; as it is written, 'He who through faith is righteous shall live.'" Rather than supplementing and "correcting" the tradition of human knowledge, as much medieval theology had attempted, Luther understood God's revelation in Christ to be a confounding of the world's wisdom in line with 1 Corinthians 1:18-25 — true also of the prologue of John's Gospel, 1:1-18. God's unique transforming wisdom is strange to the world — and the world declares its judgment upon it in the death of Jesus on the cross. But the transcendent God reverses and overrules that judgment, making it the very basis of faith, hope, and love. Faith understands God's strange wisdom and its proffered righteousness to be liberation, to be nothing less than God's promised salvation. One recalls, yet again, the special quality of God's love as Luther expressed it in the Heidelberg Disputation: "The love of God does not find, but creates, that which is pleasing to it."[90] Over the course of the

90. The Luther scholar Paul Althaus contended that Luther's "theology of the cross," with an accent upon Christ's suffering, leads on to the major theme of the "hiddenness of God" in Luther's later thought. Althaus suggested that this theme in Luther had its origin in the 20th and 21st theses of the Heidelberg Disputation (May 1518); see Paul Althaus, *The Theology of Martin Luther*, trans. Robert C. Schultz (Philadelphia: Fortress Press, 1966), pp. 28-34. While Althaus offers, in the main, an illuminating exposition of Luther's "theology of the cross" in connection with the suffering theme of the 20th and 21st Heidelberg theses, he fails — to the mind of the present writer — to make adequate connection to the climactic 28th thesis, which asserts the value-creating nature of God's love in contrast to the value-seeking nature of human love (as in Aristotle). This inadequacy in Althaus's discussion is perhaps traceable to the incompleteness of Luther's own assimilation of justification at the time of the Heidelberg Disputation, something that is more fully addressed and, as argued here, completed with the writing of the final paragraph of *The Freedom of the Christian* (November 1520). *It is in the latter that Luther brought together the otherness of the cross and the otherness of justification by faith as an expression of God's transcendence.* Althaus, however, comes close to this and is certainly on the mark when he declared: "The cross simultaneously destroys both natural theology and the self-consciousness of man's natural ethos" (p. 28).

year 1518, Luther moved ever closer to the linkage of 1 Corinthians 1 and Romans 1. It is in the concluding paragraph of *The Freedom of a Christian* that this linkage is made clear.

With this analysis it becomes possible to interpret Luther's "theology of humility"[91] of the years 1514-1516 as a personal, individualistic reading of 1 Corinthians 1. Read in this context, the passage can be interpreted as an exhortation to humility and the need also to bear the burden of suffering. Such a reading would be consistent with Luther's early personal quest for spiritual meaning in his study and exposition of the Psalms. But Luther's attack upon scholastic theology in September 1517 suggested something more than a quest for answers to his own personal trials *(Anfechtungen)*. It suggested that "the offense of the cross" had wide-ranging theological implications. In criticism of scholasticism Luther challenged one of the major, medieval goals of theology: the effort to wed philosophy and theology, Aristotle and Scripture. Subsequently, in his attack on the practice of the sale of indulgences, he displayed a pastoral concern for the people consistent with his duties as a professor of Bible, people whom he also saw as victims of patent economic exploitation. The response of high-ranking ecclesiastical authorities to the ninety-five theses convinced Luther that, along with the "wisdom" issue, economic power was at issue across the church — and this he saw as a concomitant betrayal of the essential New Testament message. With each ensuing encounter in the growing theological/political controversy, and especially in the aftermath of the Leipzig debate with Eck, Luther affirmed a prophetic/social relevance of 1 Corinthians 1 for interpreting the ecclesiastical, social conditions with which he was confronted. It provided a compelling interpretation of the times, lending further support for his belief in the reality of the Devil and giving weight to his growing conviction that he was living in the end times, with manifestations of the Antichrist.

As described above, Luther brought these evolving convictions to Worms in April 1521. Excommunicated by Rome in January 1521, Luther sought and received a hearing before the Emperor Charles V and the Imperial Diet, this through the political influence of the elector Frederick the Wise. Despite the escalating steps taken against him by the papal au-

---

91. On this phase in Luther's theological development, see Brecht, *Martin Luther,* pp. 133-37.

thorities at Rome, Luther apparently still entertained a hope that political authority, in the person of the emperor and the proceedings of the Diet, could initiate a full and open discussion of issues and a reform of the church. As Luther pointed out in his August 1520 *Address to the Christian Nobility of the German Nation:* There is "no basis in Scripture for . . . [the] claim that the pope alone has the right to call or confirm a council. This is just their own ruling, and it is only valid as long as it is not harmful to Christendom. . . . Thus we read in Acts 15[:6] that it was not St. Peter who called the Apostolic Council but all the apostles and elders. . . . Even the council of Nicea, the most famous of all councils, was neither called nor confirmed by the bishop of Rome, but by the emperor Constantine."[92]

As described previously,[93] on the first day of his hearing at the Diet Luther was confronted with the sole demand that he recant his views, this with the full weight of the emperor's authority supporting that demand. Luther, above all, had sought a *hearing.* Afterward, a decade later, looking back upon the crucial events from the posting of the theses on the Wittenberg church door through the "hearing" at Worms, Luther, in the *Table Talk,* is reported to have said that he had been excommunicated three times: first by von Staupitz who released him from his vow of obedience to the Augustinian Order and abandoned him at the Diet of Augsburg in 1518, then by the pope who cut him off from the church in January 1521, and finally by the emperor who decreed his seizure and arrest within the empire.[94] Though still committed to a concept of "Christendom," but focusing on the role of Christian princes and imperial cities, Luther, after Worms, spoke of secular authority in a more critical tone, not only in terms of its necessity (vs. Anabaptists and spiritualists) but also of its responsibilities.[95] After Worms, there was no alternative for Luther but to structure a reformed church on the basis of the preaching of the Word of God and the observance of the two sacraments (Baptism and the Lord's Supper), with expectations of its adoption at least within what was increasingly recognized as "Lutheran" ter-

---

92. *LW,* vol. 44 (1966), pp. 136-37.

93. See above, pp. 72-75.

94. See Oberman's discussion on this point, *Between God and the Devil,* pp. 186-87.

95. See the treatise "Temporal Authority: To What Extent It Should Be Obeyed" (1523), *LW,* vol. 45 (1962), pp. 81-129.

ritories. The unity of a "Christian Europe" was shattered — with many unforeseen consequences.

To review and summarize the discussion of Luther's often implicit critique of otherworldliness, we have argued that one cannot understand Luther, make sense of his thought, or do justice to the events that mark the initial stages of the Reformation without recognizing the absolutely critical role of the rediscovery of the transcendence of God, a transcendence that was/is not to be humanly restricted to the questions of life after death and is expressed also in judgment upon the world's wisdom and power. This is not to say that expressions of God's transcendence had not been preserved within some aspects of the medieval church's life, in its observances, in its preaching, and in elements of its theology. But as Luther noted in his quotation of Augustine,[96] custom and the accretions of tradition had a way of domesticating God, shading the Other with the embroidered veil of the past, in ceremony, in the aesthetics of ritual that draw upon the human sense of mystery and the wonder of existence.[97] In *The Freedom of a Christian* Luther remarks: "[T]hey [the "religiously" inclined] remain caught in *the form of religion* and do not attain unto its power [2 Tim. 3:5]."[98] Without a sense for the transcendence of God and the liberating message of grace set forth in Scripture, the critical, dynamic aspect of Luther's theology could not have come about or endured.

The whole debate about the authority of Scripture versus the authority of the hierarchically structured church hung on the issue of God's transcendence, or as Luther came to see it, on the freedom of God in his Word. In *The Babylonian Captivity of the Church* Luther cited the passage in 1 Corinthians 1:17 in which the apostle Paul declared that he had been sent not to baptize "but to preach the Gospel," a gospel that stood in contrast to the entirety of the world's "wisdom and power" (1 Cor. 1:18ff.). "The pope," Luther wrote, "should teach nothing but faith without any restrictions."[99] Luther's monastic career moved out and

---

96. See above, p. 96.

97. Martin Buber, in *I and Thou*, remarks on the way in which an original encounter with an eternal, transcendent God is subsequently ensconced in ritual and tradition. See Martin Buber, *I and Thou*, trans. Ronald Gregor Smith (New York: Charles Scribner's Sons, 1958), pp. 112-14.

98. *LW*, vol. 31, p. 376; emphasis added.

99. *LW*, vol. 36, p. 71.

away from the forms of monastic piety to a discovery of new depths of meaning in Scripture which he saw to be, humanly speaking, counterintuitive. New questions were raised; old questions lost their significance. For Luther, God, who created through the Word, created still through the Word. God's message for humankind was not conveyed chiefly in visual form or in repeated, ritual enactments. Basic always was form plus substance, form plus Word, promise. It is the latter, Luther believed, that occasioned the response of faith. The former sought repetition, containment under an established human mode, and had its terminus in death and the world beyond.

In the book of Isaiah, following almost immediately upon the assertion of divine transcendence ("For my thoughts are not your thoughts, neither are your ways my ways, says the Lord" [Isa. 55:8]) come the words: "For as the rain and the snow come down from heaven, and return not thither but water the earth, making it bring forth and sprout, giving seed to the sower and bread to the eater, so shall my word be that goes forth from my mouth; it shall not return to me empty, but it shall accomplish that which I purpose, and prosper in the thing for which I sent it" (Isa. 55:11). For Luther, God was/is active not alone in utterance, but in reception, in the human hearing as well. Thus, as noted, in the key paragraph in *The Freedom of a Christian*, one reads: "Therefore there is need of the prayer that the Lord may *give us* and *make us theodidacti*, that is, those taught by God, and himself, as he has promised, write his law in our hearts; otherwise there is no hope for us."[100] For Luther this meant that a transcendent God, who speaks through his Word and enables even the hearing of that Word, would have a human response in and for this world, addressed to life this side of death, an ethic essentially freed from otherworldly fears.

Spread abroad among a variety of hearers, an understanding of a Word preached, a Scripture read, demanded for Luther openness and conversation regardless of rank, ecclesiastical or political. In the *Address to the Christian Nobility of the German Nation* Luther quoted Paul in 1 Corinthians 14:30: "If something better is revealed to anyone, though he is already sitting and listening to another in God's word, then the one who is speaking shall hold his peace and give place." Luther then commented: "What would be the point of this commandment if we were

---

100. Quoted above, pp. 101-2; emphasis added.

compelled to believe only the man who does the talking, or the man who is at the top? Even Christ said in John 6[:45] that all Christians shall be taught by God."[101] The sovereignty of God in the Word, the freedom and unmerited favor of God's grace, along with the universality of the human condition in sin, gave rise in Luther to a radical spiritual egalitarianism which he gave expression in his own resistance to pope and emperor on behalf of the gospel of forgiveness. With Luther it is God's love of the sinner that creates the value of each and every person, not the achieved goodness of the individual assumed "by nature" to elicit God's love. Neither is humankind's supposed rational competence equated with the image of God, a supposed basic source for an understanding of God. For Luther, "the inner man . . . [is] *by faith* . . . created in the image of God."[102]

In his major work, *The Social Teachings of the Christian Churches and Sects* (1911), Ernst Troeltsch suggested in a footnote that "the history of the problem of equality would be one of the most important contributions which could be made to the understanding of the development of European Society. It is, however, still entirely unwritten."[103] It can be suggested that such a work, as envisioned by Troeltsch, remains still to be written, but what can be affirmed is that, whereas in the medieval past class was excluded as a condition for service in ecclesiastical orders, with Luther and the affirmation of the priesthood of all believers, a new sense of spiritual equality found expression in the world — not out and away from the world but by everyone in his or her vocation.[104] In the *Address to the Christian Nobility of the German Nation*, Luther wrote:

> Therefore . . . those who are now called "spiritual," that is, priests, bishops, or popes, are neither different from other Christians nor superior to them, except that they are charged with the administration of the word of God and the sacraments, which is their work

101. *LW*, vol. 44, p. 134. For John Calvin's corresponding elaboration of this point, see below, pp. 156-57.

102. *LW*, vol. 31, p. 359; emphasis added.

103. Ernst Troeltsch, *The Social Teaching of the Christian Churches* (New York: Harper & Brothers, 1960), reprint of a 1931 translation (Allen & Unwin/Macmillan) of *Die Soziallehren der christlichen Kirchen und Gruppen* (1911), vol. 2, p. 902, n. 356.

104. Troeltsch saw this as a special mark of the Reformation coming out of Geneva and especially characteristic of Calvinism; see *Social Teachings*, pp. 902-3, n. 361.

and office, so it is with the temporal authorities. They bear the sword and rod in their hand to punish the wicked and protect the good. A cobbler, a smith, a peasant — each has the work and office of his trade, and yet they are all alike consecrated priests and bishops. Further, everyone must benefit and serve every other by means of his own work or office so that in this way many kinds of work may be done for the bodily and spiritual welfare of the community, just as all the members of the body serve one another [1 Cor. 12:14-26].[105]

With equality in and through God's grace came also Luther's commitment to adulthood, to freedom. As noted above, Luther saw the Christian life as one of growth toward adulthood, adulthood in this life. While he allowed — with the apostle Paul — concessions to "weaker" brothers and sisters who remained captive to the law and to "nature," he never suggested that such "weaker" fellow Christians should dictate rules for those freed in and by grace. As he put it in *The Freedom of a Christian,* though the weak in faith (those still bound by the law) should not be condemned or rejected, neither should "the liberty of faith" be "despised by stubborn, works-righteous men." Paul, Luther says, "chose a middle way, sparing the weak for a time, but always withstanding the stubborn, that *he might convert all to the liberty of faith.*"[106]

In March 1522 Luther exemplified this very point. He left his protective ten-month seclusion at the Wartburg castle after the Worms hearing to return to Wittenberg to restrain Karlstadt and overeager, reform-minded students who had undertaken a frenzied destruction of images and attacked the observance of the mass in the churches of the surrounding area. Luther consistently rejected coercion in matters of faith; but he did not abandon the project of a this-worldly tutoring of the faithful, to the end that all might be converted "to the liberty of faith." It was thus not until October 1524 that Luther abandoned his monk's habit and in 1525 reformed the mass. He did, however, insist on obedience for all Christians to "the governing authorities" (Rom. 13:1), such authorities having been "instituted" and ordained by God — a theme that took on added emphasis following the 1525 Peasants' Revolt which

---

105. *LW,* vol. 44, p. 130. John Calvin's interpretation and further development of this passage will be discussed further below, see pp. 155-59.

106. *LW,* vol. 31, pp. 368-69; emphasis added.

contributed to the further development of Luther's "two kingdoms" teaching.[107] He did not see the adulthood of Christians applying directly to the form or structure of government, believing as he also did that he was living in the end times before the return of Christ. Wolfhart Pannenberg, in a 1969 Reformation lecture, underlined Luther's affirmation of *Mündigkeit* ("speaking for oneself," the status of having come-of-age) as a feature of any modern Christian piety. Pannenberg distinguished this Christian maturity from the later Enlightenment claim of radical self-determination, yet insisted there were still wide-ranging political implications growing out of Luther's affirmation of *Mündigkeit*. Pannenberg comments: "The coming-of-age of faith includes the right to self-rule also in the worldly, political realm, a tendency to abandon dominion and further the realization of political freedom. This, in the political sphere, is not compatible with mere submissive obedience."[108]

Luther's forceful, forthright statements of spiritual equality and the freedom and responsibility of adulthood, rooted in the message of a this-worldly transcendent grace, introduced a powerful force for change into the mix of a Western cultural tradition already undergoing significant economic and social alteration. The gospel of the sufficiency for this life of Christ's death and resurrection provided a new focus of meaning over against the then-current, increasingly complex, anxiety-ridden system of salvation that stressed and relied upon obedience to ecclesiastical office for its legitimacy and power.[109] Through his long struggle with the

---

107. See above, pp. 76-77, esp. n. 22; and below, p. 128, n. 22. In his 1522 return to Wittenberg after his stay in the Wartburg, Luther admonished the iconoclastic students and their enthusiastic compatriots to refrain from any use of coercion in instituting various reform measures. He urged the advocates of such reform to seek the approval and endorsement of the civil authorities in such further efforts, thus anticipating his more vehement, angry rejection of the use of violence in the Peasants' Revolt. The continuation of the law-bound "outer man" even in the life of faith is an important point in *The Freedom of the Christian* and later comes increasingly into play as Luther struggled with the question of social and political order in face of the rise in popularity of the spiritual enthusiasts (Anabaptists et al.) and revolutionary political advocacy. It lays lines of development for the "two kingdoms" teaching. See especially Luther's sermons of March 9 and 10, 1522: *LW,* vol. 51 (1959), pp. 70-78. For the individual Christian's continuing struggle with bodily temptations and the need for their restraint, see *LW,* vol. 31, pp. 358-65.

108. Wolfhart Pannenberg, *Reformation zwischen gestern und morgen* (Gütersloh: Gerd Mohn, 1969), p. 27; my translation.

109. See above, pp. 81-82.

meaning of Scriptures, Luther came to insist — especially in the aftermath of his 1521 hearing at the Diet of Worms — upon the disruptive presence and freedom of a sovereign Word of God. The gospel of God's creative, affirming love of the sinner in the message of justifying grace/faith precluded the "other world" as the determinant of ethical responsibility. The here/now of the gospel message constituted the proper stage for faith's encounter with God.

To be sure, Luther's conviction that he was living in the end times restricted the scope of resistance implicit in the realization of the adulthood of faith. He believed the social and political structures of his time to be ordained of God and briefly saw the in-breaking of God's grace in the life of the individual as promising also transformation of the social-political order, but without the thought of a reform or redesign of that order. Wolfhart Pannenberg writes on this point:

> Because of their bond with the Lord of All [i.e., a transcendent God], Christians need be submissive to no human lordship, but can be self-governing — a thought which belongs to the roots of modern democracy and which is not yet, in these political consequences, found in Luther. Rather, it is well known that Luther demanded obedience to the actually existing authorities. But, in the immediacy of faith in God's justification, the thought of self-rule is substantively grounded, joined, with the coming-of-age *(Mündlichkeit)* of humankind.[110]

One might add to Pannenberg's observation that in the aftermath of Worms and in his 1520 writings preceding that event, Luther was firm in an assured faith in the sovereignty and freedom of God's Word, a reality before which political authority was also responsible, at least in assuring open, public preaching of that Word. As has been argued at length above, Luther's impress by the 1 Corinthians 1 passage made clear that the Romans 13:1-7 injunction of obedience to the governing authorities did not exclude a this-worldly, critical point-of-viewing vis-à-vis all earthly power and authority. The realization of justification by faith/grace was fundamental to Luther's assessment of Christian freedom, but the this-worldly judgment of the cross upon all worldly power and wisdom also opened a process of confrontation with the structures and

---

110. Pannenberg, *Reformation zwischen gestern und morgen*, p. 20; my translation.

powers of the established order of that time — first with what Luther came to perceive as the arrogance and overreach of spiritual power in the church, then, more hesitantly, with suppressed questions about the responsible exercise of political power. After Worms, the Saxon lawyers, as noted,[111] raised the question of the duties of "the lesser magistrates" in relation to the "higher magistrates," but this was a second step, in recognition of the freedom of the Word in the emerging, ever more complex, political situation of a declining Holy Roman Empire. Clear to an ever-widening audience across Europe was the manifest resistance to entrenched ecclesiastical and political power as expressed in the person and thought of Luther — in a 1517 challenge on a church door, in 1519 in debate in Leipzig, and in Worms before an emperor in 1521. This was so whether or not people of varied persuasions perceived all of the theological bases of Luther's resistance. Certainly the peasants, who in 1525 stirred Luther's vitriolic wrath in their resort to violence, grasped potent elements of Luther's message, and this lingered even after their severe suppression. And, when Luther was forced to structure an alternative reformed church, when he refigured Europe's sacral institution in territories sympathetic to the reforming cause, erosion of divine right in political governance was given signal, if slow-building, impetus. The linkage of church and crown, as Pannenberg has suggested, became increasingly open to question in subsequent generations.

A CONCLUDING word on Luther's bold, but also at times implicit critique of otherworldliness, needs final address in the scholarly problem of his "breakthrough" to an understanding of justification by faith, referred to also at times as Luther's "tower experience." The question posed is: When did he come to his mature understanding of justification? This problem has been central to much Luther study over the past hundred and more years and has proven productive of much impressive scholarship. In the preface to the 1545 edition of his Latin writings, Luther centered the struggle for liberating faith on his understanding of "the righteousness of God." The question arises as to how he came to move beyond a dread of God's righteousness, conceived as God's moral purity and the moral demands of the law, a standard by which all per-

111. See pp. 77-78.

sons were to be judged. In the 1545 preface, Luther confessed that he entertained not only a dread, but a hatred of God's "righteousness" so conceived. It is not clear at what point and in what manner Luther attained the insight that God's righteousness was not so much the austere perfection of moral purity but rather an active, redemptive intervention on behalf of humankind. His recollection of this matter, coming towards the end of his life, does not resolve all the questions about his spiritual struggle in this regard. Most previous Lutheran scholarship on this matter fixed a relatively early date for his spiritual "breakthrough" and generally concluded that Luther's "tower experience" preceded by at least a year or more the outbreak of the 1517 indulgence controversy.

In 1953, the English Luther scholar Gordon Rupp associated Luther's key insight into the problem of God's righteousness with his first lectures on the Psalms in 1513-1514.[112] Luther's marginal notes on the 31st Psalm, at verse 1, expressed puzzlement at the psalmist's prayer that God's righteousness should be the source of his deliverance, his salvation. Rupp concluded that Luther at this point began reflection on the, for him, revolutionary thought that God's righteousness was primarily an active, saving work toward Israel and toward the individual, an act of redemption. Rupp argued that in moving on to his lectures on Romans in 1515-1516, Luther avowed that trust in God's deliverance was the only basis for confidence in personal redemption. Later, in 1961, the historian and Luther scholar Wilhelm Pauck, in a new translation of Luther's Romans lectures, remarked approvingly of Rupp's interpretation and offered his endorsement of this relatively early dating of Luther's breakthrough.[113]

Three years before Pauck's endorsement however, in 1958, the theologian and historian Ernst Bizer raised doubts about this view, and others like it, of an "early" (1513-1516) dating for Luther's breakthrough. Bizer argued that it was not until Luther achieved an understanding of faith derived through hearing that one is able to speak properly of his having firmly grasped the idea of justification by faith. Bizer suggested that it was late in 1518, almost a year after posting the theses against the sale of indulgences, that Luther came to emphasize the agency of God's Word as

---

112. Gordon Rupp, *The Righteousness of God: Luther Studies* (London: Hodder & Stoughton, 1953), esp. pp. 121-37.

113. *Luther: Lectures on Romans*, trans. and ed. Wilhelm Pauck, vol. 15 of the Library of Christian Classics (Philadelphia: Westminster Press, 1961), pp. xxxvi-xxxviii.

the basic means of justifying faith. This followed Luther's interchange with Cardinal Cajetan in October 1518, after the Diet of Augsburg and Luther's early refusal to recant. Bizer argued that in Luther's account of the exchange with Cardinal Cajetan, he went beyond one of the major points in the *Explanations* of May 1518, this in his statement that "faith is nothing other than faith in the promise or in the Word [of God]."[114] Bizer observed that for Luther this is not humility as the means to, or the condition of, faith — a briefly held post-1517 view. (And one should add that, after May 1518, Luther spoke no more of the "turtle-dove," "the groaning of the heart, which is the root of good works."[115]) Bizer concluded his analysis of Luther's theological breakthrough with an account of the latter's critique of the medieval tradition of the sacraments, pointing out that following two key sermons on God's righteousness in late 1518 and in April 1519, Luther came rapidly to the view that one does not have a sacrament without an interpreting, Scripture-based Word joined with the response of faith. Bizer concludes that, for Luther, from late 1518 onward, "the sacrament is understood on the basis of the Word, and the Word itself receives a sacramental character. The point-of-departure for both is the new understanding of Rom. 1:17: 'In the Gospel the righteousness of God is revealed,' that is, it is gifted through the Word."[116]

Over the years since Bizer's 1958 study, a relatively "late" 1518-1519 dating for Luther's reorienting, determinative understanding of justification has gained important scholarly support. In the main, Martin Brecht follows and supports Bizer's analysis of a later dating,[117] as does Heiko Oberman.[118] In a 1990 survey and briefly elaborated further proposal, the Finnish scholar Lennart Pinomaa added further argument for a later 1518 dating, stressing that the important accent upon joyful human response to the message of a transcendent grace is best fixed by Luther's 1518 lectures on the Epistle to the Hebrews — precisely with Luther's comments (student-recorded) on Hebrews 7:1.[119] Certainly the theme of

---

114. *Fides ex auditu: Eine Untersuchung über die Entdeckung der Gerechtigkeit Gottes durch Martin Luther,* 3rd ed. (Neukirchen: Neukirchener Verlag, 1966), p. 118.

115. See above, pp. 87-88, 101. Rupp responded to Bizer's *Fides ex auditu* in *Zeitschrift für Kirchengeschichte* 71 (1960): 351-55.

116. Bizer, *Fides ex auditu,* p. 178; my translation.

117. Brecht, *Martin Luther,* pp. 221-37; esp. pp. 234, 236-37.

118. Oberman, *Between God and the Devil,* pp. 151-58, 164-66.

119. Lennart Pinomaa, "Noch Einmal: Der reformatorische Durchbruch Luthers,"

a responsive, joyous spontaneity found in *The Freedom of a Christian* is basic to Luther's understanding of justification, an understanding that governs most of his subsequent delineation of "Law and Gospel."

The argument developed in this chapter addresses the importance of Luther's awareness of and interaction with a transcendent God. It suggests that the later dating for Luther's breakthrough fits with a developing understanding, in changing circumstances, which led on to the intellectually assured nature of Luther's theological arguments found in the decisive 1520 writings. What is especially striking about Bizer's analysis — which does not preclude the joyous response stressed by Pinomaa and underlies also Luther's ethics of gratitude — is Bizer's point on Luther's 1519 critique of the church's medieval teachings and practice of the sacraments. The church's sacramental system, oriented as it was toward the "other world," especially in the assertion of its nature as *opus operandi,* the assumed effective agency of sacramental ritual independent of the believer's understanding of the words used in administration of the sacrament.

Especially arresting in Luther's break with this medieval system was/is his discussion of the nature of a sacrament, with its roots in the Greek term *mysterion.* In *The Babylonian Captivity of the Church* Luther writes: "[S]acrament or mystery in Paul is that wisdom of the Spirit, hidden in a mystery, as he says in 1 Corinthians 2[:7-8], which is Christ, who for this reason is not known to the rulers of this world, wherefore they also crucified him, and for them he remains to this day folly [1 Cor. 1:23], an offense, a stumbling stone [Rom. 9:32-33], and a sign that is spoken against [Luke 2:34]."[120] Critical here is the preceding 1 Corinthians 1:18-25 passage with its description of the cross as God's decisive engagement with the world. For Luther, the sacraments of Baptism and the Last Supper, though they certainly carried meaning for life after death, were defined also very much in relation to this world, in relation to the assumed

---

Zeitschrift der Luther Gesellschaft 61, no. 2 (Göttingen: Vandenhoeck & Ruprecht, 1990), pp. 77-80.

120. *LW,* vol. 36, p. 94. It is of note that whereas Luther was concerned to center the sense of mystery on the cross and the response of faith, an expansive, one might even say, exaggerated, sense of mystery continues into the present day in the Roman Catholic tradition. A news item in the *New York Times* of October 15, 2002, sec. A, reported that Pope John Paul II had taken steps, somewhat unexpectedly and seemingly out of his own personal piety, to increase the "mysteries" of the Rosary (events in Jesus' life calling for devotional contemplation) from fifteen to twenty.

wisdom and power of the world, wisdom and power that are undone by God's "foolishness" and "weakness." The cross is set in the midst of the "certainties" of the world's knowledge and power — a new kind of mystery that scrambles and confounds the world's claimed knowledge and power. It is a this-worldly, "unbelievable" mystery, accessible through faith. And, if the apostle Paul — and following him, Luther — spoke of "God's wisdom," the wisdom intended was/is clearly not an add-on to the world's wisdom, even a refined and properly purged worldly wisdom in the work of such auspicious figures as Plato and Aristotle. It is the stumbling-block wisdom, the "offending" wisdom, of the gospel, grounded in the cross.

Bizer, at a point in his discussion of Luther's two 1518-1519 sermons on God's righteousness, speaks of faith's sharing in the very righteousness of Christ, a "foreign" righteousness. He writes: "I Cor. 1:30 now becomes important and in the following time is frequently cited."[121] First Corinthians 1:30 reads: "He [God] is the source of your life in Christ Jesus, whom God made our wisdom, our righteousness and sanctification and redemption." First Corinthians 1:30 is only further elaboration of 1 Corinthians 1:18-25. The cross, in Luther's terms, is God's wisdom made manifest, revealed, in a world that thereby becomes again God's world, freed of the overlay of human conceit and presumption. The cross is seen as God's claim upon this world, especially in the fact that it does not conform to the world's imaginings and projections of God. In contemporary intellectual parlance Luther argues that the cross is *God's deconstruction* of humanity's familiar, self-assured, even postmodern world, a reality not conceivable apart from faith's awareness of God's transcendence in both love and judgment.

This theological, spiritual revolution of Luther was a powerful force for change. It brought about reappraisals of church doctrine and church structure. To be sure, the medieval church survived, with a significant measure of its power intact and its continuing, claimed custodial command of a natural knowledge of God and natural law. But Luther's reforming revolution could not help but manifest itself in concrete forms of change and proved itself a force of the spirit that went beyond, interacted with, and leavened the play of other political and social forces of the time. Luther's reform was set within the bounds of the given social

---

121. Bizer, *Fides ex auditu*, p. 127.

and political order even though he did not consciously intend a political revision of that order. Not only did he steadfastly affirm the traditional understanding of the role of political authority as set forth in Romans 13; but his own eschatological expectations, his assumption that he was living in the last times, helped foreclose a thoroughgoing critique of inherited political and social institutions. To be sure, forced change, violence as a means of change, was beyond his tolerance, though a few of his more radical religious contemporaries entertained such means.

Beyond his ken also was any thought that an expanding human knowledge and a growing human mastery over nature could deliver materially "redemptive" change — a thought that came especially to mark the later "enlightened ones" of the eighteenth century and one that underlies much of a technologically oriented belief in progress. What Luther *did* contribute to later thought was the necessity of criticism and reappraisal of inherited conceptual schemes, theological and otherwise. The world's wisdom, for those influenced by Luther (and Paul), is always open to question. Added to this was Luther's new insistence upon the this-worldly nature of Christian ethics. Ethics, Luther argued, were no longer a human means to a heavenly reward but were loosed into and for this world as a response to God's "justifying" love of the sinner in the here and now. Ethics was response to the cross as grace and love, but also a disruptive confrontation with human self-deception and self-aggrandizement. Whatever the world might view as the source of human freedom and equality, Luther was sure it resided in the unmerited favor of God, laid hold of in faith. With faith came also freedom and the call to adulthood, perceived often only as a persistent beckoning, a possibility, an urging, making for personal spiritual change, but also, engagement with established interests and making for social and political change. Further developments along this line are the subject of the next chapter on the contributions of Martin Bucer and John Calvin to the understanding of a transcendent love of God, a transcendent gospel message, given utterance within, and amidst, the human realities of this world, yet offering assurance of life beyond death. For Luther a seeming sequentially "second word," redemption, following creation, was in faith actually the First Word — that is, the Word in the cross and resurrection. But one makes affirmation of a doctrine of the Trinity to believe and proclaim such a radical thing.

Chapter 4

Divine Transcendence and Corporate-Historical Existence: Bucer and Calvin

In the preceding discussion of Luther's theological development and faith commitment it has been argued that, far from sanctioning the religious-theological status quo, his understanding and experience of a transcendent God — with Scripture as its source — challenged the closed medieval system of salvation. This system had been presided over by a hierarchically structured church with the papacy at the apex of spiritual power, exercising also signal political and economic power. Luther's breakthrough to the freely proclaimed grace of forgiveness in Christ as the central content of the Word of God called into question this system of salvation. The message of justification, with its strong qualification of medieval otherworldliness, its critique of an ecclesiastically structured "solution" to the death question, bore with it an ineluctable affirmation of human equality and a frequently suppressed, but nonetheless restive and persistent call to growth toward the goal of "adulthood." Luther, in his own thought and experience, anticipated an impending end of history, an inclination in his thought that left undeveloped potentialities of this-worldly theological meaning. This situation — and the freedom of the gospel itself — elicited within the broadening Reformation movement the contributions of others, who, though they learned a great deal from Luther, were also moved to make their own distinctive contributions. In this chapter we address the work of two contemporaries of Luther who offered further understanding of an engaged, this-worldly form of faith: the Strassburg reformer Martin Bucer (1491-1551) and John Calvin (1509-1564) of Geneva. Each gave expression to forms of faith, interacting with traditional spiritual and political structures of power, offering criticism and redefinition as well as affirmation of this-worldly corporate existence.

Bucer

In his 1984 treatment of the life and thought of Luther, Heiko Oberman, in discussing a developing problem of anti-Judaism in Luther, makes the observation that "[w]e should not identify the Reformation movement with Luther to such an extent as to neglect the nuances of various views among a series of Luther's distinguished students."[1] And he cites as one example the figure of Justus Jonas, a close friend of Luther and fellow reformer, who departed significantly from Luther's later, increasingly harsh views of the Jews. Oberman could well have enlarged the scope of this observation by citing others who, on a variety of questions, brought readings and perspectives to Luther's work that provided significant, new, theological insight and this-worldly developments. Martin Brecht enlarges on such a view when he writes: "With Bucer, as previously with Karlstadt, we see the problem of accepting Luther's thoughts while at the same time reformulating his own concepts, a process which had a great deal to do with the Reformation's intellectual variety and richness, but which also brought tensions along with it."[2] It is important to follow up this lead and consider Bucer's thought, albeit briefly, as it gives expression to affirmations of this-worldly existence in the context of the gift of a transcendent, divine grace.

In April 1518, as mentioned earlier,[3] Martin Luther was summoned by the leadership of his Augustinian order to Heidelberg to give account and explanation of his attack upon the sale of indulgences. One of those who gained admission to the weeklong hearing was a twenty-seven-year-old Dominican monk by the name of Martin Bucer (Butzer, in German). Bucer had been chosen by his order to go to Heidelberg to further his theological studies. As a result of sitting in on Luther's elaboration

1. Heiko Oberman, *Luther: Mensch zwischen Gott und Teufel* (Berlin: Severin und Siedler, 1982); trans. Eileen Walliser-Schwarzbart, *Luther: Man between God and the Devil* (New Haven/London: Yale University Press, 1989), p. 296.

2. Martin Brecht, *Martin Luther: His Road to the Reformation, 1483-1521*, trans. James Schaaf (Philadelphia: Fortress Press, 1985), p. 216.

3. See above, pp. 86-87, 90, 99.

and explanations during Luther's Heidelberg disputation, Bucer's life was radically altered.

Bucer does not fully identify, in theological terms, what most moved him in Luther's presentation. In a letter to a friend, he cited the persuasiveness of Luther's argument and his command of the scriptural sources.[4] One can offer only a surmise about the specific theological insights he carried away from the encounter. But it is not unreasonable to suppose that Bucer found a grounding for a newfound faith as a result of personal conversation with Luther — also, perhaps, in the key last theological article in the Disputation. This surmise is proffered even though Bucer's letter-account of Luther's discussion breaks off at the fourteenth article. The twenty-eighth theological article offered a concise early theological statement of Luther's understanding of the gospel, one that consistently figured in Bucer's subsequent theological and ecclesiastical/political determinations. As cited previously,[5] that article reads, "The love of God does not find, but creates, that which is pleasing to it. The love of man [by contrast] comes into being through that which is pleasing to it."

Shortly before his death in 1551, in lectures on the book of Ephesians at Cambridge University in England, Bucer echoed and stressed just such an understanding of the gospel in treating the biblical theme of election. He remarked at the later time: "The goal of election is that we should know God, love and worship him, and live according to his will. Moreover, Paul says that God chose us 'in himself,' lest we should think there is any merit in ourselves. . . . Foreknowledge of what we were to do or of future faith in us, was in no sense the cause of our election. 'For the natural man does not receive the things of the Spirit of God, indeed they are folly to him, and he is unable to understand them' [1 Cor. 2:14]." Bucer followed with the note: "It is the mark of the anti-christ to exalt nature over against grace so that he may reign in the stead of Christ."[6] Present in these words is not only an affirmation of the twenty-eighth article at Heidelberg but a parallel to the thought expressed in the final paragraph of Luther's 1520 *The Freedom of a Christian*.[7] This was so with Bucer, as

4. See D. F. Wright, trans. and ed., *Common Places of Martin Bucer* (Appleford: Sutton Courtenay Press, 1972), pp. 19-20; cf. Brecht, *Martin Luther*, p. 216.
5. See above, p. 90.
6. Wright, *Common Places*, pp. 111-12.
7. See above, pp. 101-2.

with others, only as he believed it to be a proper reading and fundamental understanding of Scripture.

After the encounter with Luther at Heidelberg, Bucer became increasingly restless in his monastic calling. In his earlier monastic career he appeared, at the start, to have been drawn to the Dominican order out of an early love of learning, a love of learning marked by humanist, Erasmian sentiments.[8] Later, after some years in following the discipline of his order, he was allowed to pursue advanced studies at Heidelberg, receiving in the spring of 1519 the degrees of bachelor of theology and "Master of Students." His strong support of the humanist point of view within the Dominican order and then his sympathies with Luther led increasingly to his isolation and alienation among the Dominicans. His critics within the order sought to deprive him of his earned degrees after one particular forthright public defense of Luther by Bucer. And, in 1520 he was forced to flee the chapter at Heidelberg and seek refuge, through the aid of the humanist Ulrich von Hutten, in the territory of the imperial knight Franz von Sickingen, another humanist and early supporter of church reform as advanced by Luther. Bucer sought official release from his monastic vows, a difficult goal in the face of mounting enmity toward him within the Dominican order and also on the part of the papal legate Aleander. The release, however, was finally granted through quiet diplomacy and the support of a suffragan bishop sympathetic to his cause. He was granted a release from his monastic vows on April 29, 1521, and was, at that point, accorded the status of a member of the secular clergy, a status that allowed him to pursue other forms of ecclesiastical service.

For about a year he served as chaplain to Count Frederick of the Palatinate; but, growing restless with the luxury of the court, along with advice from Ulrich von Hutten against loss of purpose and effectiveness, Bucer sought a pastoral appointment in the territory of von Sickingen in order to pursue more effectively an evangelizing role. Appointment to the pastoral care of the parish of Landstuhl ensued. There, in the course of a popular preaching ministry, Bucer's life was altered by two events: the outbreak of war, initiated by von Sickingen against the elector of

8. Hastings Eels, *Martin Bucer* (New Haven: Yale University Press, 1931), pp. 1-3; cf. Wilhelm Pauck, ed., *Melanchthon and Bucer,* vol. 19 of the Library of Christian Classics (Philadelphia: Westminster Press, 1969), p. 156.

Treves, and Bucer's own decision publicly to marry a former nun, Elizabeth Silbereisen. The latter step raised new problems with regard to his status within the church. Once more he was forced to move, and he decided to resume his studies, this time at Wittenberg with Luther.

In the course of his journey to Wittenberg, Bucer and his wife passed through the city of Wissembourg, where the pastor of the church there, Heinrich Motherer, requested Bucer's aid in the reform of the church's worship and in the preaching of the evangelical message. Over the course of a few months Bucer further developed personal skills in preaching, debate, and the structuring of church reform. Though his preaching was strongly supported by the city council of Wissembourg (often cited as Weisenburg), mounting opposition from the monastic communities in the town and the threat of external attack by forces sympathetic with the bishop of Treves, a Bucer critic, led the city council to order Bucer to leave. The recent, official excommunication of Bucer by the bishop of Speyer lent weight and urgency to the council's action. For his part, Bucer recognized the threat his presence posed for his friends and sympathizers in Wissembourg, and, after offering regrets over ending his promising work there, he — and Motherer too — departed for a new place of refuge and work. They determined upon Strassburg (now Strasbourg), the home city of Bucer's parents — and, for the next twenty-six years, the city served as the locus of Bucer's reforming efforts, the place from which his fame as a reformer and as an ecclesiastical statesman spread extensively over much of Europe.

Strassburg was a free imperial city, and it had already set out on a course of religious reform prior to Bucer's arrival. Earlier, in the 1490s, John Geiler, an earnest son of the church in the city, preached forcefully against a variety of abuses. These efforts bore fruit in 1515, five years after Geiler's death, when the bishop of Strassburg addressed some of Geiler's complaints, issuing a rule "forbidding the priests to wear lay clothes, to carry weapons, to maintain concubines, or to frequent taverns."[9] Popular criticism at the time was also directed against a variety of "sin taxes," e.g., five schillings assured forgiveness for adultery. When Luther attacked the sale of indulgences, copies of his *Ninety-Five Theses* were posted in public places throughout the city. His writings were printed and widely circulated in Strassburg; and, even after the

9. Eels, *Martin Bucer,* p. 21.

Edict of Worms (1521) forbade their publication, Luther's writings continued to be printed there, but without Luther's name attached. These writings of Luther proved to be a powerful force for reform within the city.[10] At first the Luther-inspired reform message found a muted expression in the preaching of a city pastor, Matthew Zell. But by 1521 Zell had shifted his preaching from moral exhortation to a straightforward affirmation and proclamation of the message of justification. Considerable controversy and strife ensued, but the city council endorsed the preaching of Zell and rejected the demand of the bishop of Strassburg that he be dismissed and sent from the city.

Bucer arrived in Strassburg in early May 1523 in the midst of rising religious turmoil. On the 18th of May, on the basis of his parents' citizenship in the city, he requested, as the son of citizens, that the city council grant him its rights and protections. The council approved his request, though it did not at the time assign him any specific pastoral duties within the city. Nevertheless, through the help of Zell and others, he was granted limited pastoral and instructional duties as a source of livelihood since he was destitute and without means of support. In June the council gave permission for Bucer to preach one hour a day on the Gospel of John. But when his sermons attracted ever-larger public audiences, the council, fearful of political ramifications, rescinded Bucer's privilege to preach in German and limited him to instruction in Latin. Bucer obeyed, addressing small groups of students in the home of Zell. Respect for Bucer continued to grow, and the council subsequently gave tacit approval for him to take on an expanded preaching role.

In the midst of these unsettled conditions, Bucer, in the summer of 1523, published a brief work spelling out major features of his understanding of the Christian life in order to make clear to the council and the public how he understood matters of faith. His little book bore the lengthy German title, *Das ym selbs niemant sonder anderen leben soll, und wie der mensch dahyn kummen mög*,[11] — a title that has been rendered in English as "That No One Should Live for Himself but for Others, and How to Attain to This Ideal."[12] The work was translated into

10. Eels, *Martin Bucer*, pp. 21-22.

11. This work in its original German can be found in *Martin Buceri Opera Omnia*, ed. F. Wendel, E. Staehelin, R. Stupperich, J. Rott, and R. Peter, Series 1: *Deutsche Schriften*, ed. R. Stupperich (Gütersloh: Gerd Mohn, 1960), vol. 1: *Früschriften 1520-1524* (1960).

12. Wright, *Common Places*, p. 21.

English only in 1952 under the more felicitous title: *Instruction in Christian Love.*[13] This brief work by Bucer, coming at an early stage in the Reformation movement, has been accorded increased recognition for its significance in tracing the development of Bucer's thought, along with appreciation for its early widespread influence. Wilhelm Pauck, a previously cited historian, failed to note the significance of this work in a 1928 treatment of Bucer's conception of a Christian state,[14] even though the 1523 work bore the substance of much of what was later found in Bucer's final major work, *De Regno Christi* (1550). David F. Wright, in contrast to Pauck, properly observed in 1972 that the short 1523 work, with its accent upon love and service to the neighbor and concern for "the commonweal," anticipated "many features of the mature Bucer."[15] And Martin Greschat, another interpreter of Bucer's thought, has described *Das ym selbs niemant* as "the most important" of Bucer's early works for understanding the systematic/theological origins of his thought.[16]

In Wissembourg, in April 1522, and again a year later in Strassburg, Bucer had proposed debates with Catholic critics on theological matters at issue, offering to submit to death by stoning if it could be shown that he taught anything contrary to Scripture.[17] He was never taken up on these early offers, repeated again by Bucer in 1547 toward the end of his work in Strassburg, a year after the military defeat of the Protestant Schmalkaldic League had brought severe restrictions on Protestant reform activities in Strassburg as well as in other nearby locales. Bucer wrote to John Calvin that he was prepared to make "the supreme sacrifice for faith" if God demanded it.[18] The times were such that death for

---

13. *Instruction in Christian Love: 1523 by Martin Bucer the Reformer,* trans. and intro. Paul T. Fuhrmann (Richmond, VA: John Knox Press, 1952).

14. Wilhelm Pauck, "Martin Bucer's Conception of a Christian State," *Princeton Theological Review* 26 (1928): 80-88. This judgment may be made also about his later introduction to major portions of Bucer's *De Regno Christi* (1550) in *Melanchthon and Bucer.*

15. Wright, *Common Places,* pp. 21-22. Wright's claim that Bucer's accent upon love as service was grounded as much in his early humanism as in his biblical understanding is questioned in the ensuing analysis and interpretation.

16. Martin Greschat, "Der Ansatz der Theologie Martin Bucers," *Theologische Literaturzeitung* 103, no. 2 (1978): 81-96; cf. also Martin Greschat, *Martin Bucer. Ein Reformator und seine Zeit 1491-1551* (München: Beck, 1990).

17. Eels, *Martin Bucer,* pp. 15-16, 26.

18. W. Pauck, *The Heritage of the Reformation* (Glencoe, IL: Free Press of Glencoe, 1961), p. 94.

condemned heretics was a common threat; and, Bucer, no less than Luther and other reformers, lived under those threats. This atmosphere of physical danger — and also the corollary assumption of excommunication and the loss of eternal life — illumines a key passage in Bucer's *Das ym selbs niemant* in which he offered exposition of two linked passages of Scripture. In the course of describing the nature of the ministry of the preached Word, Bucer made reference to the examples of Moses and the apostle Paul:

> Such a ministry consists in this — that the one who is thereto called and ordained by God, dedicates himself to serve God the Father and our Saviour Christ in the work of making the sinner blessed. According to I Timothy 2:4, this was the unique office of our Lord and Saviour Jesus Christ. The minister therefore willingly stakes not only his body and sacrifices not only his material possessions but also his spiritual life and blessedness, if only his preaching the divine Word would lead others to a knowledge of God, to blessedness, and thereby to praise and eternally to glorify the goodness of God. Moses was so minded. When the people of Israel had sinned, he begged God to forgive them, and said: "Lord, either forgive this sin of the people or erase me from the book which thou hast written" (Ex. 32:32). Likewise Paul writes: I tell the truth in Christ Jesus and I lie not, my conscience is my witness in the Holy Spirit, I have in my heart a great sadness and a restless affliction: I have desired to be banished from Christ for the sake of my brethren (Rom. 9:1-3).[19]

Bucer followed these words by pointing up the example of Christ in such a way as to simultaneously underline the message and nature of justification: "Christ not only put up His soul and bodily life for us His little sheep (John 10:11), but was also cursed for our sake so that we might have a part in the blessing of Abraham (Gal. 3:13-14). He, who knew no sin, for our sake became sin so that in Him we might become that righteousness which is valid before God (2 Cor. 5:21)" (p. 31). Then Bucer noted: "He commits no sin, therefore, who loves God and desires to please Him to such an extent that he is ready to forfeit his own salvation in order to obtain this blessedness for his neighbors" (p. 31). At this

---

19. Bucer, *Instruction in Christian Love*, pp. 30-31. Hereafter, page references to this work will be given parenthetically in the text.

point Bucer also called attention to Paul's statement of willingness to surrender his salvation in Christ for the sake of his Jewish brethren (Rom. 9:3) and his declaration, in Romans 8, that "neither life nor death, neither angel nor domination nor power, neither thing present nor thing future, neither height nor depth nor any other creature, could cut him off from the love of God in Christ Jesus our Lord (Rom. 8:38-39)" (pp. 31-32). Bucer pointed out that Paul, in his willingness to surrender his salvation for the sake of his brethren, offered to do what God's grace in Christ basically precluded in the promise that God's will for our redemption in Christ could not be undone.

It is important to observe that Luther earlier had also cited these examples of Moses and Paul, Exodus 32:32 and Romans 9:1-3, but Luther did not develop the meaning of these references in the same way that Bucer did in his 1523 treatise. In his later elaboration of the ninety-five theses in the *Explanations* in August 1518,[20] Luther suggested that since Moses and Paul had been willing to surrender their salvation in this life, he, Luther, would not rule out the possibility that the saints Severinus and Paschal of legend might have done the same in purgatory in order to perfect their love of God. He also cited this legend in the original 1517 version of the theses but without reference to Moses and Paul, though he did not give credence at the time to the legend as such. What Luther accents in his later *Explanations* is that no one attains heaven other than by grace.[21] In Bucer's interpretation, however, a grace, no less transcendent than Luther's, allowed the believer to volunteer his/her personal salvation in this-worldly service to the neighbor along with the seeming contradictory surety that God remained lord in the promise of election in Christ.

This, for Bucer, raised the important question of vocation, or calling. In the historical context, the question of vocation in ministry was sharply raised by the situation of those who broke with the power of Rome and were threatened with death in both physical and "spiritual" terms. Bucer maintained that the vocation of the preached Word involved a willingness to surrender one's personal salvation for the sake of proclaiming the this-worldly gospel of free grace. But this in turn posed a question of Christian vocation for all believers. For Luther, to hear the

20. See above, pp. 86-87.
21. *LW*, vol. 31, p. 178.

gospel, to be justified, meant to have the message of the love and for-giveness of God "written on the heart." This meant for Luther that the believer remained in whatever occupation or position he/she previously filled in life, but now with new meaning and the overflow of a grateful heart making for unselfish works of charity and service in established occupations. Thus, for Luther, all orders of society, all levels of employment within society, were to be enriched by a vivified Christian love and a grateful, spontaneous goodness, at least to the degree that justification took root in the heart of the believer.[22]

Bucer, however, strikes a different note. In this 1523 discussion of the Christian life Bucer offered the view that everyone, pastor and layperson alike, is, in faith, endowed by grace with salvation, the promise of eternal life, and that consideration be given to how that same salvation may be "sacrificed," given up, in neighborly service. Put another way, Bucer — to use an economic metaphor — was asking each believer to consider the future course of "investing," without personal gain, his/her salvation in some form of service to the common good, the "commonweal." Salvation, for Bucer, was conflated with this-worldly service and was inseparable from it. Salvation, for Bucer, represented a this-worldly resource for expenditure, one paradoxically linked to the assured promise: "neither life nor death, nor thing present nor thing future" could separate the believer from the love of God in Christ.

In Luther's *The Freedom of a Christian* there is a line that comes close to what Bucer presents here. Luther remarked that "a Christian

22. Cf. Gustaf Wingren, *Luthers Lehre vom Beruf* (Munich: Kaiser Verlag, 1952), pp. 28-31, 154-55. Wingren stresses the paradoxical, eschatological view in Luther that the believer is always *simul justus et peccator,* justified and sinner, and that vocations are embedded in an earthly existence bound by the overlap of the "two realms," the law-bound realm and that of the Spirit and God's grace. For a 1523 brief statement of Luther's "two realms" teaching, see *LW,* vol. 45, pp. 90-92. On a visit to the chief Luther sites in the German Democratic Republic (the DDR, East Germany) in 1984 during a year-long celebration of the 500th anniversary of Luther's birth, the present writer took special note of one of many regime-sponsored banners designed to enlist Lutheran support for the existing Marxist government. A quote from Luther, the obverse of spontaneous goodness, read: "Do what you are guilty of doing in your vocation" (my translation). I have been unable, thus far, to locate the source of this quote in Luther, but it *does* reflect a major aspect of Luther's "two realms," or "two kingdoms," teaching. It points up an important feature of Luther's view of vocation: that it is essentially defined by one's employment in the socioeconomic order.

lives not in himself, but in Christ and in his neighbor. . . . He lives in Christ through faith, in his neighbor through love."[23] Certainly this parallels in some way what Bucer argued three years later. But whereas Luther suggested that the believer, with heart imprinted by the gospel message, was — even if only at times — freed up for spontaneous, selfless expressions of love for the neighbor (in whatever social, economic position the believer found himself/herself), Bucer offered that the Christian is to expend his/her salvation in a particular life work for the common good, a vocation open to choice and commitment. Thus, along with the description of the calling of pastor/preacher, Bucer identified different occupations, or vocations, that served the commonweal in greater or lesser degree. The office of magistrate, or princely ruler, was held in especially high regard by Bucer. He wrote of that office in the following terms:

> Though its office is not concerned directly with spiritual things such as preaching the Word of God, the estate nearest to the ministry is that of secular authority. It consists in keeping good order and outer peace, in protecting the godly, and, by its penalties, in keeping the ungodly from wronging the godly. The service of the civil authorities is such that it reaches the whole community, whose welfare it should procure by maintaining the common peace and law. This is much more than being at the service of particular businesses and individual men of the community. (p. 34)[24]

In line with the tradition of a *corpus christianum*, a Christian civilization, Bucer held that secular authorities were responsible for governing according to the divine law as contained in Scripture, a law which super-

---

23. *LW*, vol. 31, p. 371. P. Fuhrmann notes that in 1949 Henri Strohl, the French translator of *Das ym selbs niemant sonder anderen leben soll*, suggested that Bucer's work may have been inspired by the last paragraph of Luther's *The Freedom of the Christian*; see Fuhrmann, *Instruction*, p. 54, n. 12. This suggestion of Strohl does not take cognizance of the differing accent in Bucer on deliberative choice of Christian vocation in comparison to Luther's carryover of "the Law written on the heart" (the spontaneity of Christian love) to established, "secular" vocations as forms of service to the neighbor (see above, p. 128 and n. 22). The two forms of service are not essentially contradictory, but Bucer's emphasis suggests a more society-conscious, rationally formulated ethic.

24. In Bucer's frame of reference, the description of the calling of the magistrate would be inclusive of all those who fill bureaucratic offices in contemporary governments.

seded the inherited laws of ordinary political life, those of human law and opinion.

Next, in degree of service to the common good, Bucer named the various services/vocations essential to the practice of agriculture. Bucer wrote:

> God established these two general orders, the spiritual ministry and the secular authority, in order to further the public good. . . . Below the aforesaid two orders are the most Christian orders or professions. They are agriculture, cattle-raising, and the necessary occupations therewith connected. These professions are the most profitable to the neighbors and cause them the least trouble. Every man should encourage his child to enter these professions because children should be encouraged to enter the best profession and the best profession is the one which brings most profit to neighbors. (p. 39)

Of business enterprise, however, Bucer warned: "[Many] men wish their children to become businessmen always with the idea that they would become rich without working, against the commandment of God (Gen. 3:19), and with the idea that they will seek their own profit while exploiting and ruining others, against the divine order and the whole Christian spirit" (p. 40). Bucer concluded: "The more a profession is useful to the needs of the general neighborhood and furthering the profit of the whole community, the more that profession is honorable and Christian and should be cheerfully entered or accepted by each" (p. 40).

One should point out that there is here in Bucer, early on, as well as in the later *De Regno Christi*, a strong and consistent condemnation of idleness in forceful embrace of a "work ethic," the latter not as an expression of uncertainty about "election," as in Max Weber's well-known interpretation of "the Protestant ethic," but rather as an expression of confidence in election/justification parallel to Luther's ethics of gratitude. Love of neighbor and the realities of community demand constant and continuing commitment — but, in Bucer, in chosen fields of endeavor that are not at all points socially and economically predetermined.

Important in all of this is the general framework in which Bucer cast his thought, that of creation — creation as originally intended by God. This may in part be due to Bucer's early training among the Dominicans and a reflection of themes in the thought of the Dominican favorite, Thomas Aquinas. Some have argued the importance of this influence on Bucer, especially, most recently, Martin Greschat, though questions exist regarding the extent of such influence.[25] Bucer prefaced his discussion of neighborly love, as discussed above, with an account of God's original intent in creation. "God," he wrote, "has created all things according to His will and purpose (Prov. 16:4). Hence all things should be directed toward God and be at His service" (p. 21). In fact, Bucer's understanding of creation, and of God's purpose in creation, is a distinctive one, one that Bucer conceived to be a communal life in the form of a positive interdependence and interaction of all creatures. True, humankind was accorded preeminence among all creatures, in line with the Genesis account, and all creatures were seen to be of service and use to humankind, but never, as Bucer saw it, without the obligation to honor lesser creatures in all of their unique features and existence. Bucer cited God's purpose of creating a "helpmeet" to Adam, and saw in that particular Genesis passage a *Gestalt* for what God intended for all other creaturely relationships. He wrote: "Without contradiction this passage means that all things are directed one toward the other; all things outside of man are submitted to man so that they may be useful to him. On the other hand, man rules over all things *for their own good and usefulness*" (p. 24; emphasis added).[26] Bucer continued: "Consequently all things in their respective order are altogether very good. The Scripture, as a matter of fact, calls good only that which brings good to others, such as a good tree which brings forth good fruits" (p. 24). In God's original creation, Bucer wrote, "creatures were so directed one toward the other that they were mutually useful and doing good one to the other" (p. 24).

With the onset of human sin, however, this divinely instituted order

25. See above, p. 125, n. 16.

26. In accenting the purpose of God that Adam have a helpmeet, Bucer raised questions about the general requirement of clerical celibacy. Bucer saw celibacy only as a special gift to some. As noted above, Bucer married soon after his break with monasticism in 1519, and when he moved to Strassburg in 1523 he officiated at a number of marriages for the reforming clergy of that city (see Eels, *Martin Bucer,* pp. 28-29). Later, in *De Regno Christi* (1550), Bucer wrote expansively on marriage and divorce, and argued for the liberalization of divorce laws where marriage had lost its shared, reciprocal sexual meaning; see Wright, *Common Places,* pp. 401-6.

was disrupted, original community destroyed. When humankind, Adam and Eve, turned away from God, the order of nature also got caught up in service of self. As Bucer put it: "[M]an has become selfish. He serves only himself and seeks but his own interest" (p. 26), with the result that nature and its creatures also became alienated and turned against humankind. Bucer remarked: "[T]he whole creation, which should have been used only to the praise and glory of its Creator and for the preservation and profit of men, has been disgraced, profaned, and depraved by our diabolical misuse and self-seeking" (p. 27).

For Bucer, deliverance by Christ, redemption, pointed to a restoration of the original order of creation. Bucer's words are as follows:

All things indeed have been created through Christ Jesus our Saviour. Therefore it pleased God through Him also to bring all things again into the position and order in which they had at first been created. God's revealing of His true children (Rom. 8:19), that is the advent of . . . [persons] who are true believers, would benefit the other creatures (Is. 11:6). From men, then, must begin this universal return to the earliest and right character of creatures. Though not yet perfect, this return of men must begin here and now. (p. 42)

The centrality of this idea of community in Bucer's thought and work[27] was grounded in an ultimate fellowship and the positive, mutually beneficial relationships intended for all creatures, relationships established by God in creation. This original order, distorted by human sin, was in the process of being restored through redemption in Christ — a process under way in the "here and now," leading to a final culmination in eternity. In creation Bucer saw this communal reality prefigured in the communion of the Father, Son, and Holy Spirit in the Godhead, the ultimate ground of all creaturely existence (p. 25). And, Christ as Logos, a full participant in the original creation (John 1:1-5), was, Bucer believed, cur-

27. In 1991, in observance of the 500th anniversary of Bucer's birth, an international gathering of Bucer scholars commemorated Bucer's work with a symposium dedicated to a reassessment of his significance for Reformation studies. The papers read at this Strassburg symposium were edited by Christian Krieger and Marc Lienhard with the title, *Martin Bucer and Sixteenth Century Europe*, 2 vols. (Leiden: Brill, 1993). Selections from this Brill publication were translated into English and edited by D. F. Wright with the title: *Martin Bucer: Reforming Church and Community* (Cambridge: Cambridge University Press, 1994).

rently operative in creation's restoration through the redemptive forgiveness offered in the gospel.

In sum Bucer offered a new accent in theological discussion: the affirmation of vocation for all believers, set against the backdrop of an original interdependent and mutually affirming creation. "Vocation" could no longer be limited to those entering ecclesiastical orders, as in the medieval church, orders essentially oriented to an otherworldly redemption. Here Bucer shared themes with Luther.[28] Vocation was, for Bucer, the necessary concomitant of a restored order of creation, to wit, a disciplined service and love of the neighbor — and all creatures — in this life, one freed, as in Luther, from concern for merit, but one integrated also into ongoing judgments about service to the well-being of the commonwealth.

These themes in *Das ihm selbs niemant* were carried over into Bucer's subsequent work. As one of the more irenic of the Protestant reformers, Bucer labored indefatigably both to build up, structure-wise, the new reformed churches and to resolve developing rifts between segments of the reforming movement, especially among the followers of Luther and the Swiss Protestants influenced by Huldreich Zwingli (1481-1531). He labored equally diligently to overcome the differences between these Protestant groups and the Church of Rome. So ardent was he in seeking to work out agreements with the Roman church that many of his good friends — Luther especially — were troubled by the lengths to which he seemed willing to go to accommodate central points of reformist thought with what were perceived to be biblically questionable theological positions of the Roman church. There were concerns among friends that Bucer, in his "vocation as reconciler and healer," might cross the line where compromise would become surrender.[29] After ambitious efforts by Bucer to resolve major differences between Protestants and Catholics at the Regensburg Colloquy in 1541, an angry Luther, in a letter to a friend, described Bucer as a "toady" and "rogue."[30]

The same Regensburg Colloquy, however, seemed to have represented something of a turning point in Bucer's efforts to reconcile key

28. See above, pp. 120-22.
29. See Eels, *Martin Bucer*, p. 296.
30. Martin Brecht, "Bucer and Luther," in *Martin Bucer and Sixteenth Century Europe*, vol. 1, p. 364.

Protestant beliefs with those of the Roman church. He sensed the decline and withdrawal of the moderate center among his Catholic counterparts. John Gropper, on the Catholic side, a moderate who previously had proved willing to entertain the legitimacy of many Protestant teachings and beliefs, withdrew from dialogue and took up attack. A former trusting relationship between Bucer and Gropper broke down.[31] And early developments in the Catholic Council of Trent (1545-1563) made it increasingly apparent that the church at Rome was set on undertaking reform within itself, exclusive of Protestant participation and dialogue. Regensburg and the subsequent proceedings of the Council of Trent represented, for Bucer, a sort of corporate-historical equivalent of Luther's 1518 encounter with Cajetan and later at Worms: the simple insistence on recantation. In the light of the Bucer story, one can see warrant in H. R. Trevor-Roper's historical judgment that

> [a]t first, in the 1530's, the [Roman] Church had recognized the justice of the [Protestant] challenge. It had contemplated conciliation, appeasement. But then the mood had hardened. The Counter-Reformation papacy, abandoning all thoughts of conciliation, turned to aggression on every threatened front. Clerical wealth, it declared, must be not diminished but increased; there must be not fewer but more regular orders, more lavish propaganda, more magnificent buildings, more elaborate devotions. Moreover, since the Church, to defend itself, needed the power of the princes, the princely bureaucracy, in return, was sustained by the clerical bureaucracy.[32]

The events of Regensburg and Trent, the breakdown of efforts at conciliation, the breaking of promising ties, ended Bucer's ecumenical efforts at major compromise. Thereafter he returned to the role of outspoken advocate of the Protestant cause, less that of mediator. The defeat of the Protestant military forces of the Schmalkaldic League in 1546, along with the resolution of political differences between the papacy and Charles V, made the religious situation of the Protestants in central and southern Germany tenuous. The adoption of the Augsburg Interim of

31. Cf. Eels, *Martin Bucer*, pp. 295-301; Wright, *Common Places*, pp. 42-47.

32. H. R. Trevor-Roper, *Religion, the Reformation and Social Change*, 2nd ed. (London: Macmillan, 1972), p. 34.

May 1548 curtailed the growth of the evangelical cause in sections of Germany and threatened the reforms that Bucer had helped establish in Strassburg. In fact Bucer's own exile from Strassburg and his April 1549 departure for England soon followed. In England he subsequently carried on a reforming work — a brief work but one that nonetheless had some long-lasting effects on the Reformation underway there. Failing in health, cut off from his wide circle of friends on the Continent, he died in Cambridge on March 1, 1551.

With Bucer — as with Luther — there is manifest a continuing awareness of, and responsibility to, a transcendent God. Bucer, along with Luther, found the origin and sustenance of this faith in the Scriptures. In 1544, despite some previous differences with Luther, Bucer acknowledged the latter to have been a decisive influence in his life: Luther had helped open to him the meaning of Scripture, especially as it related to the centrality of the message of grace, a gift in all present circumstances and not alone in the hope of eternity. On this point, Bucer wrote: "As far as evidence avails, no one, since the time of the Apostle [Paul], has expounded more truly or clearly the article of the justification of mankind before God."[33] Bucer also saw in Luther one who, abandoning human safeguards and trusting in Christ, uncovered the overreach and various hypocrisies of the ecclesiastical custodians of "spiritual" power. For Bucer, no one had proclaimed true penance and pure faith with greater diligence than Luther. He viewed the Wittenberger as a singular "man of God," an "instrument of the Holy Spirit" who had accomplished a unique historical work.

But Bucer provided his own contribution as well. With his insight concerning the possible sacrifice of one's salvation in service to the neighbor, the insight that such a surrender pointed beyond itself to God's ultimate election in grace,[34] Bucer shifted the message of "martyrdom" from heavenly reward to faithfulness in earthly tasks. Vocation became the concomitant of faith. For himself vocation meant the duties of preacher, biblical exegete, organizer, and reconciler. For all believers it meant assessment of how best to expend one's gift of grace in earthly

33. Quoted by Brecht, "Bucer und Luther," p. 366; my translation.

34. See above, pp. 126-27. At a number of points, Bucer insisted that it was necessary for the believer to give over anxiety about "falling away" from election, God's enduring grace; e.g., see Wright, *Common Places*, pp. 100-101, 109-12.

tasks. Unlike Luther, who did not stress the consideration of occupational options as a fundamental dimension of faithful commitment and endeavor, Bucer encouraged each believer to maximize service in vocational choice, to consider vocation as a means to the greatest good for the greatest number. He perceived a bond between justification, election, and vocation and made room for a "rationalization" of the Christian life while at the same time holding to the work of the Holy Spirit in shaping and undergirding community. Community entailed a work of discernment and not alone a "writing" of the gospel upon the individual heart. For Bucer — and also for Calvin who followed — vocation meant a vesting of salvation in the here-now world, an engagement of faith that furthered Luther's hoped-for growth toward faithful adulthood and maturity, but one that gave rise to a different kind of engagement — in H. Richard Niebuhr's terms — of Christ with culture. The medieval, hierarchical oversight of culture was displaced by a much more interactive involvement with culture, especially on the part of the political leadership, in shaping a more this-worldly manifestation of the New Testament "kingdom of heaven."

Yet, in Bucer, there lingers ambiguity in his inclination to interpret redemption as the restoration of an original order of creation. Certainly Bucer offered new engagements with the realities of "this world" in contrast to dominant, traditional images of a pilgrimage toward the next. For Bucer salvation in Christ meant a concretion of Spirit in the world in forms other than that modeled by a hierarchically structured ecclesiastical institution. In piety it meant a departure from the medieval mystical transport to another world. Unlike Luther, Bucer saw the law as a means toward the restoration of God's original creation and not primarily as an instrument of judgment and instruction, of restraint of evil and conviction of sin. To be sure, Bucer recognized these also as functions of the law; but with his view that redemption was to be seen as a restoration of an original *communal* creation there is also a sense of movement forward, a call to reorder society, if not always on the basis of a "*new* creation" and appreciation for the spontaneity of Luther's Christian liberty.

In a discussion of marriage and divorce, a discussion in which Bucer's views are, as expected, informed by the words of Scripture, he saw the vocation of women fixed tradition-wise in childbearing, but he also held the deprivation of conjugal rights to be grounds for divorce — something of a marked development over customary belief and practice.[35] In the matter of education, Bucer argued that young girls, as well as boys, should be trained to read and write as a means of guaranteeing equal access to the Scriptures and biblical instruction. In more traditional mode, however, he advised that it was boys, at least those with requisite abilities for learning, who should be encouraged to further skills "for . . . fuller service to Church and State."[36] For the most part, however, Bucer, with his view of redemption as a restoration, seemed to suggest something of the need for a return in time, rather than an appreciation of new possibilities in the future. Nevertheless he embraced the actual world in positive, concrete ways, in ways at variance from those characteristic of medieval otherworldliness. He broke with the previous efforts of his Dominican mentors to enlist Aristotle as proctor in the discernment of a timeless *rational* order of nature. With Bucer the image of God in humankind was not reason, but a calling to community and God's original intent for an inclusive and affirming love, one lost in humankind's rebellion against God, but restated with finality in the gospel.[37] For Bucer a reading of God's intent in creation was essentially dependent upon the message of grace in Scripture. Yet it can be said that Bucer's idea of an overarching redemptive, yet binding, order of creation revealed an orientation with some limits for appreciation of new possibilities arising out of grace, possibilities of new birth and new creation.

Calvin

John Calvin was resident in Strassburg in the years 1538-1541. As a young man, Calvin had embraced the main lines of Luther's teaching

35. Cf. Pauck, ed., *Melanchthon and Bucer,* p. 327; Wright, *Common Places,* pp. 402-7.

36. Pauck, ed., *Melanchthon and Bucer,* p. 336.

37. Pauck, ed., *Melanchthon and Bucer,* p. 334. To this writer it is of note that Barth spends very little time on the contribution of Bucer to Reformation thought, especially in the latter's relationship to Calvin. For Barth the concept of the church as "the communion of saints" is of major import, yet he is strangely silent on Bucer's possible contribution to this understanding of the church in the thought of Calvin, and its obverse as well. In his late work, *De Regno Christi,* Bucer affirms mutual sharing as fundamental to the Christian life; see Pauck, ed., *Melanchthon and Bucer,* p. 183. Yet in Bucer, it should be marked, the sharing is understood chiefly in terms of material goods, whereas in Calvin it is interpreted much more in terms of spiritual gifts making for edification. See also p. 163, n. 80, below.

sometime around 1531-1532, probably while a graduate student in Paris — teachings that by this time had come to be characterized as "Protestant." (There is uncertainty among scholars about the precise "where" and "when" of Calvin's conversion.) In November 1533 Nicholas Cop, a friend of Calvin, serving as the newly elected rector of the University of Paris, delivered a pro-reform inaugural address that was followed by tumult and rioting in the city. Facing persecution and likely death for his assumed part in Cop's provocative act, Calvin fled the city. After finding temporary refuge in other parts of France, he traveled to Basel, Switzerland, where he was able to complete and publish, in 1536, a well-received early summary of Protestant belief. Over the years, with many additions and revisions, this early work, *Institutes of the Christian Religion,* came to be regarded as the leading systematic formulation of Protestant teaching of that time. It reached a final form in the edition of 1559.[38]

In the spring of 1536, Calvin left Basel for brief secret visits in Italy and France. He then set out on a journey to Strassburg, where many French Protestants had found refuge and where Calvin hoped to have conversation with Martin Bucer. Calvin had read some of the latter's works in Latin, though his lack of familiarity with the German language makes uncertain his knowledge of Bucer's German works. On the journey to Strassburg, because of the outbreak of war between the king of France and the emperor, Calvin was forced to make a detour through the French-speaking city of Geneva. There, political ties with the duke of Savoy had been severed and religious subservience to the bishop of the city had been repudiated. The bishop had had close ties, some of them political, with the ruling duke. A religious reform of the city was undertaken under the leadership of a French Protestant by the name of William Farel. When the latter learned of Calvin's arrival in the city in July/August 1536, he sought out Calvin and prevailed upon him to help in the reform effort. Calvin stayed on in Geneva and joined Farel in the work of church reform.

The political situation in Geneva was unstable. There was wide popular support in the city and surrounding areas for independence, but fac-

---

38. For a brief history of the early development of Calvin's *Institutes,* see the Introduction to John Calvin, *Institutes of the Christian Religion: 1536 Edition,* trans. Ford Lewis Battles (Grand Rapids: Eerdmans, 1985), pp. xxxvi-xlv. Hereafter cited as *Institutes (1536).*

tions and divisions within the city's two governing councils, on matters both political and religious, generated unrest. For some months Farel and Calvin pressed a vigorous religious reform, initiating a citywide catechism and seeking the adoption of a common confession of faith. In the course of events the two reformers rejected a council decree enjoining observance of certain ecclesiastical practices favored in the sister city of Bern and then also rebuffed an effort by the two councils to restrict the exercise of excommunication within the church. An election in February 1538 brought to power four "syndics" in the magistracy opposed to the religious reforms instituted by Farel and Calvin. In April 1538, after the two refused to administer the Lord's Supper on Easter Sunday as the Council of Two Hundred had ordered, Farel and Calvin were expelled from the city. Then, in response to standing invitations to come to Strassburg, Calvin decided to join the reforming work there, while Farel returned to Neuchâtel where he had previously labored. With relocation in Strassburg Calvin took on responsibilities as pastor to the city's French Protestant exiles and, in that quieter setting, was able to devote more time to his scholarly theological pursuits.

Some months — almost a year — after the expulsion of Farel and Calvin from Geneva and with the city still in an unsettled state, a letter was sent by Cardinal Jacopo Sadoleto to one of the governing councils of Geneva urging the city to return to the Roman fold. Sadoleto had not had any previous relationships with Geneva, and it is not entirely clear why he chose to intervene in the situation there.[39] His letter was designed to address the anxieties of unsettled believers and cast doubt on the integrity and motivations of the leaders of the reform movement, not only of Farel and Calvin in Geneva, but Protestant reformers in general. A ranking prelate with close ties to the papacy, Sadoleto had twice served as papal secretary. He also bore a reputation for humanist scholarship. His letter to the Geneva authorities reflected an increasingly consolidated Catholic response to Protestant reform, reaffirming set belief in the medieval system of salvation and accenting an otherworldly redemption under the guardianship/control of a hierarchically structured ecclesiastical institution.[40]

---

39. Some have suggested that the initiative may have come from circles in Rome.

40. Carl Becker, *The Heavenly City of the Eighteenth-Century Philosophers* (New Haven: Yale University Press, 1932), offers, I believe, a fair summary description of the medi-

In opening remarks clearly intended to establish a pastoral concern and his long-time commitment to such, the cardinal professed high regard for Geneva and its citizens, declaring a neighborly interest in their well-being. Sadoleto wrote that "twenty-three years ago," when he became bishop of Carpentras (in the south of France), he learned much from his people there of the Genevans and their civic pride: "[E]ven then began I to love your noble city, the order and form of your republic, the worth of its citizens, and, in particular, that quality lauded and experienced by all, your hospitality to strangers and foreigners."[41] He then proceeded to warn the Genevans of the deadly danger in which they stood if they forswore their allegiance to the Roman church. Sections of Sadoleto's extended remonstrance to the Genevans, urging them to assure the salvation of their souls, is helpful in conveying a sense of the polemical atmosphere that attended the extensive Catholic/Protestant "debates" of the times.

Sadoleto wrote:

> [It has come] . . . to my ears that certain crafty men, enemies of Christian unity and peace, [have] . . . cast among you, and in your city, the wicked seeds of discord, [have] turned the faithful people of Christ aside from the way of their fathers and ancestors, and from the perpetual sentiments of the Catholic Church, and filled all places with strife and sedition (such is always the appropriate course of those who seek new power and new honors for themselves, by assailing the authority of the Church). . . . [Such] innovators on things ancient and well established, such disturbances, such dissensions, [are] not only pestiferous to the souls of men (which,

---

eval system of salvation. "Although created perfect, man had through disobedience fallen from grace into sin and error, thereby incurring the penalty of eternal damnation. Yet happily a way of atonement and salvation had been provided through the propitiatory sacrifice of God's only begotten son. Helpless in themselves to avert the just wrath of God, men were yet to be permitted, through his mercy, and by humility and obedience to his will, to obtain pardon for sin and error. Life on earth was but a means to this desired end, a temporary probation for the testing of God's children" (p. 6). Becker might have added that "the way of atonement and salvation" was provided through the church's sacramental system of baptism, confession, penance, eucharist, extreme unction, and priestly ordination.

41. John Calvin and Jacopo Sadoleto, *A Reformation Debate,* ed. John C. Olin (New York: Harper Torchbooks, 1966), p. 30. Hereafter, page references to this book are given parenthetically in the text.

however, is the greatest of all evils) but pernicious also to private and public affairs. (pp. 30-31)

[In order that] we may begin with what we deem most seasonable, I presume, dearest brethren, that both you and I, and all else besides who have put their faith and hope in Christ, do, and have done so, for this one reason, viz., that they may obtain salvation for themselves and their souls — not a salvation which is mortal, and will quickly perish, but one which is ever-enduring and immortal, which is truly attainable only in heaven, and by no means on earth. Our task, accordingly is thus divided — having first laid the foundation of faith, we must thereafter labor here in order that we may rest yonder; we must cast seed into the earth, that we may afterward be able to reap in heaven; and in whatever works, or whatever studies we have exercised ourselves here, may ultimately obtain similar and fit fruits of our works and labors in another life. (p. 32)

We all, therefore, (as I said) believe in Christ in order that we may find salvation for our souls, i.e., life for ourselves; than this there can be nothing more earnestly to be desired, no blessing more internal, more close and familiar to us. For in proportion to the love which each man bears to himself is his salvation dear to him; if it be neglected and cast away, what prize, pray of equal value can possibly be acquired? (pp. 34-35)

Such sentiments and arguments very much convey the tone and intent of Sadoleto's letter to the Genevans. Its orientation is thoroughly otherworldly in its accent upon death and with the implicit and explicit threat of eternal damnation for all who do not return to the fold of the Roman church. In pursuit of this goal Sadoleto denigrated the spiritual integrity of the agents of ecclesiastical and spiritual reform — at least for all those who did not obediently adhere to the "traditional" teachings of the church at Rome. The reformers, Farel and Calvin in particular, but all others as well, were characterized as "innovators," their teachings as "novelties," their motives as exploitative and self-serving. At frequent points Sadoleto adjured his readership to honor the beliefs of their forebears, their parents, grandparents, and more distant ancestors, and to view the church and its hierarchy as guardian and "Mother" of their hope of eternal life.

One encounters here the classic formula that had previously proved successful in containing earlier church reform movements,[42] a formula that equated humility with obedience to ecclesiastical authority, the assertion of salvation by humility, a salvation to be realized after death. Sadoleto writes: "This Church hath regenerated us to God in Christ, hath nourished and confirmed us, instructed us what to think, what to believe, wherein to place our hope, and also taught us by what way we must tend toward heaven. We walk in this common faith of the Church, we retain her laws and precepts" (p. 37). Again, "To that place [heaven] whence the angel, a heavenly creature, was expelled because of pride, man, a creature of the earth, is exalted because of humility, making it plainly appear that humility constitutes both the chief help to our eternal salvation, and the chief support of that sweet and blessed hope with which we tend heavenward" (p. 38). This "salvation by humility" bore with it the concomitant postulate that belief, understood as assent to "traditional" teachings of the church, whether longstanding or relatively recent, was essential to hope for life after death. Here humility as obedience is called to serve the individual as the chief, if not sole, means of salvation.[43] Sadoleto insisted on assent of the Genevans to the claimed, virtually absolute, spiritual authority of the church, the very issue that Luther had confronted in the aftermath of the controversy over indulgences. This same issue had come to further clarification with Luther's more developed theological understanding of justification by faith, the issue that powerfully reinforced Luther's affirmation of the sovereignty of the Word of God and its grounding in God's transcendence.

It is important to note Sadoleto's subsequent argument wherein he stressed the inevitability of eternal damnation that would come to those who adhered to "false teaching" — "that horrid and dreadful sin, by which depraved worship is offered to God, . . . and by which false things are thought of Him, . . . a sin which not only places us in the most immediate peril of eternal death, but also leaves us almost without hope and endeavor to turn aside and shun the peril" (p. 39). He then pointed to

42. See above, pp. 99-100, with n. 79.

43. Sadoleto conjoined with this "humility of belief," humility in "confession of sins to a priest . . . which forms the strongest foundation of our safety, viz., true Christian humility" (Calvin/Sadoleto, *A Reformation Debate*, p. 41).

other theological disputes of the time and a situation of confusion among the general populace, i.e., among those "who are by nature of duller intellect" (p. 39). In this situation, Sadoleto averred that the "the least fear and danger" lay with "believing and following what the Catholic Church throughout the whole world, now for more than fifteen hundred years, or (if we require clear and certain recorded notice of the facts) for more than thirteen hundred years approves with general consent" (p. 40). Trust in the church's traditional teaching and practice is warranted, Sadoleto claimed, because the church "has a certain rule by which to discriminate between truth and falsehood" (p. 40). And this is true about the church even though "the actual manners of many prelates and ecclesiastics were such as might move . . . indignation" (p. 43). He ended his letter by charging that the reformers had rent the unity of the church, a sure sign of their malice and pride, their forsaken condition; and he again pled with the Genevans to return to the true faith in spite of the church's palpable faults in order that the hope of salvation might be restored to them. He assured his readers of his own prayers for them to this end.

Sadoleto's letter was received in Geneva toward the end of March 1539. As one might expect, it created a stir among the political leadership of the city. The magistracy turned to the clergy of the city but found no one whom they thought adequate for a proper response. Sometime in May the city council leadership requested advice on the matter from the city of Bern. And Bern, after some delay, finally recommended that Calvin, Geneva's exiled reformer, be asked to respond. Receiving this request in mid-August, Calvin, in six days' time, wrote an answer and delivered it to Geneva for transmission to Sadoleto. Calvin's reply was expansive though somewhat unstructured, expressive of the need of a hurried, long-delayed response. It reflects a depth of feeling provoked by Sadoleto's tone of spiritual condescension. Overall Calvin made five theological points of note in his rebuttal.

In the first instance, Calvin acknowledged Sadoleto's stature as a respected humanist scholar in his contributions to the recovery of ancient languages and learning. But very quickly Calvin took up Sadoleto's disparagement of the work and earnestness of the reformers in Geneva, the work of Farel, Calvin, and a third, Pierre Viret. Such disparagement was seen as nothing less than an attack upon the legitimacy of the "calling" of Calvin and others in the work of preaching, teaching, and the reform of the church. For many, for almost all, the work of reform was undertaken at great personal risk and sacrifice — and, as in the case of Calvin, even against his own personal inclinations. Calvin writes:

> I will, therefore, in entering into discussion with you, give you credit for having written to the Genevese with the purest intention . . . , and for having, in good faith, advised them to the course which you believed conducive to their interest and safety. But whatever may have been your intention (I am unwilling, in this matter, to charge you with anything invidious), when, with the bitterest and most contumelious expressions which you can employ, you distort, and endeavor utterly to destroy what the Lord delivered by our hands, I am compelled, whether I will or not, to withstand you openly. For then only do pastors edify the Church, when, besides leading docile souls to Christ placidly, as with the hand, they are also armed to repel the machinations of those who strive to impede the work of God. (p. 53)

Calvin insisted that God was at work in the world to bring about a reform of the church through persons dedicated to that end. The reform of the church meant not least the restoration of order, integrity, and rectitude in ecclesiastical office.

This first point led on then to the second: that the meaning of God for faith is more than a pursuit, by each individual, to secure the salvation of his/her own soul. Calvin remarked on Sadoleto's heavy accent upon the threat of eternal damnation, his persistent use of fear and spiritual intimidation to achieve what Calvin succinctly characterized as the chief purpose of Sadoleto's letter, to wit, "to recover the Genevese to the power of the Roman Pontiff, or to what you call the faith and obedience of the Church" (p. 53). Calvin expressed a counterview on this point with the following rejoinder:

> As to your preface, which, in proclaiming the excellence of eternal blessedness, occupies about a third part of your letter, it cannot be necessary for me to dwell long in reply. For although commendation of the future and eternal life is a theme which deserves to be sounded in our ears . . . , yet I know not for what reason you have spun out your discourse upon it here. . . . I am unwilling to divine what your intention may have been. . . . [But] it is not very sound

theology to confine a . . . [person's] thoughts so much to . . .
[himself/herself], and not to set before him [/her], as the prime motive of . . . existence, zeal to illustrate the glory of God. For we are
born first of all for God, and not for ourselves. . . . I acknowledge,
indeed, that the Lord, the better to recommend the glory of His
name . . . , has tempered zeal for the promotion and extension of it,
by uniting it indissolubly with our salvation. But since He has
taught that this zeal ought to exceed all thought and care for our
own good and advantage, . . . it is certainly the part of a Christian
. . . to ascend higher than merely to seek and secure the salvation of
[his/her] own soul. (p. 58)

Calvin added that he believed that anyone "imbued with true piety" is
likely to regard as "insipid, that long and labored exhortation to zeal for
heavenly life," a zeal that keeps a person confined within self-devotion
(p. 58).

What Calvin argued here — in line with accents found also in Bucer
— is that preoccupation with one's eternal salvation, the constant theme
and motif of Sadoleto's appeal — is an inadequate, deficient representation of the life afforded by faith in the gospel. He basically argues that
the gospel offers release from undue life-after-death preoccupations and
enjoins one to pursue the this-worldly purposes of God, purposes contained in Calvin's phrase, "sanctifying the name of God" — or quite
simply, "glorifying God" — the latter not limited to a worship of God
but expressed as well, more fully, in a life of faith directed to the well-
being of human life in this world. In Calvin's thought the human soul is
not so much an eternal sanction of selfhood, though it may in part bear
that character; chiefly, it is to be understood in its potential for this-
worldly existence in and devotion to the purposes of God.

In response to Sadoleto's charge that the reformers had introduced a
false worship of God and thereby had violated the nature of the church,
Calvin countered, in a third point, that the church is not a structure sustained by an irrevocable possession of the Spirit, a possession affixed to
hierarchical office, but that it is essentially a community of faith nurtured and governed by the Word of God, a community realized not only
in hearing and responding to the Word in worship but also in the ordering of ecclesiastical life and in corporate edification. The Spirit, Calvin
maintained, is not operative independent of the Word; the Spirit func-

tions to confirm God's Word in the hearts — and Calvin adds — also in the minds of believers. He writes to Sadoleto:

> When you describe . . . [the Church] as that which in all parts, as well as at the present time in every region of the earth, being united and consenting in Christ, has been always and everywhere directed by the one Spirit of Christ, what comes of the Word of the Lord, that clearest of all marks, and which the Lord himself, in pointing out the Church, so often recommends to us? For seeing how dangerous it would be to boast of the Spirit without the Word, He declared that the Church is indeed governed by the Holy Spirit, but in order that that government might not be vague and unstable, He annexed it to the Word. For this reason Christ exclaims that those who are of God hear the Word of God — that His sheep are those which recognize His voice as that of their Shepherd. (p. 60)

Calvin insisted that God continues to rule — continues, transcendent and sovereign, in the preaching and hearing of the Word, confirmed through the agency of the Holy Spirit.

Calvin's inclusion of the mind with the heart of the believer in the latter's coming to faith suggests something of a variance from Luther. Calvin sees the issue of righteousness and faith not only in terms of an inspired, grateful heart, engendering freedom and spontaneous goodness in the life of the believer; he held also for a renewed and deepening understanding of the faith, an understanding in process, which grows toward maturity within the community of faith. The work of the Holy Spirit in its linkage with the Word brings with it "edification," an edification that is constituted and furthered in the context of an interacting community of the Word. Against Sadoleto, Calvin argued that there can be no simple subscription to the "teachings and doctrine of the church," even for those of "duller intellect," no final fallback on what parents or grandparents may have believed. He rejected the medieval formula of "humility equals obedience to the church equals salvation/eternal-life." Humility, for Calvin, was marked, fundamentally, by a present openness to, and edifying awareness of, the Word of God, an openness that carries over also to the future. "Away, then, with that nugatory simplicity (which you say becomes the rude and illiterate) of looking up and yielding to the beck of those more learned!" (pp. 79-80). "All that you leave to the faithful is to shut their own eyes, and to submit implicitly to their teachers" (p. 77). Rather, with Paul (2 Cor. 13:10), to speak with authority means to adhere to "the proviso that [such speaking] was to avail only for edification, was to wear no semblance of domination, was not to be employed in subjugating faith" (p. 77). "[The] Church of the faithful does not force you into any other order than that in which the Lord wished you to stand . . . , [one in which] a Prophet holding the place of teacher should be judged by the congregation (1 Cor. xiv.29)" (p. 77).

(In this connection it should be noted that, earlier in the 1536 edition of the *Institutes*, Calvin spoke already of the church as "the communion of saints" in which all believers were bound together by the mutuality of shared spiritual gifts.[44] And, in a later edition of the *Institutes*, Calvin remarks: "The highest wisdom, even of him who has attained the greatest perfection, is to go forward, and endeavor in a calm and teachable spirit to make further progress. . . . God . . . [assigns] to each a measure of faith, that every teacher, however excellent, may still be disposed to learn."[45])

In this light and context, Calvin offered rejoinder to Sadoleto's contention that the reformers were intent on violating the unity of the church and that, according to John 17, this represented prima facie evidence that disruptive controversy within the church was disobedience to Christ. Calvin insisted that silence in the face of manifest abuses within the church was itself "to connive" in that evil. He argued that to be open to instruction in the Word cannot possibly be regarded as "derogating from the majesty of the Church . . . , [that there is a] great . . . difference . . . between schism from the Church and studying to correct the faults by which the Church herself was contaminated" (pp. 88-89). Far from seeking schism, the reformers, Calvin averred, labored solely for "the edification of the Church." As the prophets of old, who sought to restore the religion of Israel, had been persecuted and killed by the rulers of the church of that day, so too the prophets of Calvin's time suffer "fires, swords, and gibbets," but they cannot be "regarded as schismatics" (p. 85).

44. *Institutes (1536)*, p. 63.

45. John Calvin, *Institutes of the Christian Religion*, trans. Henry Beveridge (Grand Rapids: Eerdmans, 1953), vol. 1, pp. 471-72 (3.2.4). Hereafter cited as *Institutes (1559)*. I have added book, chapter, and section numbers to allow tracking in other editions of the 1559 edition of the *Institutes*.

Calvin's fourth counterpoint was a reply to Sadoleto's charge of "novelty" in the reformers' teaching. Sadoleto had contrasted the long 1,300/1,500-year history of the church's teaching with what he termed "innovations introduced within these twenty-five years, by crafty or, as they think themselves, acute men" (pp. 40-41). The issue posed here was that of the authority of "tradition" vis-à-vis that of Scripture (the Word of God). In response, Calvin argued that far from innovating, the reformers were intent on recovering what was substantively at the heart of the church's faith but that had been distorted through neglect, ignorance, and superstition over the centuries, distorted gradually, incrementally, so that the average believer had come no longer to discern, let alone grasp, the message of redemption. Calvin wrote: "You know, Sadoleto, . . . not only that our agreement with antiquity is far closer than yours, but that all we have attempted has been to renew that ancient form of the Church, which, at first sullied and distorted by illiterate men of indifferent character, was . . . almost destroyed by the Roman Pontiff and his faction" (p. 62). Calvin then asked Sadoleto to place "before your eyes, that ancient form of the Church, such as their writings prove it to have been in the age of Chrysostom and Basil, among the Greeks, and of Cyprian, Ambrose, and Augustine, among the Latins; after so doing, contemplate the ruins of that Church, as now surviving among yourselves" (p. 62).

Calvin offered critical example of this kind of distortion in the church's teachings and practices in regard to purgatory. He wrote:

> As to purgatory, we know that ancient churches made some mention of the dead in their prayers, but it was done seldom and soberly, and consisted only of a few words. It was, in short, a mention in which it was obvious that nothing more was meant than to attest in passing the affection which was felt toward the dead. As yet the architects were unborn by whom your purgatory was built, and who afterwards enlarged it to such a width, and raised it to such a height, that it now forms the chief prop of your kingdom. You yourself know what a hydra of errors thence emerged; you know what tricks superstition has at its own hand devised, . . . you know how many impostures avarice has here fabricated, in order to milk men of every class; . . . how great detriment it has done to piety. . . . For . . . while all, without any command from God, were

vying with each other in helping the dead, they utterly neglected the congenial offices of charity . . . [for the living]. (p. 73)

Calvin charged that the church's teachings on purgatory represented a serious distraction by otherworldly fears, enhanced by religious fancy and subject to exploitation by the church hierarchy. The end result was frequently the neglect of the believer's this-worldly responsibilities and possibilities. These distractions had grown over time to the point that the stress on purgatory had become a major source of the church's power and wealth and led to a destructive loss of focus on the gospel of Christ.

Such a process of progressive neglect and obfuscation had also contributed, Calvin charged, to the transformation of the "sacred Supper" into the reenactment of a ritual "sacrifice," — "by which the death of Christ," a once-for-all event, was "emptied of its virtues" (p. 74). Instead of freeing the faithful for engagement in vocation in the midst of the world, it was reduced chiefly to a means of access to the other world, waiting finally on the coming of death. Rather than providing the trusting believer with a body of truth approved "throughout the whole world . . . for . . . fifteen hundred years . . . with general consent," the church, over the course of time, had in fact furthered its own innovations and "novelties," which had brought the church, through ignorance and through the exploitation of its power, to its present state of confusion and moral decay.

Calvin's critique of "tradition" included a discussion of the then relatively recent introduction — during the papacy of Innocent III (1198-1216) — of required annual auricular confession to a priest. Far from instilling a "saving humility,"[46] this practice brought in its train a variety of new legalistic abuses. Auricular confession to a priest, Calvin wrote, "was neither commanded by Christ, nor practiced by the ancient Church. . . . [The Scriptures do not support the practice] . . . while the common books on ecclesiastical history show that it had no existence in an earlier age. The testimonies of the Fathers are to the same effect" (p. 72). Calvin added that the worship of the saints showed similar development to the point "that the intercession of Christ was utterly erased from men's thoughts"

---

46. On the theme of humility Calvin commented: "[I]t is very far from being true that every kind of abasement, which assumes the name of humility is commended by God. Accordingly, Paul teaches (Col. ii.18) that that humility only is genuine which is framed in conformity with the Word of God" (Calvin/Sadoleto, *A Reformation Debate*, p. 72).

(p. 72). Against Sadoleto's charge of twenty-five years of innovation and novelties by the reformers, Calvin pressed the counterargument of decades, centuries, of ecclesiastical innovations that condoned, and furthered, superstitious practices. Such practices served to enhance clerical power at the expense of a freely proclaimed gospel of forgiveness. The extent and the degree of such innovation, for Calvin, was made apparent by the Word of God, the source of awareness of God's present rule over the consciences of the faithful (p. 91).

A final major point, the fifth, in Calvin's rejoinder to Sadoleto was restatement and clarification of the nature of justification by faith. Sadoleto had offered in his letter a summary of his understanding of Luther's teaching on this matter. In his letter he offered, in the form of a prayer, caricature of a typical Protestant believer making affirmation — after rejection of church-imposed obligations such as confession, fastings, etc., "that we should trust to faith alone, and not also to good works (which are particularly extolled and proclaimed in the Church), to procure us righteousness and salvation — seeing, especially, that Thou hadst paid the penalty for us, and by Thy sacred blood wiped away all faults and crimes, in order that we, trusting to this our faith in Thee, might thereafter be able to do, with greater freedom, whatsoever we listed" (p. 44). Calvin, in response, rejected "[this] calumny, . . . that we take away the desire of well-doing from the Christian life by recommending gratuitous righteousness. . . . We deny that good works have any share in justification, but we claim full authority for them in the lives of the righteous. For if he who has obtained justification possesses Christ, and at the same time, Christ never is where His Spirit is not, it is obvious that gratuitous righteousness is necessarily connected with regeneration" (p. 68).[47] Calvin continued with the point that union with Christ in faith, the acceptance of Christ's righteousness in place of one's own, bears with it "the Spirit of holiness, who regenerates the soul to newness of life." Here Calvin linked justification with sanctification. In relation to Luther, this represents, in Calvin's terms, an affirmation of Luther's "ethics of gratitude" wherein the motivation for ethical action is grounded in grace rather than the threat of an impending punishment and the need of satisfaction, with continuing anxiety about final resolution at death.

47. Calvin's affirmation of "gratuitous righteousness" parallels Luther's exposition of "spontaneous goodness" in *The Freedom of a Christian*.

Similarly Calvin argued a close bond between justification and election. Calvin's own words best express his meaning, words that shed light on the nature of Calvin's understanding of predestination.

> Paul . . . says (Eph. i.4) that we were chosen in Christ, before the creation of the world, to be holy and unblameable in the sight of God through love. Who will venture thence to infer either that election is not gratuitous, or that our love is its cause? Nay, rather, as the end of gratuitous election, so also that of gratuitous justification is, that we may lead pure and unpolluted lives before God. For the saying of Paul is true (I Thess. iv.7): we have not been called to impurity, but to holiness. This, meanwhile, we constantly maintain, that . . . [humankind] is not only justified freely once for all, without any merit of works, but that on this gratuitous justification the salvation of . . . [humankind] perpetually depends. . . . [Who] can assign any other cause of our adoption than that which is uniformly announced in Scripture, viz. that we did not first love . . . [God], but were spontaneously received by Him into favor and affection? (p. 69)

Calvin followed with an observation to Sadoleto: "Your ignorance of this doctrine leads you on to the error of teaching that sins are expiated by penances and satisfactions" (p. 69).

As noted, Calvin sent his reply to Sadoleto via the magistracy of Geneva, to be forwarded then to the cardinal. Little is known of its receipt by Sadoleto. Calvin's letter, along with that of Sadoleto, was published in Strassburg in September 1539. Calvin's own French translation of both letters was published in Geneva in 1540 (pp. 26-27). Sadoleto entered into no further exchanges or efforts to win back the Genevans to the medieval church; rather, he spent considerable energy over the following years on the problem of internal Catholic reform, especially in relation to the education of its clergy. In 1542 he was called back to Rome to help formulate a reform agenda for the Council of Trent (1545-1563).

THERE IS little question that close ties were established between Calvin and Bucer over the course of Calvin's stay in Strassburg in the years 1538-1541. What is not clear is the degree of Calvin's acquaintance with Bucer before 1538. Uncertainty surrounds the question whether he had actually met Bucer before 1538. The question is not crucial, but it speaks to the matter of the nature and degree of Bucer's influence on the younger man. As observed above,[48] Calvin seems to have been familiar with some of Bucer's writings at an early stage of his own theological development. A passage in Calvin's *Institutes* of 1536 — no doubt dated to at least 1535 — suggests that Calvin had become familiar in some form with the content of Bucer's early work *Das ym selbs niemant sonder anderen leben soll, und wie der mensch dahyn kummen mög;* for in a passage in the first edition of the *Institutes* Calvin offers a parallel to the main theme of that work:

> In the entire law we do not read one syllable that lays down a rule . . . on the things . . . [one] may or may not do for his/her own advantage. And obviously, since . . . [we] were born in such a state that . . . [we] are completely inclined to self-love, there was no need of a law gratuitously to enkindle further that already immoderate love. Hence it is very clear that we keep the commandments not by loving ourselves but by loving God and neighbor. . . . *[No one] lives in a worse or more evil manner than . . . [one] who lives and strives for him[/her]self alone, and thinks about and seeks only his own advantage.*[49]

These 1535 words also anticipate Calvin's indignation at Sadoleto's recurring injunction that the first duty of everyone is to seek and secure the salvation of his/her own soul — a view which Calvin characterized as "insipid" in the face of the assurance of grace bestowed in the gospel.

In a manner similar to Bucer, Calvin fashioned a link between justification and election. Bucer, as discussed above, presented this link most strikingly in his interpretation of the relationship of Romans 9 to Romans 8, making reference to the fact that in the ninth chapter the apostle Paul offered to surrender his salvation in Christ for the sake of his brethren, an action, a separation, which the grace of Christ precluded in the eighth chapter ("[Nothing] can separate us from the love of Christ. . . .").[50] Calvin picks up on Bucer's 1523 linkage of Moses' will-

---

48. See above, p. 138.
49. *Institutes (1536)*, pp. 28-29; emphasis added.
50. See above, pp. 126-28.

ingness to surrender his own blessedness for the sake of Israel (Exod. 32:32) with Paul's in Romans 9:3 and similarly affirms a purpose, God's "glory," the doing of God's will in this life, that beckons beyond the quest for one's own personal, eternal salvation. In 1536, three years before the exchange with Sadoleto, Calvin wrote: "[I]f all hope of our own private good were cut off, still we should not cease both to desire and entreat with prayers . . . [the] hallowing [of God's name] and the other things that pertain to God's glory. In the examples of Moses and Paul, we see them turning their minds and eyes away from themselves . . . in order that, despite their own loss, God's glory and Kingdom might be advanced [Exod. 32:32; Rom. 9:3]."[51] For Calvin, appreciation of God's gratuitous election prior to birth coincides with God's imputed righteousness in justification, its reception and affirmation by the believer in faith — and, in turn, the adoption by the believer of freedom to live in a different way in the world. It removed the burden of trying to prove oneself acceptable before God through lifelong penance. Rather than focusing upon a priestly administered confession/penance practice, the life of faith, the life of the believer, was to be lived in vocation.

The reformers' teaching on election — and its further, later development in Calvin's teaching on predestination[52] — besides underlining the message of gratuitous salvation/faith, voided the medieval church's stress upon purgatory, prayers and masses for the dead, and the mediating and intercessory role of "the saints," along with the latter's supposed contributions to a "treasury of merit" overseen and administered by a hierarchically structured church. As Luther had critiqued the church's various claims to power over individuals' eternal destinies via its interpretation of "the keys of the Kingdom,"[53] so Calvin also discussed the question of

51. *Institutes (1536)*, p. 75.

52. For a brief interpretation of Calvin's teaching on predestination, see Wilhelm Pauck, *The Heritage of the Reformation*, revised and enlarged edition (Glencoe, IL: Free Press of Glencoe, 1961), pp. 66-70. Of special note in Pauck's interpretation is his statement that "Predestination . . . was for Calvin merely an appendix to the doctrine of justification by grace. He was a predestinarian because he believed absolutely in the initiative of the God of mercy" (p. 69). Pauck does not see Calvin's linkage of predestination and justification informed by Bucer's thought in the manner suggested above. For other of Pauck's insights into the Reformation and the nature of Protestantism, see esp. pp. 91, 96-98, 102-4, 109-10, 139-41, 213-17, 236-38.

53. See above, pp. 89-92.

"the keys" at five different points in the 1536 edition of the *Institutes*.[54] His discussions on the subject affirmed Luther's contention that the gift of the keys was a gift to the corporate body of the church and was not posited in any assumed ecclesiastical office. He accented the text in John 20:22-23 where the gifts of forgiveness and "binding/loosing" were granted to all of the disciples at the outset of a preaching mission. They were bestowed on Peter alone only in connection with a specific occasion. Notable in Calvin's treatment — drawing on John's account of the disciples' preaching mission — was his insistence that the preaching of God's Word, the gospel of forgiveness, was itself the "binding/loosing." Calvin wrote: "This command concerning forgiving and retaining sins and that promise made to Peter concerning binding and loosing have to be referred solely to the ministry of the Word. . . . For what is the sum total of the gospel except that we all, being slaves of sin and death, are released and freed through the redemption which is in Christ Jesus [cf. Rom. 3:24]."[55] Again: "We conclude that the power of the keys is simply the preaching of the gospel, and that with regard to men it is not so much power as ministry. For Christ has not given this power actually to men, but to his Word, of which he has made men ministers."[56]

Insisting that service to the Word precludes an exercise of power which confuses the purpose of edification with domination, Calvin stressed the primacy of the Word also in his reinterpretation of "the last days." We have noted above that Luther believed he was himself living in the end-time, the impending end of history. Luther marveled that he had gotten caught up in such an expanding, Europe-wide theological controversy. As a simple monk he had been summoned to a hearing at Worms before the emperor — the embodiment of imperial political power — to testify on matters of faith. All of this Luther saw as foreshadowing a culminating work of God. It was suggested earlier that this sense for the end times may have constricted the scope of Luther's criticism of the structures of social/political power. A Christian quietism seems to have emerged from his injunction that "Christian vocation" was to be exercised within the established orders of employment and political office present in society. No doubt, as a second-generation reformer, Calvin

54. *Institutes (1536)*, pp. 60-61, 143-44, 146-47, 157-58, 185-86.
55. *Institutes (1536)*, pp. 143-44.
56. *Institutes (1536)*, p. 144.

gained distance from the immediacy of Luther's sense of an approaching end-time. It can be argued that Calvin's removal from such an immediate end-time contributed to the shaping of a new Christian consciousness of historical existence. Writing in criticism of what he regarded as past "innovative" teachings of the church, teachings that obscured and distorted trust in the gospel, Calvin argued the finality of the biblical witness to Christ. In the process he declared that every encounter with the Word of the gospel represented experience of "the last days." He observed: "God has so filled all functions of teaching in his Son that we must regard this as the final and eternal testimony from him. In this way the whole New Testament time, from the point when Christ appeared to us with the preaching of his gospel even to the Day of Judgment, is designated . . . by 'the last hour' [1 John 2:18], 'the last times' [1 Tim. 4:1; 1 Pet. 1:20], 'the last days' [Acts 2:17; 2 Tim. 3:1; 2 Pet. 3:3]."[57]

What needs to be added to this heightened sense of decisive encounter with God in the written and preached Word was Calvin's sense of the inexhaustible character of God's wisdom in the Christ event, in the "foolishness" of the cross. In his later commentary on 1 Corinthians,[58] Calvin offered insight into this central, paradoxical expression of God's transcendence, which gave support to a forward-movement in time, one marked by the necessity of reckoning with inherited and clouded human visions and understandings. Calvin spoke throughout his theological works of the incomplete nature of the human assimilation of the gospel truth. He wrote in this sense also in the letter to Sadoleto:

> [Though] . . . the faithful soul is never so destitute as not to have a straight course to salvation . . . I do not, however, dream of a perspicacity of faith which never errs in discriminating between truth and

57. *Institutes (1536)*, p. 187. One must note an interesting similarity here in Calvin with the twentieth-century thought of Rudolf Bultmann, who stressed encounter with God in the eschatology of the Word. See Rudolf Bultmann, *Jesus Christ and Mythology* (New York: Charles Scribner's Sons, 1958), p. 44.

58. See *Calvin's Commentaries*, ed. David W. and Thomas F. Torrance, *The First Epistle of Paul the Apostle to the Corinthians*, trans. John W. Fraser (Grand Rapids: Eerdmans, 1960). Calvin writes: "When the Lord deals with us in such a way that He seems to act in an absurd way because He does not make His wisdom plain to see, nevertheless what appears to be foolishness surpasses in wisdom all the shrewdness of men. Further, when God hides His power and seems to act in a weak way, what is imagined to be weakness is nevertheless stronger than any power of men" (p. 42).

falsehood, is never deceived; nor do I figure to myself an arrogance which looks down as from a height on the whole human race, waits for no man's judgment. . . . On the contrary, I admit that pious and truly religious minds do not always attain to all the mysteries of God, but are sometimes blind in the clearest matters. (p. 79)

Essential at this point is the observation above[59] with regard to Calvin's understanding of the church as "the communion of saints": "The highest wisdom, even of him who has attained the greatest perfection, is to go forward, and endeavor in a calm and teachable spirit to make further progress. . . . God . . . [assigns] to each a measure of faith, that every teacher, however excellent, may still be disposed to learn."[60] Calvin saw the community of faith as one in process. Edification, the need of it by every believer, was ongoing. Not only the heart imprinted by the Spirit, but a mind renewed — understanding — was also a component of faith. As Calvin put it: "[Scripture teaches] . . . that with faith understanding is conjoined."[61]

Fundamentally indebted as he was to Luther, Calvin went on to develop more fully a sense for the corporate-historical nature of the church. For Calvin maturity and adulthood bore with it not only a sense of responsible freedom, but also a mutual sharing in the understanding of faith. Whereas Luther saw the need always to come back to and gain renewed inspiration/motivation in justification,[62] Calvin saw growth and development for the believer in the linkage of justification and sanctification. He remarked: "We do not obtain salvation either because we are prepared to embrace every dictate of the Church as true, or leave to the Church the province of inquiring and determining, but when we recognize God as propitious Father through the reconciliation made by Christ, and Christ as given to us for righteousness, sanctification, and life."[63]

59. See above, p. 147.

60. *Institutes (1559)*, vol. 1, pp. 471-72 (3.2.4).

61. *Institutes (1559)*, vol. 1, p. 471 (3.2.4).

62. Lennart Pinomaa makes this point in *Faith Victorious*, trans. Walter J. Kukkonen (Philadelphia: Fortress Press, 1963), p. 143: "Rightly understood Luther's ethics is an ethics of gratitude. The righteousness which is received again and again as a gift becomes again and again the reason for gratitude, and from this is born the desire to help and serve one's fellowman again and again."

63. *Institutes (1559)*, vol. 1, pp. 470-71 (3.2.4).

To be sure, Christ was known in the gospel, but along with this founding grace there was also within the fellowship of the church an accompanying variety of gifts and graces — the plural is of note here. For Calvin, the priesthood of all believers was marked not alone by care and the bestowal of loving acts upon the neighbor (out of gratitude, "spontaneous goodness") but by mutual, ongoing edification as well. Critical to Calvin's understanding of the church was the Pauline image of the body and its parts, with every part contributing to the well-being of the whole and every part in turn being nurtured and sustained by all the other parts. The key role of Romans 12:3-8, 1 Corinthians 12:4-14, and Ephesus 4:4-13 in setting forth this understanding of the church is basic throughout his writings. Far from the stereotypical image of the isolated, "elect" individual, Calvin's individual believer, with his/her unique spiritual gift(s), was understood as one who "fitted in" to a shared, communal life. Each is, and must be, a participant. Calvin wrote: "No member has its function for itself, or applies it for its own private use, but transfers it to its fellow members; nor does it derive any other advantage from it than that which it receives in common with the whole body. Thus, whatever the . . . [believer] can do, [that individual] is bound to do for . . . [the] brethren, not consulting . . . [individual] interest in any other way than by striving earnestly for the common edification of the church."[64] "All the elect of God are so joined together in Christ, that as they depend on one head, so they are as it were compacted into one body, being knit together like its different members; made truly one by living together under the same Spirit of God in one faith, hope, and charity."[65]

Again, perhaps some measure of Bucer's influence upon Calvin is to be found in this description of the faith community. Calvin shared with Bucer the need to understand faith in terms of corporate responsibilities and interactions — and not in terms of the attainment of personal merit. There is possibly echo of Bucer's early words: "[Before] all creatures, man must so direct his being that in all his doings he seeks not his own, but only the welfare of his neighbors and brethren for the honor of God."[66] With Calvin, however, as distinct from Bucer, it is the redemptive community, rather than a pristine creation, that served as the context and

64. *Institutes (1559)*, vol. 2, p. 11 (3.7.5). See below, p. 229.
65. *Institutes (1559)*, vol. 2, p. 282 (4.1.2).
66. Bucer, *Instruction in Christian Love*, p. 29.

model for ethical response. Bucer too accented redemption; but, with Bucer, this was mirrored back onto creation; and it was from this "redeemed order" of creation that Bucer read off a world-embracing ethical mandate, a new post-medieval version of the natural order and its "law." With Calvin, however, ethical thought took off from the present reality of an edifying, growth-committed, faith community. Ethics was nurtured in faith and edification, in heart and mind together, a maturing process of growth in Christ, growth in the body of Christ.

This difference of Calvin from Bucer is paralleled by still another difference of Calvin from Luther, one that furthered the heightened sense of corporate-historical existence. In his 1536 *Institutes* Calvin showed familiarity with the key point of Luther's 1520 treatise on Christian freedom: Luther's discovery/assertion that the hearing of the gospel was the occasion, through the Spirit, of God's writing "the law upon the heart," the originating source of "spontaneous goodness" in the believer. For Luther, this was assumed/expected to carry over into each believer's place of employment in society. Here, however, Calvin, in some variance from Luther, accented a "third use of the law" in addition to Luther's stress upon both "conviction of personal guilt" and "restraint of evil." Calvin proffered:

> [To] the believers, too, in whose hearts the Spirit of God already lives and reigns . . . [the law] provides no unimportant use, warning them as it does, more earnestly what is right and pleasing in the Lord's sight. For even though they have the law written and engraved upon their hearts by the finger of God [Jer. 31:33; Heb. 10:16], that is, have been so moved and quickened that they long to obey the Lord's will, they still profit by the law because from it they learn more thoroughly each day what the Lord's will is like.[67]

Luther recognized the ongoing purpose and use of the law, in its condemnatory (conscience) and social functions (restraining evil), but he also saw it as a continuing threat to a conscience freed by faith, a temptation to seek merit. Calvin saw this danger also but argued that a conscience nurtured in faith need not shun positive social uses of the law, that in fact the law could serve as a guide to the doing of God's will, individually and collectively. Though he maintained, with Luther, that the law was not a means to salvation, an instrument of merit or of saving

---

67. *Institutes (1536)*, p. 36; cf. *Institutes (1559)*, vol. 1, p. 309 (2.7.13).

good works, Calvin held that the law could serve the end of helping point up the goal of God's will for both the individual and the community. The law, Calvin wrote, "does not now perform toward us the part of a hard taskmaster; . . . but . . . points out the goal,"[68] a goal that bore within it a sense, as well, of an eternal destiny.

From this understanding Calvin garnered insight into, and formed his views of, corporate, political life and the nature and forms of government. In the circumstances of the times, there was a pressing need that this question be addressed. As a second-generation reformer, Calvin recognized the breakdown of the unity of Christendom, both theologically and politically. Hierarchical structure had failed in the test of its adequacy vis-à-vis ecclesiastical reform under the Word of God. And, to be sure, Calvin also carried over some of that old order into Geneva, where he and the city council resorted to the power of government to repress "heretical" and socially disruptive forces while at the same time seeking to realize new possibilities of social existence. The persistent question of religion's role as the assumed moral and ethical ground of civil society came expectedly to the fore in Geneva, a question that sees resurgence again in our own times.[69] But for his part, Calvin shared a growing sixteenth-century humanist awareness of historical development and diverse political structures. He carried to his discussion of government the conviction that varied forms of government were analogous to the Spirit's bestowal of the variety of gifts/graces within the community of saints. For Calvin, God's providential ordering of history bestowed gifts also in forms of government. He wrote in 1535-1536: "[As] you will surely find if you fix your eyes not on one city alone, but look around and glance at the world as a whole, or at least cast your sight upon regions farther off, divine providence has wisely arranged that various countries should be administered by various kinds of government."[70] And, in the

---

68. *Institutes (1559)*, vol. I, p. 310 (2.7.13).

69. For example, in the mid-twentieth century the philosophical theologian Paul Tillich offered the view that political, social, and religious/ideological systems over time lose their capacity to instill a sense of vital meaning and then generally resort to the use of power to try to preserve the old structures of meaning for an uncertain, changing future. Tillich characterized attempts to impose a declining order of meaning upon a new emerging era as "heteronomy"; see Tillich's collection of essays *The Protestant Era* (Chicago: University of Chicago Press, 1948), esp. pp. 55-58.

70. *Institutes (1536)*, p. 211.

later 1559 edition of the *Institutes* he declared: "The authority possessed by kings and other governors over all things upon earth is not a consequence of the perverseness of men but of the providence and holy ordinance of God. This is clearly taught by Paul when he enumerates government *(proistamenos)* among the gifts of God, which, being variously distributed according to the diversity of grace, ought to be employed by the servants of Christ to the edification of the Church."[71] This positive reading of government and historical development as a dimension of God's grace is further underlined when Calvin observed that in 1 Corinthians 12:28 Paul uses the same Greek word for the office of rule in society, i.e., government, that he uses to denote the office of rule by the elders in the church. "There can be no doubt," Calvin argues, "that [Paul] is recommending every kind of just government."[72]

In relation to the different forms of government, Calvin described three main types: monarchy, aristocracy, and democracy. He interpreted monarchy to be rule vested in one person, aristocracy as "dominion of the principal persons" of a community or nation, and democracy as rule by the general populace. While indicating that Christians were to be respectful and grateful for every form of just rule, he offered his own view that each had flaws that could lead to abuse. He offered his own preference for aristocracy, or better, a mix of aristocracy and democracy, on the principle that human imperfections are such that it is "safer and more tolerable when several bear rule, that they may thus mutually assist, instruct and admonish each other, and should any one be disposed to go too far, the others are censors and masters to curb . . . excess."[73] One does not need to point out that this admonition on rule in government parallels his view on the nature of ministry and instruction in the church that all should be open to the insights of others to the purpose of general edification[74] and also, one might add, justice.

This train of thought in Calvin points to new, this-worldly concerns

71. John Calvin, *On God and Political Duty* (Indianapolis: Bobbs-Merrill, 1950), p. 48; cf. *Institutes (1559)*, vol. 2, p. 654 (4.20.4).

72. *Institutes (1559)*, vol. 2, p. 654 (4.20.4).

73. *Institutes (1959)*, vol. 2, p. 657 (4.20.8).

74. There is much in Calvin's theology that supports the theory of checks and balances in government, especially in its insistence on the need for openness to instruction/edification and correction at the highest levels of political power, even as it derives from lower levels in the magistracy.

and projects leavened by commitment to an interactive process of correction and growth. Calvin, through his Strassburg/Geneva experiences, was able to fashion a long-lived ecclesiastical structure that offered an alternative to the medieval, hierarchical model, one different also in principle from the classical republican model. Calvin adhered to the longstanding Christian prohibition against the overthrow of government in accord with Romans 13:1-7, but his discussions in this regard also heightened the sense of need, if not "right," for effective, responsive government. The "third use of the law" represented for Calvin no simple adoption of the Mosaic code; rather, the "third use" called for thoughtful engagement with new social, economic realities.[75] He pointed out that much of the law provided in God's dealings with Israel was of a nature unique to that people in their times, but, like the forms of government, the laws of Israel were not binding upon all peoples and all times. This was not to say that the substance of the Ten Commandments did not apply to peoples beyond ancient Israel, but that Christian rulers and peoples in different times and places were obliged to shape their own societies to the needs of justice and the divine will as they were variously confronted by different circumstances.

With Calvin, the diversity of gifts in the communion of saints made for an enriched experience and appreciation of the one grace (justification). In lesser degree, but nonetheless analogously, the historical-political realm of peoples and nations were to make their way in an interactive, historical encounter. In 1536, in the first edition of the *Institutes*, Calvin warned against being offended by providential historical diversity since such "diversity [was] perfectly adapted to maintain the observance of God's law. . . . For utterly vain is the boast of some, that the law of God given through Moses is dishonored when it is abrogated and new laws preferred to it. For either others are not preferred to it when they are more approved, not by simple comparison, but with regard to the condition of times, place, and nation; or that law is abrogated that had never been enacted for us."[76] Calvin continued: "For the Lord through the hand of Moses did not give that law to be proclaimed among all nations;

---

75. See Andre Bieler, *The Social Humanism of Calvin*, trans. P. T. Fuhrmann (Richmond, VA: John Knox Press, 1964) for Calvin's social and economic views. This work is dated in some particulars, but still good on economic questions. See also Jane Dempsey Douglass, *Women, Freedom, and Calvin* (Philadelphia: Westminster Press, 1985) on gender issues.

76. *Institutes (1536)*, p. 217.

but when he had taken the Jewish nation into his safekeeping, defense, and protection, he also willed to be a lawgiver especially to it: and — as became a wise lawgiver — he had special concern for it in making those laws."[77] Here Calvin spoke to a corporate justification and freedom for peoples and nations in history, one that went beyond a humanly assigned role for God as gatekeeper of the "other world" beyond death. At this point, corporate-historical existence was given meaning in fresh awareness of God's reigning sovereignty in history, a meaning with an altered apocalyptic and eschatology.

It is appropriate to cite again in this context the phrases and accents in the vision and calling of John Winthrop and those who shared with him the journey to a New World almost a hundred years after Calvin recorded his own testimony.[78] In a shipboard sermon on the voyage to New England in 1630, Winthrop declared:

> We must entertaine each other in brotherly affection, wee must be willing to abridge ourselves of our superfluities, for the supply of others necessities, wee must uphold a familiar Commerce together in all meekeness, gentlenes, patience and liberality, we must delight in eache other, make others condicions our own, rejoyce together, mourne together, labour, and suffer together, always haveing before our eyes our Commission in the worke, our Community as members of the same body; soe shall wee keep the unitie of the spirit in the bond of peace, the Lord will be our God and delight to dwell among us . . . so that we shall see much more of his wisdome, power, goodness and truthe than formerly wee have been acquainted with . . . that men shall say of succeeding plantacions: the Lord make it like that of New England; for wee must consider that wee shall be as a City upon a hill.[79]

In a monumental work, published at the end of the first decade of the twentieth century, the social-ethical historian Ernst Troeltsch presented

77. *Institutes (1536)*, p. 217.

78. The present writer has cited these words in a previous work, *Technology, Theology and the Idea of Progress* (Louisville: Westminster/John Knox Press, 1991), in anticipation of the fuller theological/historical background provided in the present work.

79. Darrett B. Rutman, *John Winthrop's Decision for America* (Philadelphia: Lippincott, 1975), p. 100.

a summary of the historical development of Calvinism in contrast to that of later Lutheranism. The present study suggests that, rather than Troeltsch's largely socio-historical analysis, quoted below, the differences of Calvin from Luther hinged on a perceived, continuing, communal interaction with a transcendent God, which moved Reformed communities of faith still further out of the valley of the shadow of death and "otherworldly" preoccupations, into creative and often subversive roles in relation to inherited social, economic, and political structures. For communities leavened by Geneva, eschatology and apocalyptic notions were absorbed into the actualities of the present realities of God's lordship and were less confined to past forms and traditions. God's sovereignty was seen to involve the social order in a way that carried further Luther's earlier qualification of spiritual inwardness.[80] In modification of Luther's affirmation and anticipations of "spontaneous goodness," edifying and liberating as they continued to be, Calvin spoke freely and persistently of a "voluntary obedience" that summoned up corporate social responsibilities, even when they became absorbed, at times, in restrictive "blue law" propensities, an aspect of Calvinism's subsequent historical program. Though certainly not beyond challenge at points, Troeltsch's summary account of differences between the ethos which came out of Wittenberg and that which came out of Geneva offers perspective on, and need for, continuing reflection and assessment. Writing in 1911, Troeltsch observed:

> After a period of initial success Lutheranism ceased to advance. This must be attributed, in the main, to its stress on personal piety,

---

80. Karl Barth writes on this point: "[T]he *communio sanctorum* is the event in which the *sancti* [believers] participate in . . . [the] *sancta* [gifts of the Spirit]. . . . It takes place, in relationship to the world as the fellowship of those who are moved by the burdens of the world, and the promise given to it, as their own inmost concern; yet also, in this relationship, as the fellowship in arms of those who are determined, in order to be true to the world and meaningfully to address themselves to it, not in any sense to be conformed to the world. It takes place as the fellowship of service in which the saints assist and support one another, and in which they have also actively to attest to those outside what is the will of the One who has taken them apart and sanctified them." Barth continues: "[The gifts of the Spirit] . . . are not entrusted to any of us as private individuals. They are entrusted to us all only in conjunction with others. In this way, but only in this way, are they entrusted to each of us personally" (Karl Barth, *Church Dogmatics* IV/2, *The Doctrine of Reconciliation*, trans. G. W. Bromiley [Edinburgh: T. & T. Clark, 1958], p. 643).

its acceptance of the existing situation, its acquiescence in the objectivity of the means of grace, as well as to its lack of capacity for ecclesiastical organization, and its non-political outlook. It was the destiny of Calvinism to extend the Reformation of the Church throughout Western Europe, and thence out into the New World. . . . [A reason for this] . . . lies in the active character of Calvinism, in its power for forming Churches, in its international contacts, and in its conscious impulse towards expansion, and most of all, in its capacity to penetrate the political and economic movements of Western nations with its religious ideal.[81]

Consideration will be given in the following chapter to Troeltsch's suggestion for the "penetration" of a Reformation "religious ideal" into subsequent "political and economic movements" — though not in the form of Troeltsch's "idealistic," Kantian supposition. This will be done in relation to a brief review of the English Reformation as the context for an exposition of the thought of Francis Bacon, who played a formative role in the development of the idea of progress and was frequently cited in connection with the discussion of that idea in Chapter 2 above. Bacon, as the source and occasion of significant new thinking in the Western intellectual tradition, was a blend of various influences, some difficult to trace. A uniquely creative thinker, Bacon provided important intellectual grounding for the modern, post-medieval "culture of change." Certainly he serves as a prime example of "the change in the attitude toward change," the initiation of a positive view of change markedly different from the inherited Greek and medieval Christian disposition which viewed change as a "deficiency of being." This shift in outlook is apparent, theologically, in the Reformation heritage of Luther, Bucer, and Calvin, and is, as we have argued, distinctly associated

81. Ernst Troeltsch, *The Social Teachings of the Christian Churches*, vol. 2, trans. Olive Wyon (New York: Harper Torchbooks, 1960), pp. 576-77. One of the basic presuppositions that influences Troeltsch's work throughout is his assumption of a "religious a priori," the source of "religious ideals," an innate human impulse or disposition that underlies the "history of religions." Such a presupposition, as appealing and seemingly reasonable as it may appear, disposes one to read the particularities of historical religions as manifestations of a general human faculty or propensity. It hardly needs pointing out that both Luther and Calvin would have rejected such an assumption. In our time, the common use and embrace of the term "spirituality" fits well with Troeltsch's anthropocentric (via Kant) supposition.

with the rediscovery of divine transcendence as a prime factor in the human understanding of God's relation to the world, leading on to expression of new responsibilities of faith in the light of newly perceived realities. The discussion of Bacon suggests positive links between the sixteenth-century theological revolution and the emergence of subsequent, even "secular," expressions of continuous new insight and edification in relation to this-worldly developments.

Chapter 5

The English Reformation: The Ripple Effect of Reformation in Francis Bacon

I t cannot be denied that processes of change had already begun to accelerate throughout Europe in the century and more before the Reformation. New worlds had been discovered; the growth of commerce was contributing to the expansion of city and town life. Social and economic pressures were building against the feudal system. Technological breakthroughs in timekeeping, military warfare, navigation, and printing had made for new confidences and configurations of power. The Renaissance had accomplished major advances in art, along with the recovery of ancient languages and literary traditions. The question that needs to be asked is whether and in what ways the change engendered by the Reformation had an effect upon the changes already under way. That Luther, Bucer, and Calvin were all in some degree influenced by the humanist recovery of long-neglected linguistic skills and an accompanying well of classical learning made them part of an intellectual movement already under way. But they also left the company of many, if not most humanists, in identifying and giving expression to a crisis of spiritual meaning, one that saw in change the work of an active Providence. If a fractured Christendom was forced to address the issue of how and in what ways religion played a constitutive role in the maintenance of a viable social order, a new question also arose as to the degree to which order and direction within change were expressive of divine purpose. In the Reformation, faith took on a historical purpose and commitment not only because the world was changing but also because a transcendent God was believed to be actively present in that world and its times. The scope of God's sovereignty was perceived in a larger, more dynamic frame — or, put another way, a renewed sense of God's active lordship provoked faith's free embrace of an emerging world and concomitantly loosed it from the totalizing grip of a humanly envisioned "other world." In allowing God to exercise free lordship over grace and life, important elements of Reformation faith came to recognize new realities in the concrete, experienced world.

In his 1536 *Institutes* Calvin had noted this larger frame in its import for government and the Christian's response to government. For Calvin, government was an expression of "common grace," which came in diverse forms. As noted above,[1] Calvin affirmed diversity in the forms of government — and also in the matter of law, arguing that in God's providence the laws that are designed to uphold and guide society are not, and cannot be, a simple imposition of the laws of Israel; rather, aspects of the laws of Moses were expressions of God's special legislation for Israel in its own particular times and places. Calvin argued that God has no less concern and love for people in "the conditions of other times, places, and nations" and that government and law must thus be understood in terms of diverse circumstances. To quote Calvin again on this point: "[D]iversity [was] perfectly adapted to maintain the observance of God's law. . . . For utterly vain is the boast of some, that the law of God given through Moses is dishonored when it is abrogated and new [i.e., Christian] laws preferred to it."[2] Not only individuals within the faith community were recipients of God's special providence and accorded special responsibilities, but nations as well were caught up under this divine governance. Thus Christian social and political responsibilities were assumed to vary with the forms of government and the locales of human community. What was commonly shared was the one redeeming, justifying grace in Christ. But Christian social and political responsibilities in Wittenberg were of one order, those in Geneva of another — and those in London, in England, were of still another.

The story of the Reformation in England is, naturally, distinctive and unique.[3] It was, as one might expect, a worried one. In England the Ref-

1. See above, pp. 159-62.
2. Quoted above, p. 161. Cf. Karl Barth, *The Theology of John Calvin*, trans. G. W. Bromiley (Grand Rapids: Eerdmans, 1995) for an early 1922 Barth reading of Calvin.
3. G. R. Elton, *Reform and Reformation in England, 1509-1558* (Cambridge, MA: Harvard University Press, 1977), and A. G. Dickens, *The English Reformation*, 2nd ed. (Uni-

ormation encountered a long-established church and church structure, one closely linked with the monarchy and with most of the usual ties with Rome. In Germany the Protestant churches were established under the sanction of princes, dukes, and free municipal governments. In the break with Rome various levels and forms of government were often regarded as active sponsors of reform. In Switzerland, within cantons dominated by certain cities and towns, elected municipal councils were, most frequently, the chief agents of reform, this often in response to public preaching that garnered support among the general populace. In England there were some parallels to this in the spread of evangelical preaching and pamphleteering. But in England reform was peculiarly entwined with issues of state associated with the rule of Henry VIII. Henry VIII happened also to be an interested lay theologian, initially strongly opposed to the teachings of Luther. In 1521, Henry circulated — whether he wrote it entirely himself is a question — a short treatise in which he defended traditional church teaching and excoriated Luther's reform teachings. For such loyalty, the pope, Leo X, bestowed on him the title "Defender of the Faith," a title that has ever since attached to the bearer of the English crown.

Later, however, as Henry's concern for a male heir and continuity in succession to the throne became increasingly the focus of his attention, he sought in 1527 a papal annulment of his marriage to Catherine of Aragon, an aunt to Charles V, the Habsburg Holy Roman Emperor and also king of Spain. Henry's case for annulment was weak but not unreasonable when weighed against earlier papal practice.[4] It was also complicated by a political power struggle between France, the papacy, and Spain. Initially, the case was brought to an ecclesiastical council of the English church, but the issue was regarded of such moment that it was decided to send the case first to Rome for determination. Strategy and maneuvering in the case were managed by Cardinal Thomas Wolsey, primate of England, the papal legate, and powerful chief minister to the king. After delay and equivocation, Pope Clement VII, successor to Leo X, refused Henry's request for divorce and remarriage. Then, when

---

versity Park: Pennsylvania State University Press, 1989), offer scholarly accounts of the English Reformation.

4. See A. G. Dickens, *The English Reformation* (New York: Schocken, 1987), pp. 125-29.

efforts to find a religious sanction for divorce elsewhere in Europe's universities — also in Wittenberg — failed, Henry turned again to the council of the English church for approval of his divorce. In the process he essentially declared himself to be the head of that church, the overseer of ecclesiastical power in England. As a further step, he reasserted a 1353 English law of praemunire.[5] This law allowed the king to forbid, without his personal approval, the appeal of questions of dispute beyond the borders of England. As a result of his failure to persuade the papacy in the matter of the king's divorce and also in the face of growing royal financial problems, Cardinal Wolsey fell from favor and was disgraced, charged with major acts of malfeasance, and imprisoned. Never politically popular, Wolsey died before his scheduled trial in 1530 and was succeeded in the role of lord chancellor by Thomas More, a loyal son of the Roman church. More had been a leading parliamentary critic of Wolsey; but then he himself soon resigned the office of lord chancellor in 1532. As a devout Catholic, More refused to acknowledge any but the authority of the pope as supreme in the church. In 1534, he was executed for treason for his refusal to affirm the king's authority under the 1533 act of Restraint of Appeals.[6]

Except for the pope's claim of supreme authority in the English church, Henry remained generally committed to basic Catholic beliefs and practices, especially transubstantiation, the invocation of saints, purgatory, and masses for the dead. In the course of general political and religious turmoil, Henry turned to a commoner, Thomas Cromwell, for political advice and direction in dealing with Parliament. The Parliament in elected office from 1529 to 1536 came to be known as the "Reformation Parliament," since it was this parliament which passed into law a series of ecclesiastical reforms that historians term the "Henrician reform," a nationalization of the church under the English crown, even though many traditional church beliefs and practices were preserved. Cromwell guided many of these changes through Parliament, laws that formalized and extended the break with Rome by forbidding payment to the papacy of annates (one year's diocesan income for newly appointed bishops), laws that closed most of the smaller monasteries along

---

5. Elton, *Reform and Reformation,* p. 51.
6. For a brief account of More's career — and as a "controversial saint" — see Dickens, *English Reformation,* pp. 160-66.

with confiscation (for the royal treasury) of their endowments. Parliament, guided by Cromwell, established the practice of the appointment of bishops only upon the king's nomination and cancelled clerical oaths of obedience to the papacy. The Supremacy Act of November 1534 explicitly declared the English monarch to be the supreme authority in the English church. And then, in 1537, permission was given for the sale of the Bible in English, followed a year later by Cromwell's decree that an English-language Bible was to be made accessible to the public in every church, a decree that was given active support by the archbishop of Canterbury, Thomas Cranmer. In 1539 the lands and endowments of the larger remaining monasteries were also confiscated.

Despite his own conservative religious beliefs, Henry allowed Thomas Cromwell, who seems to have had Lutheran leanings,[7] some latitude in introducing Protestant-type reforms, especially the above-mentioned promotion of the English Bible. In other matters of state Cromwell refashioned the operations of government, laying the foundations for a modern state. However, he, too, fell from favor after the failure of an arranged marriage of Henry to Anne of Cleves — also in conjunction with aristocratic intrigue against the commoner Cromwell. The latter was charged with both heresy and treason and was executed in July 1540.

In the aftermath of Cromwell's downfall, conservative religious sympathies regained ground in governing councils until Henry's death in 1547. Then, with the succession to the throne of Edward VI (1537-1553), a new phase of the English Reformation began. Edward was the only son of Henry, the offspring of the marriage to Jane Seymour, who had died shortly after Edward's birth. Henry provided a classical education for Edward. But, after Henry's death, Edward Seymour, later the duke of Somerset, requested and was accorded the role of Edward's "protector" by the governing council assigned to oversee matters of state during the early years of the young monarch's reign. Under the guiding hand of Somerset, Edward was provided an education in the tenets of Protestant belief. Broader tolerance of differences in religious belief was also furthered throughout the kingdom. Over the three years of Somerset's status as protector, Parliament enacted a number of measures favorable to

---

7. Dickens discusses these leanings in Cromwell; see Dickens, *English Reformation,* pp. 130-35.

Protestantism, all of which moved beyond the Henrician reform. In the Holy Communion, the cup was administered to the laity, images were removed from the churches, the marriage of priests was allowed, and the rule of orthodox belief under Henry was repealed. (Henry's earlier "Six Articles" had officially decreed punishment by fire for denial of transubstantiation and had affirmed masses for the dead, auricular confession, a celibate clergy, and private masses.) In 1549 an Act of Uniformity decreed the use of a book of common prayer — printed in English — in churches throughout the kingdom. Archbishop Cranmer oversaw the work on the prayer book — and also offered sanctuary in England for persecuted Protestants from Europe, many of them preachers forced from their pulpits by Emperor Charles V's institution of the Interim Settlement. Martin Bucer was among those who found refuge in England at the time. Bucer, along with others among the emigrés, was enlisted in a further revision of the English prayer book, bringing it into greater conformity with leading continental Protestant teachings — but also leaving ambiguous certain wordings in the service of Holy Communion to make room for elements of traditional Catholic belief.

Political and economic circumstances led to domestic unrest under Somerset, and he proved unsuccessful in checking the spread of French influence in Scotland, chiefly accomplished through the betrothal of the Scottish princess Mary, later "Mary Queen of Scots," to the heir of the French throne, later to become Francis II. The earl of Warwick, the duke of Northumberland, conspired against Somerset and displaced him in October 1549, arranging, after a brief delay, for the latter's execution. Northumberland proved more politically ruthless than Somerset. In religious affairs, often with the advice and influence of Cranmer, he pressed additional reforms in Parliament. Another Act of Uniformity in 1552 adopted a second, revised prayer book, one that eliminated prayers for the dead, replaced the altar with a communion table, and replaced the special communion wafer with common bread in the service of Holy Communion. A set of forty-two articles of belief and instruction, articles even more distinctively Protestant than any found in the 1552 prayer book, was authorized by King Edward shortly before his death in June 1553.

This account of the Reformation-come-to-England through the reign of Edward VI suggests a very unsettled progression, very much caught up in the play of political interests and forces. Yet, one should not suppose that Henry VIII and his special interest in a male heir (and suitable wives) were the chief, or the sole, factor in establishing a Bible-centered faith and church in England's break with papal authority. G. R. Elton, for example, in his interpretation of the origins of the English Reformation,[8] lays important emphasis upon a lay reform movement dating to the late fourteenth century that also stressed the centrality of the Bible in matters of faith. Though consistently harassed by ecclesiastical authorities and condemned as heretical, the Lollard movement persisted into the sixteenth century despite the martyrdom of many of its adherents. So also did the memory and influence of John Wyclif (1328?-1384), an Oxford don and founding spirit of the Lollards. Wyclif was posthumously declared a heretic at the Council of Constance (1415), along with the Bohemian reformer John Hus. As noted earlier Wyclif's bones were exhumed and burned as a result of his heretical condemnation. This history, joined with other issues such as corruption among the clergy, contributed to a strong undercurrent of anticlerical feeling which fostered a widespread, indigenous feel for the need of religious reform.

For hundreds of years Europe had been home to a broad, varied movement favoring local control of regional churches. Economic issues, especially the papal drain on national wealth, fed restlessness. A political struggle over control of the church and economic resources was present during much of the Middle Ages. At points in the past, this became a struggle over ultimate authority between the papacy and various European monarchs. The church at first fought for its own independence in the appointment of bishops. This was especially the case under Pope Gregory VII (in office 1073-1085).

But, after Gregory (Hildebrand), the struggle of the church for independence from political control often became an assertion of papal dominance over political rule throughout Europe. This was largely the case under popes Innocent III (in office 1198-1216) and Boniface VIII (in office 1294-1303). The assertion of papal supremacy over all secular power ("caesaro-papism") reached its high point under Boniface. In effect, Boniface made assertion of this-worldly rule for the church on the basis of its claim to control access to the life hereafter, the life beyond the grave. It utilized the instruments of excommunication and interdict as threats to opposing rulers and people, this in addition to claiming

8. See n. 3, above.

oversight of political rule based on the previously discussed "Donation of Constantine."

For their part, many political figures sought to establish or enhance their own local rule through control and appointment of bishops, bishops who would then be expectedly pliant to the interests and desires of their political patrons. "Erastianism," the term for such political dominance over the ecclesiastical institution, was also a phenomenon in Europe through much of the Middle Ages. Such was the policy among many of the Holy Roman emperors of the eleventh and twelfth centuries and was notably successful under the French monarchs of the fourteenth century, particularly Philip IV (reigned 1285-1314), who was able, with the election of a French pope, to have the papal seat moved for a time from Rome to Avignon. English kings in the thirteenth and fourteenth centuries pursued similar efforts to enhance regal and national power through the appointment of subservient church officeholders. Marsilius of Padua (1290?-1342?) in his notable *Defensor Pacis* offered a persuasive statement of the Erastian position, one that also found sympathetic expressions in the works of the Italian poet Dante Alighieri (1265-1321) and John of Paris (1265-1306), a Dominican. It is noteworthy that Henry VIII, after his accession to the throne, gave pointed expression to this Erastian point of view some years before he sought annulment of his marriage to Catherine. In 1519 he is reported to have spoken of "kings of England as monarchs who had never had any earthly superior but God alone."[9] A large measure of the Henrician religious reform in England can be read in the light of this Erastian background as well as Henry's own conservative theological views. Henry's break with papal authority was subsequently joined with popular access to an English translation of the Bible, to the spread of a vernacular liturgy, and to a growing emphasis on preaching. These developments moved beyond what Henry seemed to have originally intended and embraced.

After the death, at age sixteen, of Edward VI in 1553, the rule in England fell to Mary Tudor, daughter of Catherine of Aragon, Henry's first wife. An effort was made by the chief minister, Northumberland, to divert the succession to a grandniece of Henry, Lady Jane Grey, wife to

9. Elton, *Reform and Reformation,* p. 56; see his n. 14 for brief discussion of the authenticity of Henry's remark.

one of Northumberland's sons. The move failed, largely as a result of popular support for the right of succession, seen properly to belong to Mary, even though she remained an ardent Catholic. Mary was a cousin of Charles V, the Holy Roman Emperor, to whom she turned for advice in the first year of her rule. Basic among Mary's goals was the restoration of Catholicism as the established religion of England.

There is no need, for our purposes, to dwell long upon the details of Mary's rule. Her five-year reign (1553-1558) proceeded cautiously at first in religious matters. She succeeded in getting Parliament to declare Henry's marriage to her mother, Catherine, a valid one and then to repeal most of Edward's religious reforms. This step basically returned England to the situation of Henry's earlier religious reforms. Then in 1554 she sought to fashion strong political ties with Spain through marriage to Philip, heir to the throne of Spain. But initiation of this foreign tie proved unpopular at many levels of English society.

With the agreement of the papacy, Mary refrained from an effort to restore to the church its former monastic properties and endowments, a move that would have stirred strong opposition from the new landholders and other beneficiaries of Cromwell's earlier steps. The arrival in England of the new papal legate, Cardinal Reginald Pole (1500-1558), gave further direction to Mary's religious reforms, and they took on an increasingly restrictive character. Even though Pole bore a reputation for humanist learning and was a close colleague of Cardinal Sadoleto in framing a 1537 program of Catholic church reform,[10] he came to champion an increasingly harsh policy of repression of Protestant views in England. Protestant-leaning bishops and clergy were removed from their ecclesiastical positions, many of them forced to seek refuge on the Continent. Pole announced the nation's papal absolution from heresy; then, on November 30, 1554, Parliament voted to reinstitute papal authority in the English church. Parliament passed measures to repeal Henry VIII's ecclesiastical reforms and restore severe laws against heresy. This move was followed by active pursuit and prosecution of declared heretics, a number of them former prominent bishops and clergy. Cranmer was one

10. John Calvin and Jacopo Sadoleto, *A Reformation Debate,* ed. John C. Olin (New York: Harper Torchbooks, 1966), p. 10. A number of the reforms in the 1537 proposal to Pope Paul III were adopted at the Council of Trent (1545-1547, 1551-1552, 1562-1563); see Steven Ozment, *The Age of Reform: 1250-1550* (New Haven: Yale University Press, 1980), pp. 402-3.

of these. Among those who fell victim to the repression were also many laypeople: tradesmen, merchants, and ordinary citizens.

Altogether, 280 or more persons were declared heretics and burned at the stake from early February 1555 until Mary's death on November 17, 1558. Most authorities agree that the burnings had the opposite effect of the one intended. Along with Mary's Spanish marriage, they projected an image of an alien rule. Mary herself was given the sobriquet "Bloody Mary." To this day historians speculate whether a more humane policy on the part of Mary and Pole could have won back England for Catholicism. But some, like G. R. Elton,[11] argue that the seeds of Protestant belief were already deeply rooted in English soil from the fifteenth-century Lollard movement onward. Also, the decades of religious discussion and controversy during Henry's rule were too much to be undone during Mary's brief reign. Cardinal Pole died on the same day as Mary — an incidental fact that historians are prone to note. The deaths closed a traumatic chapter of history for many in England.

However one assesses Mary Tudor's brief, unhappy rule, the accession to the throne of Elizabeth I, queen from 1558 to 1603, marked a change in the tenor of English national life. Early in the first parliamentary session under the new queen (January-May 1559), her chief minister, Lord Keeper Nicholas Bacon (1510-1579), offered a statement of policy on behalf of the queen that set forth a new sense of national purpose. With the consent of the queen, Bacon declared on that occasion:

> Now the matters and causes whereupon you are to consult are chiefly and principally three points. Of those the first is of well making of laws, for the according and uniting of the realm into an uniform order of religion, to the honour and glory of God, the establishing of the Church, and tranquility of the realm. . . . For [this] first, the queen's majesty having God before her eyes, and being neither unmindful of precepts and divine councils, meaneth and intendeth in this conference, first and chiefly there should be sought the advancement of God's honour and glory . . . whereupon the policies and of every good common-wealth are to be erected and knit. . . . And . . . the well and perfect doing of this cannot but make good success in all the rest. . . . Wherefore her highness

---

11. See Elton, *Reform and Reformation*, pp. 388-89.

willeth and most earnestly requireth you all . . . that in this consultation, you with all humbleness, singleness and pureness of mind, confirm yourselves together, using your whole endeavour and diligence by laws and ordinances to establish that by which by your learning and wisdom shall be thought most meet for the well performing of this godly purpose.[12]

Although addressing, in the first instance, the need for a post-Marian reform of the English church, Nicholas Bacon also spelled out in this address the goal of fashioning a more viable, participatory "commonwealth." Whereas for the Roman church England remained a prize to be regained, a people to be restored to papal authority and to the Roman church's proprietary status as guardian and dispenser of an otherworldly salvation, for Bacon and a majority in Parliament under the reign of Elizabeth, England had become a *project* rather than a prize, a project in which members of Parliament were to become participants in framing "laws and ordinances," both private and public.[13] Though in the first instance Parliament was enlisted in the reform of the church, the message of reform embraced the communal nature of the commonwealth's well-being. There is some, perhaps chance, parallel in Nicholas Bacon's words at this point with Calvin's rebuttal of Cardinal Sadoleto that, for humankind, the purposes of God go beyond each person's effort to secure his/her salvation, to wit, the affirmation and betterment of corporate existence.

Thus, along with the call to reform the church, Bacon pointed to a second but equally necessary task of reviewing and revising the laws of

---

12. Simonds D'Ewes, *A Compleat Journal of the notes, speeches & debates of both the House of Lords & House of Commons, the whole Reign of Queen Elizabeth* (London: Paul Bowles, 1693), p. 11.

13. In a discussion of Parliament's legislative record during the reign of Elizabeth, Michael Graves, in his *Elizabethan Parliaments 1559-1601*, 2nd ed. (London/New York: Addison Wesley Longman, 1987, 1996), seems to see a fundamental conflict between Parliament's attention to "public" and "private" [i.e., local] legislation. He does not address the question of the degree to which both broad public policy and local legislation helped play roles in shaping a commonwealth. Though he cites evidence that concentration on national policy questions frequently revolved around matters of royal succession and alliance with Catholic continental powers (France, Spain), Graves does not address the issue/question of how "England-as-project" may have been grounded in a new religious perspective or consciousness.

the land. Bacon commissioned Parliament to review "whether the Laws before this time made be sufficient to redress the Enormities they were meant to remove, and whether any Laws made but for a time, be meet to be continued for ever, or for a Season. . . . To be short, you are to consider all other imperfections of Laws made, and all wants of Laws to be made, and thereupon to provide the meetest Remedies, respecting the Nature and Quality of the disorder and offence; the inclination and disposition of the people; and of the manner of the time."[14]

A third task that Nicholas Bacon assigned to Parliament, as a commission from the queen, was consideration of the financial needs of the nation, the need to raise new taxes and levies. England, Bacon pointed out, had fallen into dire straits as a result of commitments and losses abroad, especially the recent loss of its important cross-channel territorial holdings in and around the port of Calais. England was confronted with new security needs, the strengthening of its naval forces and garrisoning its northern border with Scotland against a French presence there. In regard to the requested new levies, Bacon urged upon the members of Parliament "the well-looking to the whole universally . . . [as] the only sure preservation of every one particularly; so seemeth it of all congruence and reason meet, that every one particularly, by all ways and means readily and gladly, according to his power, should concur, and joyn to relieve and assist the whole universally."[15] For her part, the queen, through Bacon, gave assurance that she "is not, nor ever meaneth to be, so Wedded in her own will or Fantasie, that for the satisfaction thereof, she would do any thing that was likely to bring any servitude or Bondage to her people, or give any just occasion to them of any Inward Grudge, whereby any Tumult or stirs might arise, as hath done of late days, things most pernicious and Pestilent to the Common-Wealth."[16]

To ensure a religious settlement, a renewed reform of the church, which Bacon offered as the queen's first charge to Parliament, laws were enacted in the form of a new Act of Supremacy and an Act of Uniformity. By the former act, Queen Elizabeth was declared "the supreme governor" of the Church of England, rather than "the supreme head" as denoted earlier under Henry. This rewording mollified many of the reli-

14. D'Ewes, A Compleat Journal, p. 12.
15. D'Ewes, A Compleat Journal, p. 14.
16. D'Ewes, A Compleat Journal, p. 13.

gious conservatives in the House of Lords and many of the bishops who had been appointed during Mary's reign. The Act of Uniformity affirmed virtually all of the 1552 prayer book but produced a wording for the communion service that allowed interpretation of a special presence of Christ in the elements of bread and wine, both of which were again, as in Edward's time, to be distributed to the laity. Also affirmed was the retention of clerical vestments, a move again to assuage the concerns of more conservative elements in the House of Lords and other segments of the population, especially in the north and west of England. Over the following decade, Catholic resistance to the Elizabethan settlement persisted in some areas among elements of the nobility and general populace.[17] But a visitation of the churches by a royal commission with a set of "injunctions" in the summer/fall of 1559 laid the basis for local reform of the churches (e.g., the substitution of a communion table for an altar, elimination of images, allowance for clerical marriage, etc.). Then, in 1663, Parliament adopted the Thirty-Nine Articles, a doctrinal statement of belief that further defined a Protestant, biblically oriented, though hierarchically structured, national church. After the rule of Elizabeth, the adoption of an English Authorized Version of the Bible in 1611 helped to confirm the form and nature of a Protestant Anglican Church.

Catholicism during the first decade of Elizabeth's reign resisted the settlement, primarily in the more conservative House of Lords and among some of the gentry. On the Continent of Europe the Roman church was largely caught up in the effort of religious reform instituted at the Council of Trent (1545-1563), but also in balancing the political rivalries of France and Spain. The papacy was deeply involved in these latter political struggles. In England, local, scattered Catholic communities were served by a number of devoted survivors of the Marian priesthood. The eventual resignation of many of the Marian bishops allowed for the reconstitution of a hierarchy supportive of the Elizabethan Protestant Settlement. Yet, within the newly reformed church many voices also agitated for further reform on such matters as episcopal structure, church courts, and clerical vestments. These "Puritan" voices posed a significant source of unrest and struggle within the English church in the ensuing years.

17. W. J. Sheils, *The English Reformation 1530-1570* (London/New York: Longman, 1989), offers a concise account of the difficulties of carrying through the Settlement; see pp. 53-57. For the geographical areas of strongest Catholic and Protestant loyalties, see pp. 69-70.

In the late 1560s the Church of Rome — after the Council of Trent — was able to establish a center at Douai, in France, for the training of English seminarians for the purpose of re-evangelizing England and serving the Catholic communities there. A period of early, broad tolerance of Catholic belief in England was undermined by aggressive efforts on the part of Rome to reclaim England for Catholicism. Not long after Elizabeth's ascent to the throne, the papacy declared her birth to have been illegitimate, and Mary Stuart, granddaughter of the sister of Henry VIII — raised Catholic in France — was declared to be the rightful heir to the English throne. Encouraged by the papacy, many who were loyal to Rome sought to destabilize Elizabeth's rule and provided support to foreign political opposition to her government. This created increasing suspicion and distrust among Elizabeth's ministers, members of Parliament, and the Protestant clergy. The historian W. J. Sheils comments in this regard: "The work of the missionary priests created a new revived Catholicism which either emerged as a household-based spirituality distinct from the mainstream of English life or was actively hostile, if not subversive, to the Elizabethan regime."[18] As early as 1566, the growing atmosphere and concern about a conspiratorial Catholicism was expressed in Parliament by a privy councillor, Sir Ralph Sadler, who, in pleading for new taxes for the nation's defense, remarked: "[W]e hear daily of secret conspiracies and great confederacies between the Pope, the French King and other princes of the popish confederacy against all princes [who are] protestants and professors of the gospel, of the which the Queen's Majesty is the chief patroness. . . . [T]herefore her Majesty never had greater cause, never more need to arm herself, . . . whereby she may be the more able to defend her realm and subjects and to encounter and meet with the malice of her enemies."[19]

In a 1570 papal bull excommunicating Elizabeth, Pope Pius V declared:

> He that reigneth on high, to whom is given all power in heaven and in earth, hath committed his one, holy, Catholic and apostolic church, out of which there is no salvation, to one alone upon earth, namely to Peter, the chief of the apostles, and to Peter's successor, the bishop of Rome, to be by him governed with plenary authority,

18. Sheils, *The English Reformation 1530-1570*, p. 61.
19. D'Ewes, *A Compleat Journal*, pp. 192-95.

Him alone hath he made prince over all people and all king-doms. . . . [W]e do, out of the fulness of our apostolic power, declare the aforesaid Elizabeth, as being an heretic and favourer of heretics, and her adherents . . . , to have incurred the sentence of excommuni-cation, and to be cut off from the unity of the body of Christ. And moreover we declare her to be deprived of her pretended title to the kingdom aforesaid, and of all dominion, dignity, and privilege whatsoever. . . . And we do command and charge all and every the noblemen, subjects, people, and others aforesaid, that they presume not to obey her, or her orders, mandates and laws: and those which shall do the contrary, we do include them in the like sentence of anathema.[20]

The bull of excommunication stood not only as an act excluding Eliza-beth from the church's sacraments and the assumed hope of salvation but as an invalidation of her government and an incitement to its over-throw. The decree offered legitimacy to an earlier Catholic rebellion in England in 1569, a quickly suppressed rebellion led by the earls of Northumberland and Westmorland.

The St. Bartholomew's Day Massacre of Protestants in Paris and other areas of France in August and September of 1572 played an impor-tant part in the mix of unrest and threat. This event created much anxi-ety not only in England, but in all Protestant territories of Europe. An arranged, proposed reconciling marriage between the Protestant Henry of Navarre and Marguerite of Valois, the French king's sister, became the occasion for a plot to assassinate a key French Protestant leader, Gaspard de Coligny. Catherine de Medici, mother of the French king, Charles IX, fearing the growing influence of Coligny over Charles, joined in a conspiracy to have Coligny murdered. The failure of a first assassination attempt on the 22nd of August precipitated a general mas-sacre of assembled Protestant nobles and other Protestants in Paris on the 24th of August. Upwards of 8,000 died in Paris alone, and the massa-cre spread to the provinces in still higher numbers.[21] Henry of Navarre

20. Quoted in Sheils, *The English Reformation 1530-1570*, pp. 106-7.

21. There is divergence among historians regarding the estimated casualty numbers, but there is little doubt about the significant after-effects of the event in the deepened an-tagonisms and suspicions that it spawned, especially in Protestant lands and territories throughout Europe. In his biography of the German mathematician/astronomer Johannes

survived by abjuring Protestantism. There was rejoicing in Rome and Madrid over the event, and the conspirator Catherine de Medici was later awarded a papal medal for her loyalty to the Catholic faith.[22] But Protestant peoples in Europe were appalled and alarmed by the event. In England, the sense of a nation under siege was sharply heightened. A. G. Dickens has noted the considerable attention given to the St. Bartholomew's Day Massacre in English publications in the aftermath of the event. On its impact Dickens writes:

> If one sought to describe the most obvious and immediate effects of St. Bartholomew on the mass of Elizabethans, one would doubtless have to say that it confirmed to the hilt the ugly conclusions they were drawing from the latest exploits of the political Counter Reformation — from Pius V's "roaring Bull" deposing the queen, from the northern rising of 1569, from the presence of a French garrison in Edinburgh Castle, from the savagery of Alva in the Netherlands, from the Ridolfi Plot [to poison Elizabeth] and the endless conspiracy turning around Mary Stuart alias Guise. And should any have thought that the Massacre could not recur in England, John Foxe stood ever at hand [in his *Actes and Monuments of the English Church* (1563)] to remind them in lurid detail of the fires lit by Mary Tudor. . . . It requires no lengthy research to show that the Massacre nourished their fear and hatred of Catholic rulers and politicians; that they did not merely believe in an immense international conspiracy but mistakenly supposed it to be a well-integrated plan organized from Rome, whence the *Te deums* soon resounded to celebrate the slaughter.[23]

Some sixteen years after the massacre, in 1588, Philip II of Spain, who had earlier sought to gain the hand of Elizabeth in marriage, attempted to

---

Kepler, Arthur Koestler notes that many in the flood of pamphlets that followed the appearance in the heavens of a bright new star (a supernova) three months after the St. Bartholomew's Day Massacre saw the astronomical phenomenon as an evil omen; see Arthur Koestler, *The Watershed* (Garden City, NY: Anchor Books/Doubleday, 1960), p. 93.

22. J. E. Neale notes that, after the event, "in her communications with Catholic rulers, Catherine took full credit for a clever and meritorious, not to say holy deed"; J. E. Neale, *The Age of Catherine de Medici* (New York, Harper & Row, 1962), p. 80.

23. Quoted from A. G. Dickens, *Reformation Studies* (London: Hambledon Press, 1982), p. 486.

conquer England by force and restore Catholicism there. However, his great armada was defeated in one of the decisive sea battles in history, one that assured the survival and religious independence of England.

At the time of the Elizabethan religious settlement, a good many English Protestants, a number of whom had spent years in exile on the Continent during Mary Tudor's rule, expressed dissatisfaction with the retention of a hierarchically structured church and pressed for further change. One historian observes: "The Protestants in 1559 had supported the Queen and government, but at the same time many influential clergy expected that the terms of the settlement would be revised in due course. In 1563 a new Parliament and a Convocation [of bishops] were called, and it was in the course of their meetings that the determination of the Queen to stay with the terms of the 1559 settlement became apparent."[24] The religious advocates of more radical reform constituted a "Puritan" party within, and outside, the hierarchically structured church. This opposition was most frequently rooted in Calvinist tenets favoring a form of corporate governance, a point of view represented also within the government, chiefly in Parliament.[25]

In an influential speech in February 1575, the Puritan Peter Wentworth raised the issue of freedom of speech as it related to members of Parliament. Wentworth argued that the freedom to discuss all issues pertaining to good governance was essential to the well-being of the commonwealth and should not be limited to those questions that the queen chose to bring to Parliament. Underlying Wentworth's stance was the apparent Calvinist adaptation of the original Lutheran "doctrine" of the duty of the "lesser magistrates" to offer correction of abuse of power by the "higher magistrate."[26] Whereas Luther saw the doctrine applied primarily to the relation of the electors to emperor in the Holy Roman Em-

---

24. Sheils, *The English Reformation 1530-1570*, p. 59.

25. The historian J. E. Neale argued that growing opposition to a conservative Queen Elizabeth, jealous of her royal prerogative, came to center in the House of Commons and contributed to the decline of the House of Lords. Though Elizabeth survived the Puritan/Calvinist criticism with her powers intact, subsequent restiveness about the powers of the monarchy continued. J. E. Neale, *Elizabeth I and Her Parliaments, 1584-1601* (London: Jonathan Cape, 1957), pp. 18, 434-36.

26. See above, pp. 77-78, 113. Neale notes in the previous reference that Sir Thomas More had earlier also spoken out in Parliament in support of freedom of speech for its members, but lacked the policy overtones of the Puritan-leaning Parliaments under Elizabeth.

pire, Calvin adapted it to the elective bodies of the Swiss city councils and worked from the model of openness to the Word of God within the believing community. In his speech in the House of Commons, Wentworth described the roles and duties of members of Parliament as office-holders under God who share oversight for the well-being of both the monarch and the state. Wentworth embraced the doctrine of vocation and calling in government as a responsibility before God, one that should not be abridged in the face of the arbitrary will of the monarch. Wentworth remarked: "He that hath an Office let him wait on his Office or give diligent attendance upon his Office. It is a great and special part of our duty and office, Mr. Speaker, to maintain the freedom of Consultation and Speech, for by this, good Laws that do set forth God's Glory, and for the preservation of the Prince and State are made."[27]

In relation to Elizabeth's insistence that the House of Commons refrain from discussion of matters of religion not addressed to them by the Convocation of Bishops, Wentworth responded that the burden of the religious settlement, at the beginning of Elizabeth's reign, did not come from the bishops but was essentially the initiative and achievement of the Commons. In his conclusion, Wentworth declared:

> Wherefore God for his great mercies sake, grant that we may from henceforth shew our selves neither Bastards nor Dastards therein, but that as rightly begotten Children, we may sharply and boldly reprove God's Enemies, our Princes and State; and so shall every one of us discharge our Duties in this High Office, wherein he hath placed us, and shew our selves haters of Evil, and Cleavers to that, that is good, to the setting forth of God's Glory and Honour, and to the Preservation of our Noble Queen and Common-Wealth: for these are the marks that we ought only in this place to shoot at.[28]

The recorder D'Ewes reports that Wentworth, twice during his speech, cautioned "that Will may not stand for a Reason"[29] — a not very subtle, but, for England, an increasingly persuasive assault upon "the royal prerogative" and other forms of arbitrary rule. Wentworth and many Puritans in Parliament felt impelled to challenge the right of the monarch to

27. D'Ewes, *A Compleat Journal*, p. 240.
28. D'Ewes, *A Compleat Journal*, p. 240.
29. D'Ewes, *A Compleat Journal*, pp. 238-39.

dictate, or alter, the newly won and expected further development of the religious order, a concern that extended to the matter of the royal succession and to Elizabeth's possible marriage to a Catholic prince or king.

For his remarks, regarded as offensive by the queen and some of her strong supporters in the Commons, Wentworth, as D'Ewes reports, was "sequestered" by Elizabeth — sent to the Tower. Subsequently, however, pressure from members of Parliament led to Wentworth's release and his restoration to his seat in the Commons. Freedom of speech within Parliament became an argued rule and principle. Under the Tudors, however, this was never a principle extended beyond the halls of Parliament to society at large.

Four years after Wentworth's challenge in the House of Commons, an ardent Puritan, John Stubbs, wrote a political pamphlet, *The Discovery of a Gaping Gulf,* which criticized Elizabeth's exploration of a possible marriage to a French prince, François, Duc d'Alençon. Stubbs warned against any alliance with a royal line tainted by the blood of the St. Bartholomew's Day Massacre and the complicity in that event of the queen mother Catherine de Medici, the "Italian Athaliah." At the order of the queen, Stubbs and his publisher were convicted under a questionable Marian law and had their right hands chopped off in the marketplace at Westminster. An eyewitness account by William Camden — which became legend — reported that Stubbs, after the imposed penalty, "raised his hat with his left hand, and before he fainted cried out in a loud voice, 'God save the Queen.'"[30] Stubbs, at least in the popular retelling of the story, fostered on the level of the ordinary citizen what Wentworth had argued in 1575 as the particular vocation of elected members of the Commons: the affirmation of both freedom of speech and loyalty to the queen.

The contagion of free speech and its crucial role in religious dissent in England — even under the "Protestant" Queen Elizabeth — was underlined again in the late 1580s and early 1590s with the "Martin Marprelate" incident. Puritan dissidents both within and outside the state church continued agitation against the retention of a hierarchical ecclesiastical structure for the church. During the years 1588 to 1589 a series of pamphlets appeared attacking the prelacy as unbiblical. Most of the pamphlets were

---

30. A. G. Dickens cites this Stubbs incident in his discussion of the impact of the St. Bartholomew Day's Massacre on the general English populace in *Reformation Studies*, pp. 287-89.

written anonymously, some bitingly satirical, especially those ascribed to "Martin Marprelate." The presses of England were, at the time, very much overseen and controlled by the government and the church. The Marprelate pamphlets, however, were printed on a clandestine press that was moved from place to place to avoid discovery. The pamphlets created a major stir, and both government and church sought to uncover the agitators responsible for them. The queen issued a special decree on February 13, 1589, which declared that the "Bookes, Libels, and writings tend by their scope, to perswade and bring in a monstrous and apparaunt daungerous Innouation within her dominions and Countries, of all manner Ecclesiasticall Gouernement now in vse, and to the abridging, or rather to the ouerthrowe of her Highnesse lawfull Prerogatiue, allowed by Gods lawe, and established by the Lawes of the Realme, and consequently to reuerse, dissolue, and set at Libertie the present Gouernment of the Church."[31] The queen declared that these attacks upon the established church represented an attack upon her own authority and thus were also an act of sedition. Suspects were seized and subsequently two dissenting Puritan clergymen were charged with treason — one, John Udall, died in prison; the other, John Penry, was hanged on May 29, 1593, on the evidence of "seditious" notations in his private journal.

The Church of England at the time still exercised many of the institutional powers and prerogatives of the medieval church. The ecclesiastical courts were able to wield considerable civil power and authority, utilizing the power of excommunication (in matters even of personal debt) and imprisonment for a variety of other offenses. In matters of "heresy" they were able also to impose the death penalty. Under Elizabeth, ecclesiastical officials frequently characterized attacks upon their own authority as attacks upon the state and the monarchy itself. The 1879 editor of the Marprelate papers, Edward Arber, observed that church authorities at the time essentially laid claim to a "Divine Right . . . [for] their temporal position and power."[32]

What is clear from the history of these times — on the European Continent as well as in England — is the assumption of an essential role for religion in undergirding the moral and social authority of the state. It

31. Edward Arber, ed., *An Introductory Sketch to the Martin Marprelate Controversy 1588-1590* (London, 1879), pp. 109-10.

32. Arber, ed., *An Introductory Sketch*, p. 11.

was difficult in the sixteenth and seventeenth centuries, as earlier, to contemplate a fragmented religious situation as an adequate basis for social order. This anxiety was operative in resistance to Luther's original break with the medieval church and played a major role in the formula used to bring an end to the later, bloody Thirty Years' War (1618-1648): *eius regio, cuius religio,* the formula that the religion of the people of a territory should conform to that of the prince or ruler of the territory. What is especially illuminating in the history of the Reformation in England is the undercurrent of Puritan protest against such a formula and the affirmation of the counter-idea that royal authority cannot be the guarantor of the authenticity or legitimacy of religious faith. In Luther's effort to reform the church, when he deemed the church unwilling to reform itself, he turned to the "Christian prince" as the agent of reform. What takes place at a later time in England is the phenomenon that uncertainty and/or restiveness about the religion of the king or queen began to alter perceptions of the ultimate legitimacy of monarchical rule, at the least, growing sentiment to set limits to such rule. In discussion of the impact of the 1572 St. Bartholomew's Day Massacre in fostering English mistrust of Catholic rulers and politicians, A. G. Dickens offered the observation:

> I shall venture to suggest that the Massacre . . . did something to promote a more creative and far-reaching attitude within the nation itself — a disillusion with authoritarian monarchy in general, a disillusion which started to rub off on the shining surface of Tudor monarchy. Here was a reaction which can be shown to have contributed not merely to the drama but to the origins of free speech. Alongside all its shortcomings, misconceptions, arrogant dogmatism and other historical disadvantages, the Reformed phase of the Protestant Reformation fostered the critical adulthood, the civil courage of Europeans. It gave . . . many men a capacity to commit themselves to an international creed, quite irrespective of their local rulers. We have only to read the martyrologists — Foxe, Crespin, or Haemsted — to see how it bestowed this strength upon the middle and lower orders of society. Begun in the religious sphere, the defiant spirit swiftly spread to fields which nowadays we should regard as predominantly political.[33]

33. Dickens, *Reformation Studies,* pp. 486-87.

Questions can be raised at two points in this provocative judgment by Dickens. First, it attempts to account for the challenge to national and local authority on the basis of a major new initiative for freedom of speech arising out of the "international creed" of Calvinism, or as Dickens phrases it: "the Reformed phase of the Protestant Reformation." By contrast, what has been accented in our current study is the argument that the dynamic of the Reformation and the political restiveness of its "Reformed phase" had much to do with the sense of the present reality of a transcendent God which underlay the international appeal of its "creed." It was arguably a sense for God's transcendence that inspired the "international" nature of Reformed statements of faith.

It can be suggested, further, that along with the attendant Protestant "martyrology" consideration should be given to then-current religious meaning that qualified heavenly reward as the preeminent, even sole goal of Christian faith. Implicit in the vision of purpose beyond martyrdom and the prize of "eternal reward" was a new, class-negating commitment to vocation, which simultaneously called forth active individual and corporate involvement with God in a not infrequent challenge to the world's inherited, "natural" order. The right hand of an author and printer may be sundered, at times heads and necks as well; but this was seen by many as testimony to a Divine Presence and to faithfulness in vocation (a grace-inspired duty and service) and not alone as source of hope for a heavenly reward.

The ethos of this faith-inspired outlook was reflected over a century later, in Boston, when the Puritan Josiah Franklin instilled in his children the proverb: "Seest thou a man diligent in his calling, he shall stand before Kings." His famous son, Benjamin Franklin, toward the end of his life noted that in confirmation of his father's admonition, he himself had stood before five kings.[34] Over the course of his life, and despite his other great accomplishments, when called upon to claim status, an identity for himself, Franklin frequently offered the simple response, "Printer." In the aftermath of the Reformation, vocation could no longer be confined to, or defined primarily as, service in an ecclesiastical institution, even though the medieval church's call to vocation allowed

---

34. Walter Isaacson, *Benjamin Franklin: An American Life* (New York/London: Simon & Schuster, 2003), p. 12. See above, p. 16.

many — women, men, commoners, nobility — to break from "confining" social stations to embrace vocation within the church.

The second point of note in Dickens's observation is his delineation of the broader, cultural contagion of important Reformation themes. He ascribes to "the Reformed phase" of the Reformation, in conjunction also with the impact of the St. Bartholomew's Massacre, a growing, general disillusionment with "authoritarian monarchy," a contribution "not merely to the drama but to the origins of free speech," to "critical adulthood" and "the civil courage of Europeans." The point to be pursued in the remainder of this chapter — against the backdrop of the English Reformation — is an exploration of this contagion of change, which extended beyond the political sphere, as underlined by Dickens and historians such as J. E. Neale, Christopher Hill, and Michael Walzer.[35] In describing this widening impact — what might be termed the "ripple effect" of the Reformation — attention will center on the intellectual contribution of the influential Francis Bacon (1562-1627).

WHILE THE origins of Bacon's creative thought still puzzle interpreters, there is little question about the reach of that thought. Thomas Jefferson numbered Bacon among the three greatest minds that ever lived, joining his name with those of Isaac Newton and John Locke.[36] And philosopher/historian Ann Richter writes:

> There is a sense in which the work of Francis Bacon . . . has served the centuries as a quarry. One piece is mortised into the Royal Society. Others help to compose the post-medieval structure of English prose, of English historiography, of English law. Fragments of Baconian architecture turn up on all sides: in Hobbes, and Locke, Descartes, Leibniz, Voltaire, Mill, Kant, Shelley, Coleridge, and

35. For further discussion of the political impact of the Reformation in England, especially Puritanism, see Christopher Hill, *Puritanism and Revolution* (New York: Schocken Books, 1964) and *The World Turned Upside Down* (New York: Penguin Books, 1975), and Michael Walzer, *The Revolution of the Saints: A Study in the Origins of Radical Politics* (New York: Atheneum, 1974).

36. Noble E. Cunningham, *In Pursuit of Reason: The Life of Thomas Jefferson* (Baton Rouge/London: Louisiana State University Press, 1987), p. 129. This opinion about Jefferson is cited in many Jefferson studies.

Marx. Technology, the experimental method, inductive reasoning, linguistic analysis, psychology: all of them appear to incorporate some elements of Bacon's thought, although it is usually difficult to identify these elements precisely, or determine their real importance. . . . His published work is a bell to call other wits together, a collection of sparks flying out in all directions to kindle a general conflagration.[37]

Of special import for the present study is Bacon's influential role in helping to frame the modern doctrine of progress and identifying the critical, expanding role of technology in the Western, now worldwide, culture of change. Philosophically, Bacon is renowned for his formulation of the inductive method and the central role of experiment in the discovery of new scientific truth. This project of Bacon laid the groundwork for later formulations of empiricism, positivism, and pragmatism in the modern philosophical tradition. The question posed in the context of this study is the degree to which Bacon in his philosophical work assimilated and transformed fundamental affirmations of Reformation theology, Lutheran and Reformed, in the development of his special project: the "Novum Organum," a new ordering of knowledge. This is a question not usually emphasized in studies of the origins of Bacon's thought — a question about Bacon's theological literacy. It is a question also of the usefulness, the need, for a theological perspective in attempting to decipher points of origin for some basic ideas in Bacon's philosophical work, a project that properly deserves a more extended examination than can be afforded within the framework of this study.

It must be noted at the start that Bacon's life work was divided between his philosophical work and a political career in which he finally gained the long-sought, high office of lord chancellor of England, a goal he achieved under James I, king of England from 1603 to 1625, the successor to Queen Elizabeth. Rising in various offices under James I, Bacon was appointed lord keeper in 1617, the same position that his father, Nicholas Bacon, had filled under Elizabeth for twenty years. Then, in January 1618, he was promoted to lord chancellor, a position he filled until May 1621, when he was accused and convicted of bribery by the

---

37. Ann Richter, "Francis Bacon," in *Essential Articles for the Study of Francis Bacon,* ed. Brian Vickers (London: Sidgwick & Jackson, 1968), p. 300.

House of Lords. With his conviction he was removed from office. The machinations of Bacon's political enemies had a role to play in his fall from power,[38] but most historians agree that Bacon handled his personal business poorly, failed to exercise oversight of his financial affairs, and contributed to his own disgrace. A recent intellectual biography of Bacon by Perez Zagorin provides a brief, critical review of Bacon's political career, a career diminished in the minds of some by his long, persistent courting of patrons in the quest for high office.[39] During the reign of Elizabeth, his family tie with Lord Burghley (William Cecil), an uncle through marriage and closest advisor at the time to Elizabeth, failed to produce the kind of appointment and political recognition he sought. Later, a cultivated alliance with the earl of Essex gained him appointment as solicitor general under Elizabeth. But it was only during the reign of James I that Bacon achieved his political ambition of appointment to the high office of lord chancellor. James Spedding, the nineteenth-century editor of Bacon's literary works and letters, offered a more positive appraisal of Bacon's political career than Zagorin, less prone, in spite of Bacon's impeachment, to draw a sharp contrast between achievements in the latter sphere and those in the intellectual/philosophical area. Accordingly Spedding played down Bacon's later statements of regret about not having devoted himself earlier, and more fully, to a philosophical vocation. Spedding suggests that, if he had followed that latter course, his talents were such that he would probably also have regretted not having served in the political arena.[40]

Scholarly efforts to identify the roots and sources of Bacon's thought are confronted by at least three major problems. The first is Bacon's consistent avoidance of citing the names of others who may have influenced and helped shape the course of his philosophical thought. Bacon was

---

38. See Perez Zagorin, *Francis Bacon* (Princeton: Princeton University Press, 1998), p. 22.

39. Zagorin, *Francis Bacon*, pp. 5, 7-10.

40. See James Spedding, Robert L. Ellis, and Douglas D. Heath, eds., *The Works of Francis Bacon* (London: Longmans, Green, Reader & Dyer, 1853-1874), vol. 14, pp. 569-74. Also, see below, pp. 233-34. Hereafter cited as *WFB*, with volume designation. I have added Roman numeral section designations in parentheses for references to passages in Bacon's *Novum Organum* in order to facilitate locating these citations in American and other editions of Bacon's works.

critical of the fashion of quoting "authorities,"[41] a practice he regarded as a sort of game-playing among scholars, intended more to impress others than to establish quality of thought. Bacon's whole project of the "new ordering of knowledge," yet to be discussed, involved a critique of "authoritative," inherited modes of thought. He made this point in broad terms especially in discussion of "the Idols of the Theatre" in the *Novum Organum*.[42] Criticism of the prior philosophical tradition, which takes place most thoroughly in this latter work, was central to his project for reordering knowledge on new methodological foundations. When he does cite authors, mostly literary notables of classical Greece and Rome, he does so usually in a non-authoritative fashion to draw out meanings he was in process of formulating in his own work.[43] Bacon frequently mentions Aristotle, but almost always in criticism, never as an authority.[44] In the main, however, he felt free to draw out insight and understanding in past intellectual endeavors as he deemed warranted.

It would certainly have been helpful to those interested in the course of Bacon's intellectual development to have had access to the books that made up his considerable personal library. This is a second problem in any effort to explore the presuppositions and sources of his thought. Upon his death in 1627, Bacon bequeathed his library to his brother-in-law, Sir John Constable, a man he held in high regard. This library, however, was not kept intact and was scattered after his death. Very few volumes from Bacon's library have been identified and preserved.[45] This is a crucial loss to any assessment of Bacon's theological literacy, equally true for tracking his philosophical roots.

A third problem, a problem attaching to Bacon's fundamental mindset, was his inclination in his key philosophical works, not present in his historical studies, to an aphoristic mode of expression, a prefer-

---

41. Zagorin, *Francis Bacon*, p. 104. The text for n. 110 in Zagorin should be weighed against the text for n. 111. For Bacon's words on this matter, see *WFB*, vol. 4, pp. 15-16, 108 (cxxii).

42. *WFB*, vol. 4, pp. 62-64 (lxi, lxii).

43. See Zagorin's treatment of this question in *Francis Bacon*, pp. 68-73, esp. p. 73.

44. Cf. Zagorin, *Francis Bacon*, pp. 60, 62-65. Zagorin seems to struggle in his effort to set out the specifics of Bacon's interactions with Aristotle.

45. *WFB*, vol. 14, p. 542; cf. also comment of Spedding, *WFB*, vol. 14, p. 552. For an update on Bacon's extant library books, see A. N. L. Munby, *Essays and Papers* (London: Scholar Press, 1977), p. 108.

ence for abbreviated summary statements of insights and interpretations. This can, in part, be traced to Bacon's education in the humanist tradition and his attraction to the literary form found in Erasmus's *Adagia* or *De copia* and in the ancient wisdom tradition found, for example, in the book of Proverbs. In this regard one must note Bacon's love of conversation and discussion, in which ideas, without "authoritative" ascription, were the major focus of his interest and interchange. In a 1930 work on Bacon, Byron Steel quotes Bacon's earliest biographer and chaplain, Dr. William Hawley, to the effect that

> [Bacon was] . . . no dashing man in conversation, as some men are, but ever a countenancer and fosterer of another man's parts. Neither was he one that would appropriate the speech wholly to himself; or delight to out-vie others. He would draw a man on, and allure him to speak upon such a subject as wherein he was peculiarly skilful, and would delight to speak. And for himself he condemned no man's observations, but would light his torch at every man's candle.[46]

This dialogic approach to truth fits well with a fundamental tenet of the *Novum Organum:* "For rightly is truth called the daughter of time, not of authority."[47]

Early in his political/literary career, Bacon was concerned with the question of history and its meaning, along with attending religious questions. Like his father Nicholas Bacon before him, Francis embraced the idea that England was a project, with a history set within the framework of the providence of God. In 1592 Bacon published one of his earliest works, *Observations on a Libel,*[48] a reply to an anonymous Catholic polemical tract, *Responsio ad edictum Reginae Angliae,* which sought to

---

46. Byron Steel, *Sir Francis Bacon: The First Modern Mind* (New York: Doubleday, Doran & Co., 1930), p. 129. Steel also quotes Ben Jonson, a contemporary of Bacon: "The fear of every man that heard him was lest he should make an end" (p. 130). Bacon's description of "Salomon's House" in *New Atlantis* carries on this dialogic model for the discovery of truth. It has been pointed out that Bacon's idea of "Salomon's House" likely had a role to play in the later founding of the Royal Society of London in 1662; cf. D. S. L. Cardwell, *Turning Points in Western Technology* (New York: Science History Publications, 1972), pp. 33-34.

47. *WFB*, vol. 4, p. 82 (lxxxiv).

48. *WFB*, vol. 8, pp. 146-208.

project a desperate historical-religious plight for England. Believed by some to have been written by the English Jesuit Robert Parsons,[49] the Catholic pamphlet denigrated England's recent history and its then-present condition. It projected for the English people a kind of earthly purgatory. Bacon countered by declaring: "I mean not after the manner of a panegyric to extol the present time. It shall suffice only that those men that through the gall and bitterness of their own heart have lost their taste and judgment, and would deprive God of his glory and us of our senses in affirming our condition to be miserable and full of tokens of the wrath and indignation of God, be reproved."[50] In calling up memory of the past and making comparison with other peoples, Bacon asserted that

> we need not give place to the happiness either of ancestors or neighbours. For if a man weigh well all the parts of state, — religion, laws, administration of justice, policy of government, manners, civility, learning and liberal sciences, industry and manual arts, arms and provisions of wars for sea and land, treasure, traffic, improvement of soil, population, honour and reputation, — it will appear, taking one part with another, the state of this nation was never more flourishing. (p. 154)

Bacon offered further description of England's improved material conditions of life: "There was never so many excellent artificers, nor so many new handicrafts used and exercised, nor new commodities made within the realm; as sugar, paper, glass, copper, divers silks, and the like; . . . singularities and particulars . . . unknown and untasted heretofore" (p. 159). And, in defense of Queen Elizabeth whom the pamphlet openly attacked, Bacon asserted that in comparison with previous English monarchs, "her Majesty . . . hath reigned" with special "felicity" (p. 154).

Bacon singled out four libels that demanded answer. To the first, that England was "rife with religious turmoil," he responded by admitting controversy in the English church, not alone occasioned by outside Catholic opposition and conspiracy. He denied, however, that such internal controversies were related to essential articles of faith but rather chiefly concerned practices and rituals left over unreformed from earlier

---

49. Steel, *Sir Francis Bacon*, p. 29.

50. *WFB*, vol. 8, pp. 153-54. Page references given parenthetically in the text in this section refer to this volume of *WFB*.

times. Bacon regarded some measure of this controversy as a positive sign consistent with the apostle Paul's descriptions of church troubles in his own times. He remarked that "reason teacheth us that in ignorance and implied belief it is easy to agree, as colours agree in the dark" (p. 165). "Our Saviour Christ delivereth it for an ill note to have outward peace; saying, when a strong man is in possession of the house (meaning the devil) all things are in peace" (p. 165).

Regarding a second libel, that England had many external enemies, Bacon pointed out that other nations, especially Spain, were even more troubled by external enemies. Bacon expressed confidence that for England "we shall depend upon God and be vigilant; and then it will be seen to what end these false alarums will come" (p. 170).

After affirming the present trust in God's providence, Bacon turned to rejection of a third libel put forth by the pamphlet writer, one that explicitly predicted disasters for England in the future. Here Bacon simply mocked the author's credibility, questioning whether one who "hath so singular a gift in lying of the present time and times past, had nevertheless an extraordinary grace in telling truth of the time to come; or as if the effect of the Pope's curse of England were upon better advice adjourned to those days" (p. 171). Highlighting the note of trust in God's providential command of history, Bacon observed: "It pleaseth God sometimes, to the end to make men depend upon him the more, to hide from them the clear sight of future events, and to make them think that full of incertainty and difficulty which after proveth certain and clear; and sometimes on the other side to cross men's expectation, and to make them find that full of difficulty and interruption which they thought to be easy and assured" (p. 171).

Of the fourth and final libel, which declared an "overthrow of the nobility and the oppression of the people" (p. 172), Bacon suggested that the decline of the nobility and their wealth was largely in the "humour of the time" [the "spirit of the times"], though he also acknowledged that royal policy in England had a role to play in this development. As to the "oppression of the people" in war, justice, and taxation, Bacon rejected the contention out-of-hand, suggesting that England's recent wars had brought "strength to the realm," being "wars of exercise and not of peril" in which "so many of our people are trained, and so many of our nobility and gentlemen have been made excellent leaders both by sea and land" (p. 174). While in the matter of a purported heavy burden of taxation, he countered that "he that shall look into other countries, and consider the taxes and tollages and impositions . . . that are everywhere in use, will find that the Englishman is the master of his own value, and the least bitten in his purse of any nation of Europe" (p. 177).

In summing up his rejection of the pamphleteer's "libels," Bacon underlined a this-worldly purpose to affirm nationhood as a project in process, this, under the providence of God. He wrote: "Thus much in answer of these calumniations I have thought good to note touching the present state of England; which state is such, *that whosoever hath been an architect in the frame therefore, under the blessing of God and the virtues of our sovereign, needs not to be ashamed of his work*. [I pray God we may be thankful for his benefits and use them in his fear]" (p. 177; emphasis added). Bacon's theological commitment, accompanying his sense of a this-worldly goal and purpose, is revealed further in his later rejection of the anonymous writer's conditions for peace, conditions tantamount to a restoration of papal authority in England. Remarking on the critic's proposal of peace, Bacon wrote: "And these articles being accorded, he saith, mought follow that peace which passeth all understanding, as he calleth it, in a scurrile and profane mockery of the peace which Christians enjoy with God by the atonement which is made by the blood of Christ, whereof the Apostle saith that it [alone] passeth all understanding" (p. 197).

Bacon's concluding remarks at the end of *Observations on a Libel* deserve note as anticipations of his later analysis of the idols of the mind, the kinds of distortion of truth that are resident in virtually all intellectual endeavors, especially those of the past that come to constitute a "tradition" and that he later interprets as a problem even for his own then-incomplete efforts at setting a course for scientific truth. The nature of these remarks in this particular context should not becloud the depth of his insight that truth, in human terms and in human endeavors, is constantly prey to prior prejudice and habits of thought. Bacon offered the comment that the author of *Responsio* "hath handled a theme above his compass" and is of a sort who "have a dispensation dormant to lie for the Catholic cause" (p. 206). He observed that libelers in that cause, as in this instance, "must now hold by lying slanders, and make their libels successors to their legend" (p. 208).

These remarks, uncharacteristic of Bacon's more general irenic disposition, display a critical spirit extended and applied later to inherited systems of philosophical thought ("legend") that similarly obscure ("slander") otherwise discernible truth. Bacon, in this early theological/political tract, offered a preview of the already noted maxim that truth is a critical, future-oriented process, a "daughter of time, not of authority." In this early statement one should not suppose that Bacon is simply an English Protestant apologist, though he is clearly that to an important extent. But he also showed himself capable of acute criticism of England's own Protestant religious scene, while maintaining against the author of the *Responsio* that theological discord did not center upon the essential articles of Christian faith. Whether or not Bacon was fully convinced and convincing on this point, he knew well the gamut of theological/religious issues left unsettled in the English church by the 1559 Acts of Supremacy and Uniformity.[51]

As evidence of this point, one notes that, three years prior to his reply to the *Responsio,* Bacon had undertaken to address and mediate divisive issues in the church as a result of persistent calls by many within the church for a more thoroughgoing religious reform. In 1589, he treated these issues in a short treatise titled *An Advertisement Touching the Controversies of the Church of England.*[52] This particular piece bears significance because it not only sheds a good deal of light on Bacon's early theological-ecclesiastical interests but also spells out some of the parameters and early suppositions of his thought. Of first note in the *Advertisement* is Bacon's expression of the broadly accepted view of his times that a wide measure of religious unity was essential to social-political order within the nation, a point of view expressed also in *Observations on a Libel.* In the latter work he argued against both a subversive, conspiratorial Catholicism and a fractious Protestantism and declared that "causes of conscience when they exceed their bounds and grow to be matter of faction, leese [lose] their nature" (p. 178). Thus also, in the *Advertisement,* he sided with the hierarchical English church against its Puritan critics. He cited with favor an injunction of Solomon ("Salomon") that "the rulers . . ." — in this case the bishops of the church — "be not reproached; no, not even in thought, but that we draw our very conceit into a modest interpre-

---

51. See above, pp. 178-79.

52. *WFB*, vol. 8, pp. 74-95. Page references given parenthetically in the text continue to refer to this volume of *WFB*.

tation of their doings" (p. 81).[54] He rejected a critical "zeal" that was lacking in love (p. 76), noting that some people were "of the nature, not only to love extremities, but also to fall to them without degrees" (p. 86), an expression of Bacon's own preference for national order and conciliation. Bacon's criticism of the more outspoken Puritan agitators, both inside and outside the church, did not, however, preclude a forthright critique of the ecclesiastical authorities. Giving voice to thoughts expanded later in philosophical observations in the *Novum Organum,* he wrote: "[I]t is hard for them [i.e., many of the bishops] to avoid blame (in the opinion of an indifferent [unbiased] person) in standing so precisely upon altering nothing. . . . Laws, not refreshed with new laws, wax sour. Without change of the ill, a man cannot continue the good. To take away abuses supplanteth not good orders, but establisheth them. . . . [A] contentious retaining of custom is a turbulent thing, as well as innovation" (p. 88). Lacking proposals of reform from the bishops, Bacon asked: "Is nothing amiss?" And he then held up for question the abuse of excommunication in such matters as the failure to pay "duties and fees" and the sorry neglect of better training for the clergy in preaching. In a passage that recalls Luther's criticism of the nobility in the course of the 1525 German Peasants' War, Bacon remarked that he does not enumerate the offenses of the ecclesiastical authorities in order to arm the opposition but rather to urge the former's "compassion and remorse," for "'. . . injuries come from them that have the upper hand [i.e., power]'" (p. 88). Bacon observed: "The wrongs of them which are possessed of the government of the church towards the other [i.e., their critics], may hardly be dissembled or excused. They have charged them as though they denied tribute to Caesar and withdrew from the civil magistrate their obedience which they have ever performed and taught. . . . Their examinations and inquisitions have been strait [i.e., severe]" (p. 89).

It is interesting that Bacon, despite his basic affirmation of the English church and the importance of the church in maintaining religious and social order, should have been as critical and explicit as he was in identifying the tendency of the top leadership in the church to arrogate

---

54. Bacon rejected the view he ascribed to the radical Puritans that "that is ever most perfe3t which is removed most degrees from that church [Rome] and that is ever polluted and blemished which participateth in any appearance with it" (p. 84).

to itself political power and prestige: he observed that they seem at times to claim for themselves the "tribute to Caesar." This point by Bacon suggests a further theme in his overall argument, a second theological-political linkage. He makes a point that the English church and the church structures of other nations follow an ordering of variety under God's providence, a view reflective of Calvin's contention that God's providence provided variety in forms of government in ordering human societies.[54] Criticizing the importation of a church polity derived from European reformed churches, chiefly Calvinist, Bacon remarked:

> For many of our men, during the time of persecution [Mary Tudor's reign] and since, having been conversant in churches abroad, and received a great impression of the form of government there ordained, have violently sought to intrude the same upon . . . our Church. But I answer . . . let us agree in this, that every church do that which is convenient for the estate itself. . . . Although their churches had received the better form, yet many times it is to be sought, . . . not what is best, but of good things what is next and readiest to be had. Our church is not now to plant; it is settled and established. It may be, in civil states, a republic is a better policy than a kingdom: yet God forbid that lawful kingdoms should be tied to innovate and make alteration. . . . *[He] that bringeth in evil customs, resisteth the will of God* revealed in his word; he that bringeth in new things, resisteth *the will of God revealed in the things themselves.* . . . *[Take] counsel of the providence of God, as well as of his word.*[55]

It is apparent that Bacon parallels here Calvin's discussion of the forms of government in the closing section of the *Institutes*, a section found in the early 1536 edition of the *Institutes* and carried over into the later editions with relatively minor subsequent elaboration and expansion.[56] The passage in Calvin, cited and discussed above,[57] underlines the

---

54. See above, p. 168.

55. *WFB*, vol. 8, pp. 84-85; emphasis is Bacon's in Spedding text.

56. Cf. John Calvin, *Institutes of the Christian Religion: 1536 Edition*, trans. Ford Lewis Battles (Grand Rapids: Eerdmans, 1985), pp. 209ff. Hereafter cited as *Institutes (1536)*.

57. See above, pp. 159-60.

ruling providence of God which makes for different forms of govern-ment conforming to the peculiar historical conditions of different peo-ples. As stated by Calvin: "[You] will surely find if you fix your eyes not on one city alone, but look around and glance at the world as a whole, or at least cast your sight upon regions farther off, divine providence has wisely arranged that various countries should be administered by vari-ous kinds of government."[58] What is different in Bacon — in a way not found in Calvin — is the point that the governance and structure of the church is also to be regarded as in part a feature of historical conditions. It should be noted in this context that Heinrich Bullinger, a leader of Swiss Protestantism after Calvin, lent support to this line of thought, ad-vising the more radical wing of English Protestants that vestment issues and a hierarchical structure for the church could be regarded as "indif-ferent" — not critical for faith — if provision were made for the central role of the Bible and the preaching of the gospel.[59]

The concept of "things indifferent" — from the Greek word *adiaphora* — constituted a third major theme in Bacon's *Advertisement,* one with ramifications also in his later thought and one that parallels earlier discussions in Luther and Calvin. The concept found usage also among scholastics and humanist scholars, but a crucial expression of it came in the thought of Calvin, who built upon its important use in Lu-ther's discussions of Christian freedom in relation to the ethical de-mands of the law. Luther rarely, if ever, used the Greek word itself;[60] but certainly he was far removed in his use of the concept of "things indif-ferent"[61] from early, classical Greek or Stoic teachings of resignation vis-à-vis a fixed order of the world.[62] For Luther — in line with the apostle Paul — things were viewed as "indifferent" because faith in an unantici-

58. *Institutes (1536)*, p. 211.

59. See Sheils, *The English Reformation 1530-1570*, pp. 63-64; Patrick Collinson, *The Elizabethan Puritan Movement* (Berkeley and Los Angeles: University of California Press, 1967), p. 79.

60. See Jane Dempsey Douglass, *Women, Freedom, and Calvin* (Philadelphia: West-minster Press, 1985), pp. 16-17. Douglass provides references for further discussion of "adiaphora" in Calvin; see p. 124, nn. 27, 28.

61. Luther cites the apostle Paul's stance on circumcision as an example of Christian freedom; see above, p. 100. Cf. also Paul's attitude toward the eating of meat offered to idols, 1 Corinthians 8:4-13.

62. Zagorin notes briefly that Bacon does not fit a pattern of Stoic indifference in ei-ther his life or writings; see Zagorin, *Francis Bacon*, p. 132.

pated, transcendent gift of grace provided a new freedom from old, seemingly absolute, ethical prescriptions. It is the neighbor and the neighbor's well-being that became, for Luther, the referent for unscripted, loving action. God's transcendent grace, for Luther, made relative many of the assumed "enduring verities" of a historical tradition and inspired in their stead a creative, loving initiative.

In development with Calvin there was no single, divinely ordained, historical order of hierarchical rule. The forms of government were "relativized," except that, in Calvin, the Christian owed obedience to whatever form of government he or she lived under — with the exception of an ungodly tyranny. And in such an instance, he warned lesser magistrates, serving under a wicked ruler, that they ought not to connive or "wink at kings who violently fall upon and assault the lowly common folk. . . . [Such] dissimulation involves nefarious perfidy, for by it they dishonestly betray the freedom of the people, of which they know that they have been appointed protectors by God's ordinance."[63] At the very least, this warning presented for the lesser magistrates a perspective different from resignation to or simple acquiescence in the powers that be.

Bacon, as noted, saw the form and structure of the church to be, to an important extent, the result of a providential order, one to be carefully assayed in discerning the will of God, but one also to be addressed in terms of its need for improvement. He cautioned the more radical English reformers not to try to impose an alien, foreign structure upon the church or advocate other "arbitrary" innovations. As quoted above,[64] he warned that "he that bringeth in new things, resisteth the will of God revealed in the things themselves. . . . [Take] counsel of the providence of God, as well as of his word." Bacon did not reject further reform in the church; he warned only that zeal for an imported reform could obscure a potential good already present. As he expressed himself on the point: "Neither do I admit that their form (though it were possible and convenient) is better than ours, if some abuses were taken away."[65]

Bacon's pairing of a will of God manifest in Scripture with a will of God manifest in providential historical conditions represents, again, a

63. *Institutes (1536)*, p. 225.
64. See above, p. 199.
65. *WFB*, vol. 8, p. 85.

form of Bacon's later maxim that "truth is the daughter of time." Apparent here is Bacon's later epistemological concern that truth is to be sought "in the things themselves," and the latter should be open always to further examination. He may, at this stage, already have been considering some application of this principle to the whole realm of "natural philosophy," or "science." At the least what is evident at this early point in his intellectual development is the view that the church, in its structure, is grounded in history and needs to be looked at in that context. One should observe that on this point Calvin would not have agreed that the form of the church is determined by history and/or "providence" in Bacon's terms. The nature and the form of the church were perceived by Calvin to be an expression of the gospel. He saw the form of the church ordered by both Scripture and faith as "the communion of saints."[66] One can also grasp Bacon's contention that if governments were providentially established by God in history — a point affirmed in Calvin, why not then the various forms of church governance? In advocating that the form of the church should be given appraisal in its historical setting and that reform be undertaken from that point, Bacon shifted the context of the discussion of "indifferent things" from a dominantly ethical one in Luther, centered in individual freedom from the law, to an inherently historical one in which analysis of "the things themselves" provided another point-of-viewing in defining the call and limits of "reform." There are anticipations here, in 1589, of Bacon's later more extensive vision of reform in knowledge of the natural world and its possible applications. In the *Advertisement* Bacon wrote: "But we contend about ceremonies and *things indifferent,* about the extern policy and government of the church";[67] and he then went on to plead for healing among those involved in the English church controversy with the assertion that "the diversity of ceremonies doth set forth the unity of doctrine." A deeper truth, Bacon argued, underlies historically determined conditions and affords a basis for affirmation as well as correction and future action.

As previously suggested, it is possible to see in this line of reasoning the form of Bacon's "natural philosophy," the idea that in the "providence" of "the things themselves" there is embedded a "unity of doc-

66. See above, pp. 157, 163, n. 80 (a rendering of Calvin by Barth).
67. *WFB,* vol. 8, p. 75.

trine," expressive of a divine "word," amidst the actualities of history and nature. That Bacon should later speak of nature as a "book" bearing its own "word" is illustrative of this line of thought. If Scripture was the book of God's will, nature was to be seen and understood as the book of "God's works." He writes: "Natural philosophy is after the word of God at once the surest medicine against superstition, and the most approved nourishment for faith . . . since the one displays the will of God, the other his power. For he did not err who said 'Ye err in that ye know not the Scriptures and the power of God,' thus coupling and blending in an indissoluble bond information concerning his will and meditation concerning his power."[68] Bacon, like Luther and Calvin, was intent on activating the ethical will of the believer, redirecting it from otherworldly fears and hopes, pointing it to this-worldly possibilities and responsibilities. Unlike Luther and Calvin however, Bacon was concerned to energize the will by enlisting human curiosity and engaging it in discovering the potential for good which God had vested in nature — "hidden" and "concealed" there,[69] but discernible to a newly directed and disciplined human inquiry which would open the way for a divinely empowered "kingdom of man." The obstacle to be overcome on this course had chiefly to do with the conceits and deceptions of the human mind, the problem of the "idols" which, in Bacon's view, had clouded and continually threaten human perception.[70]

IN CONSIDERATION of this latter matter in Bacon's later *Novum Organum*, also termed "The New Organon," a word needs to be said about the course of Bacon's religious understanding and commitments,

---

68. *WFB*, vol. 4, p. 89 (lxxxix).

69. Bacon ascribes to King Solomon the proverb (Prov. 25:2): "[T]he glory of God *is to conceal a thing, but the glory of the king is to find it out*" (emphasis is Bacon's) and then continues with the comment: "as if according to the innocent play of children the divine Majesty took delight to hide his works to the end to have them found out; for in naming the king he intendeth man, taking such a condition of man as hath most excellency and greatest commandment of wits and means, alluding also to his own person, being truly one of those clearest burning lamps"; *WFB*, vol. 3, p. 220. Cf. also p. 299 and vol. 4, p. 20.

70. Bacon links "the interpretation of nature" (the "book of nature") with the "kingdom of man" in the title of the second book of the *Novum Organum*; but the freeing of the human mind for inquiry into nature is related to a prior, broader cleansing of false idols in all human reasoning; see *WFB*, vol. 4, p. 69, and below, pp. 208-13.

perspectives that accompanied and did not contradict, as some have suggested, his emerging scientific interests and concerns.

A common feature of Bacon studies, especially among persons with primarily philosophical or scientific interests, is the acknowledgment, but then usually the neglect, of Bacon's religious/theological affirmations in analysis and assessment of the substance of his thought. Any role that theological commitments may have had in the framing of Bacon's thought are often left unexplored, their possible significance generally passed over. When philosophers or historians of science seek to assess Bacon's thought from their separate perspectives, there is, as one might expect, a tendency for them to play down, or ignore, ideas in Bacon's work that reflect important theological roots. While perhaps acknowledging his ongoing religious views, most frequently characterized as Calvinist,[71] interpreters seldom explore the nature of this influence upon his scientific/philosophical ideas, perhaps preferring to avoid theological thickets where, on the surface, they might seem of marginal significance. But theological suppositions in Bacon help to spell out the roots of his critical contention that "truth is the daughter of time."

With this point, however, one should not ignore in Bacon a deep disaffection with theological disputation, something especially apparent in the aftermath of his frustrated efforts to mediate controversies among English Protestants during the late 1580s and into the 1590s, efforts he pursued up to the failure of the Hampton Court negotiations in 1603. Bacon deplored the "zealotry" of theological controversialists while himself persistently accenting "love" and reconciliation as the foremost expressions of Christian faith. With regard to the nurturing of that faith in Bacon, certainly the piety and commitments of his father, Nicholas Bacon,[72] and his mother, Anne, had important roles to play. This can be

---

71. See esp. Virgil K. Whitaker, *Francis Bacon's Intellectual Milieu* (Los Angeles: William Andrews Clark Memorial Library, UCLA, 1962). The lecture is included also in *Essential Articles for the Study of Francis Bacon*. Whitaker writes that Bacon, by "equating the glory of God and the betterment of man . . . betrayed the practical bent of the Calvinistic Protestantism that he absorbed as a boy" (p. 22). Zagorin sees a confused, conflicted Calvinism in Bacon; see pp. 45-46.

72. Paul Kocher argues for the strong influence of Nicholas Bacon on the thought of his son Francis, but fails to note shared theological views. Kocher offers a psychoanalytic interpretation of Bacon's relation to his father; see Paul H. Kocher, "Francis Bacon and His Father," *Huntington Library Quarterly* 21 (1959): 133-58. Whitaker, *Bacon's Intellectual Mi-*

said also of Francis's older brother Anthony. The mother especially —
one of five daughters of Anthony Cooke, a Calvinist tutor of Edward VI
— worried over the spiritual state and observances of her two sons, especially of Francis, whom she regarded as more lax in spiritual discipline
than Anthony.[73] The father, Nicholas, may also have shared this concern. Nicholas may have been acquainted with Martin Bucer during the
latter's brief Cambridge years, and he revealed in his public utterances a
Bucer-like commitment to the betterment of the social-political order, an
outlook that Francis shared with his father.[74]

The depth of Francis Bacon's own faith commitment and its role in
his life is manifest early and late. Whereas a few interpreters of Bacon
have sought to represent him as an agnostic or an "irreligionist,"[75] it is
rather the case that Bacon consistently showed concern about the negative impact of inadequately trained preachers upon the English people's
faith and the unease generated by ongoing theological controversy
within the church. These he viewed as obstacles to the furtherance of
faith. In a 1603 essay, "Certain Considerations Touching the Better Pacification and Edification of the Church of England," Bacon wrote:

> And surely it may be justly thought, that amongst many causes of
> Atheism which are miserably met in our age, as schisms and con-
> troversies, profane scoffing in holy matters, and others, it is not the
> least that divers do adventure to handle the word of God which are
> unfit and unworthy. And herein I would have no man mistake me,
> as if I did extol curious and affected preaching, which is as much
> on the other side to be disliked, and breeds atheism and scandal as
> well as the other (for who would not be offended at one who co-
> mes into the pulpit as if he came upon a stage to play parts or

lieu, p. 22, emphasizes Bacon's relationship to his mother. In his will, Bacon asked to be
buried in the same cemetery as his mother; *WFB*, vol. 14, p. 539.

73. See Anne Bacon to Anthony Bacon, February 3, 1591; *WFB*, vol. 8, p. 113.

74. See above, pp. 172-78.

75. See, for example, Robert K. Faulkner, *Francis Bacon and the Project of Progress*
(Lanham, MD: Rowman & Littlefield, 1993). By contrast Stephen A. McKnight argues
strongly against a secularist reading of Bacon's work and offers a brief review of its
sources; see Stephen A. McKnight, *The Religious Foundations of Francis Bacon's Thought*
(Columbia: University of Missouri Press, 2006), pp. 1-2, esp. p. 162, n. 7, The analysis of
Bacon's religious thought in the present work varies at major points from McKnight's
reading of Bacon's "religious foundations." See below, p. 209, n. 83, 216, n. 94.

prizes?) neither on the other side as if I would discourage any who hath any tolerable gift.[76]

Bacon's affirmation of "any who hath any tolerable gift" recalls Calvin's admonition that among the clergy there was always need to allow for instruction in the Word even from those who might be regarded as of lesser intellectual weight. His judgment that ongoing theological controversy was an incitement to atheism reflected in part Bacon's frustration with his own efforts to mediate and resolve theological disputes within the English church.

Additional expression of Bacon's concern to counter "irreligion" can be found in his impassioned rejection of religious conspiracy and violence as a means toward any positive religious purpose. In the second, enlarged edition of his *Essays* in 1612, Bacon introduced a chapter "On Religion," a subject not addressed in the much shorter, initial 1597 edition of the *Essays*. A passage from this chapter warrants special note. In it Bacon makes reference to the classical story of Agamemnon's sacrifice of his daughter Iphigenia to the cause of war and then quotes the words of the poet Lucretius, who had observed how "powerfully could religion prompt a man to evil deeds." He comments:

> What would he [Lucretius] have said if he had known of the massacre in France [the 1572 St. Bartholomew's Day Massacre], or the powder treason of England? He would have been seven times more Epicure and Atheist. Nay hee would rather have chosen to be one of the Madmen of Münster [the apocalyptic-inspired Anabaptist seizure of the city of Münster, 1534-1535] than to have been a partaker of those counsels. It was a great blasphemie, when the Devil said; I will ascend, and be like the highest: but it is a greater blasphemie, if they make God to say, I will descend, and be like the Prince of Darkness: and it is no better, when they make the cause of Religion descend, to the execrable accions of murthering Princes, butchery of people, and firing of States. . . . Neither is there such a sinne against the person of the Holy Ghost, (if one should take it literally) as in the stead of the likeness of a Dove, to bring him downe in the likeness of a Vulture, or Raven; nor such a scandal to their Church, as out of the Barke of Saint Peter, to set forth the

76. *WFB*, vol. 10, p. 119.

flagge of a Barke of Pirats and Assassins. Therefore since these things are the common enemies of humane society; Princes by their power, Churches by their Decrees; and all learning, Christian, morall, of whatsoever sect, or opinion, by their Mercury rod, ought to join in the damning to Hell for ever, these facts, and their supports: and in all Counsells concerning Religion, that Counsell of the Apostle would be fixed: "Human anger does not discharge the judgment of God."[77]

Bacon's passion on this point no doubt arose in part from his own early exposure to the extremes of religious fanaticism. In 1576, at the age of fourteen, after two years of study at Trinity College in Cambridge, Francis was sent off to Paris by his father in an apprenticeship to the English ambassador to France, the Calvinist Sir Amias Paulet. It cannot be doubted that as a member of Paulet's household the young Bacon was exposed to numerous accounts of the St. Bartholomew's Day Massacre four years earlier. Likely personal testimonies and stories about that event left their mark upon Bacon and subsequently armed him against the dangers of religious fanaticism.

Added to this early exposure to religion-inspired violence was Bacon's experience of the attempt to destroy Parliament and assassinate Queen Elizabeth's successor James I. In 1604 Bacon had finally gained appointment to important political office as counsel to James I. The 1605 effort by Guy Fawkes and a circle of Catholic conspirators to carry off an English massacre and return that nation to papal authority further impressed Bacon with the potential evils of religious extremism. After his own failures to allay the politically destabilizing controversies in the English church, he increasingly saw the path to positive religious good resting most surely in the discovery of the order in nature, its enlistment in invention, and the application of the latter to improvement of the human condition. Bacon's concern that Catholic-Protestant controversy and armed conflict, along with Protestant internal dispute in England and elsewhere, would occasion growing atheism, a concern that anticipated later intellectual revulsion at the devastating destruction attending Germany's Thirty Years' War (1618-1648),[78] which helped stir the call for "enlighten-

---

77. WFB, vol. 6, p. 543.
78. See above, pp. 46-47.

ment" throughout the latter part of the seventeenth century and through most of the eighteenth. The rise of modern science and the rationality it instilled offered to many informed persons in society a better hope than religiously inspired strife. A later Europe-wide attack upon "religious superstition" seemed fully justified by the years of tragedy suffered by much of Europe during the sixteenth and seventeenth centuries. Here ground was laid for a more secular orientation of society in the West.

In the case of Bacon, his concerns to allay "atheism" through a positive mission of scientific discovery and technological innovation, viewed as gifts and purposes of God in creation, was overtaken by the passions of the later religious-political civil war in England and such wars elsewhere in Europe. But in the aftermath of those tragedies, advances in knowledge about the world and awareness of increasing technological competence were widely seen as alternatives to religious controversy, independent of Bacon's own hoped-for redirection of religious commitments. "Enlightenment" claimed the loyalties of growing numbers of influential, educated persons within the different societies of Europe during much of the seventeenth and eighteenth centuries.[79]

Bacon's own efforts to reorder the patterns of human knowing in the *Novum Organum,* with his proposal of an inductive/empirical method for the discovery of truth in nature, sought to instill new thought into the human quest for knowledge. It pressed the need for experiment and curiosity[80] in the attainment of new knowledge, followed by the application of such knowledge to invention and technological innovation. Deficiencies in Bacon's method of knowledge have been the subject of dis-

79. In recent years, in Europe and America, the Enlightenment has been subjected to much criticism for engendering a "hegemonic" mindset that has worked to the detriment of other less developed, less "rational," cultural traditions. But it seems also to be the case that much postmodern criticism of the Enlightenment lacks appreciation for the "oppression" and chaos to which the Enlightenment was at least a "reasonable," humanistic response.

80. Peter Harrison in a 2001 article ascribes a key role to Bacon in the early modern rejection of a previous scorn of curiosity and its later, fuller embrace. Harrison adopts a "history-of-ideas" approach to the subject of curiosity in scientific inquiry. He pays little heed to Bacon's treatment of the "idols of the mind," which this interpreter views as having significantly unshackled curiosity for a new look at the world. Harrison fails to credit Bacon's contribution to the critical tradition in Western thought, a development that warrants mention even within the limits of his own study of curiosity in modern scientific inquiry. See Peter Harrison, "Curiosity, Forbidden Knowledge, and the Reformation of Natural Philosophy in Early Modern England," *Isis* 42 (June 2001): 265-90.

cussion in philosophical-scientific circles over the years, deficiencies similar to twentieth-century critiques of positivism for its failure to provide adequate criteria to manage the abundance of empirical "facts" and allow for the creative, constructive role of hypothesis.[81] Bacon's early statement of the inductive method nonetheless provided a major, ongoing stimulus to scientific inquiry. An equally significant contribution to the intellectual mindset of the modern world lay in his searching critique of inherited knowledge, a contribution that underlay, as supposition, his central maxim about the temporal nature of truth.

Perez Zagorin offers judgment on this matter in his analysis of Bacon's thought. The latter's critique of the barriers to human understanding is most thoroughly set forth in his discussion of the "idols" of the mind in the *Novum Organum,* a development anticipated earlier in the *Advancement of Learning* (1605). Zagorin comments on this feature of Bacon's thought: "His examination of the idols stands out as his most significant and original contribution to the philosophy of mind, with little if any precedent in the work of prior thinkers."[82] The obstacles to truth ingrained in the human mind (the "idols") are what Bacon described as those of the "tribe," the "cave," the "market-place," and the "theatre." In his treatment of these "idols" Bacon revealed a striking, clearly modern awareness of the need for ongoing criticism of habitual and self-deceptive dispositions in the human thought process. He remarked: "The idols and false notions which are now in possession of the human understanding, and have taken deep root therein, not only so beset men's minds that truth can hardly find entrance, but even after entrance obtained, they will again in the very instauration of the sciences meet and trouble us, unless men being forewarned of the danger fortify themselves as far as may be against their assaults."[83]

81. For an account of Albert Einstein's break with positivism in the first two decades of the twentieth century, see Gerald Holton, *Thematic Origins of Scientific Thought: Kepler to Einstein* (Cambridge, MA: Harvard University Press, 1973), pp. 219-59.

82. Zagorin, *Francis Bacon,* p. 82.

83. *WFB,* vol. 4, p. 53 (xxxviii). Page references given parenthetically in the text in this section refer to volume 4. In McKnight's treatment of Bacon's thought (see above, n. 75), *instauration* is treated chiefly as a restoration of a pre-Fall (pre-lapsarian) order of human knowing. He seems to think that a pre-Fall Adamic rationality is equivalent to, interchangeable with, the rationality and "recall" of the Socratic/Platonic preexistent "soul," a supposition that seeks to lay the basis for a "natural theology" and speculation about

A summary of Bacon's insights into these barriers to understanding is essential to an understanding of the expansive, subsequent impact of his thought: In exposition of the idols of the "tribe," Bacon identifies anthropomorphism as a chronic human failing. Human beings appear impelled to project their own image upon the world. He writes: "[I]t is a false assertion that the sense of man is the measure of things. . . . [T]he human understanding is like a false mirror, which, receiving rays irregularly, distorts and discolours the nature of things by mingling its own nature with it" (p. 54 [xli]). He later illustrates the point in relation to Aristotle's concept of "final causes," saying of them: "[They] have relation clearly to the nature of man rather than to the nature of the universe; and from this source have strangely defiled philosophy" (p. 57 [xlviii]).

Bacon ascribed to the idols of the "cave" the corrosive distortions of individual life in distinction from those attributable to the tribe. Everyone, Bacon writes, "[besides the corporate 'tribal' failures], has a cave or den of his own, which refracts and discolours the light of nature; owing either to his own proper and peculiar nature; or to his education and conversations with others" (p. 54 [xlii]). The unique and distinctive experiences that help mark value in an individual life also frequently distort. After citing Heraclitus as an early exponent of his view, Bacon remarked and warned that people "look for sciences in their own lesser worlds, and not in the greater or common world" (p. 54 [xlii]).

If false perceptions derive from the idiosyncrasies and obsessions to be found in an individual life, so others arise from the practicalities and usages common to the day-to-day social milieu. These idols Bacon described as those of the "market-place." It is in the context of social interactions that word usages arise, which, when uncritically utilized "wonderfully obstruct . . . the understanding." Words, Bacon comments, can "plainly force and overrule the understanding, and throw all into confusion, and lead men away into numberless empty controversies and idle fancies" (p. 55 [xliii]).

"pure philosophy"; see, e.g., McKnight's too brief reference to anamnesis, *The Religious Foundations*, pp. 136-37. It appears that it is on this basis that McKnight interprets Bacon as a sort of apocalyptic prophet and millenarian; cf. McKnight, *The Religious Foundations*, pp. 8-9, 13, 41, 46-47, 50-51, 56, 65, 70-71, 87-88, 97-98, 102, 106, 129, 136. McKnight fails to establish the historical context for Bacon's *New Atlantis* or the rationale for the primacy McKnight gives to the work as the touchstone for McKnight's own largely literary/textual analysis and commentary on only selected Bacon writings.

The fourth and last of Bacon's idols are those of "the theatre." These he described as having "immigrated into men's minds from the various dogmas of philosophies, and also from wrong laws of demonstration." They can be called idols of the theatre, Bacon declares, "because in my judgment all the received systems are but so many stage-plays, representing worlds of their own creation after an unreal and scenic fashion" (p. 55 [xliv]). He adds: "Nor is it only of the systems now in vogue, or only of the ancient sects and philosophies, that I speak; for many more plays of the same kind may yet be composed and in like artificial manner set forth; seeing that errors the most widely different have nevertheless causes for the most part alike" (p. 55 [xliv]). He made clear that in this matter he spoke not alone of philosophical systems and tenets, but also of "many principles and axioms in science."

In so offering assessment of the impact of the idols upon human understanding, Bacon warned against a tendency of mind to "suppose the existence of more order and regularity in the world than it finds" (p. 55 [xlv]). This fault, he argued, leads to the framing, in support of theory, of all sorts of "conjugates" that "do not exist" in order to satisfy a longing for coherence. The significance of negative instances that might invalidate particular systems or theories is more difficult for the mind to discern and entertain. Bacon put the matter in the following words:

> The human understanding when it has once adopted an opinion (either as being the received opinion or as being agreeable to itself) draws all things else to support and agree with it. And though there be a greater number and weight of instances to be found on the other side, yet these it either neglects and despises, or else by some distinction sets aside and rejects; in order that by this great and pernicious predetermination the authority of its former conclusions may remain inviolate. (p. 56 [xlvi])

In elaboration of the idols of the cave Bacon noted that all thought is distorted in some degree by "an infusion from the will and affections." He observed that "what a man had rather were true he more readily believes. Therefore he rejects difficult things from impatience of research; sober things, because they narrow hope; deeper things of nature, from superstition; the light of experience, from arrogance and pride" (p. 57 [xlix]). And in relation to his own effort to define a more disciplined, inductive-experimental method of knowledge, Bacon warned against a superficial empiricism of the senses, suggesting that the latter are inordinately subject to "dulness, incompetency, and deceptions" due to their enslavement to immediacy. An important aid to understanding, he argued, is found in the capacity to suspend judgment so that aspects of a phenomenon not immediately apparent may come to the fore and be properly assessed, especially "subtle changes of form." It is precisely experiment, Bacon believed, that helps to discipline the senses and free them to uncover the "changes of form" (p. 58 [l]). He wrote: "Matter rather than forms should be the object of our attention, its configurations and changes of configuration, and simple action, and law of action or motion; for forms are figments of the human mind, unless you will call those laws of action forms" (p. 58 [li]).

The chief purpose of Bacon's discussion of the idols was to free the understanding that it might "see" the world with new eyes. By fixing upon the veiling of mind associated with the idols, Bacon held out the prospect of a new, potentially redemptive viewing of the world, not only in relation to the understanding of nature and the new inventions that would follow from it, but also in relation to the whole tradition of human thought. He wrote:

> So much concerning the several classes of Idols, and their equipage: all of which must be renounced and put away with a fixed and solemn determination, and the understanding thoroughly freed and cleansed; the entrance into the kingdom of man, founded on the sciences, being not much other than the entrance into the kingdom of heaven, whereinto none may enter except as a little child. (p. 69 [lxviii])

And further:

> There remains but one course for the recovery of a sound and healthy condition, — namely, that the entire work of the understanding be commenced afresh, and the mind itself be from the outset not left to take its own course, but guided at every step; and the business be done as if by machinery. (p. 40)

Bacon's reference to the mind being guided "as if by machinery" was his proposal for an inductive-experimental method. The purging of the idols would allow new eyes to discern God's design in the natural world and lead on to new "instruments," technologies, for the improvement of the human condition. In a metaphor he likened his proposed method to the discovery of the compass. Prior to the compass, Bacon suggested, humankind hugged the shores of knowledge or traversed only bounded seas; but with the advent of the compass people gained access to the vast oceans. This led to all kinds of new discoveries and to all the promises of a new world.

Thus did Bacon lay bare the underlying perceptions and arguments that informed his fundamental insight that truth was dependent upon a temporal process. He thus also helped lay the intellectual foundations for the emergent belief in progress, a belief grounded not only in the awareness of advancing truth but in a contagion of conscience reflective as well of an awakened appreciation for equality and freedom. It should be emphasized that Bacon's espousal of a critical mindset never came to rest in skepticism; for he always affirmed the existence of attainable truths about the world, truths he believed God had implanted or "hidden" in the natural order, discoverable truths that could lead on to a this-worldly "kingdom of man." In matters of social and political equality and freedom, Bacon was at best ambiguous, less venturesome. Politically and in church affairs, Bacon was far from espousing broad, democratic principles. He most characteristically expressed elitist or aristocratic inclinations. One biographer has observed: "Bacon showed what seemed an inborn reverence for authority and paternalism in government."[84]

Yet he also, on occasion, could speak out on behalf of those lacking privilege and power. He seems to have derailed his own political ambitions under Queen Elizabeth, when, as a member of Parliament in 1593, he spoke out against a crown tax levy that fell disproportionately upon the poor. He refused to apologize for his stand; and, though a young favorite of the queen, he was subsequently passed over for important political appointment throughout the remainder of Elizabeth's rule.[85] And in relation to his proposed inductive-experimental method of knowledge, he consciously rejected an elitist point of view. The method, he

---

84. Catherine Bowen, *Francis Bacon: The Temper of a Man* (Boston: Little, Brown & Co., 1963), p. 49.

85. Bowen, *The Temper of a Man*, pp. 69-71; cf. Zagorin, *Francis Bacon*, pp. 8-9.

wrote, "leaves but little to the acuteness and strength of wits, but places all wits and understandings nearly on a level."[86] About his own philosophical gift and achievement, Bacon declared such to be more the occasion of God's providential historical provision than a mark of his own genius. In the preface of the *Novum Organum*, dedicated to James I, Bacon wrote: "[T]o say truth, I am wont for my own part to regard this work as a child of time rather than wit; the only wonder being that the first notion of the thing, and such great suspicions concerning matters long established, should have come into any man's mind."[87] He continued: "But for this accident which I speak of, I wish that if there be any good in what I have to offer, it may be ascribed to the infinite mercy and goodness of God and to the felicity of your Majesty's times."[88]

Bacon seemed to stand in wonderment at the uniqueness and radical character of his own thought, a self-discernment confirmed centuries later by Perez Zagorin's previously cited estimate of Bacon's "idols of the mind": "examination of the idols stands out as his most significant and original contribution to the philosophy of mind, with little if any precedent in the work of prior thinkers."[89] Yet, on this point one must ask if there was not, in fact, precedent for some of these ideas in the theological revolution that stirred Europe from the time of Luther. Reticent as Bacon generally was to cite "authorities" as sanctions for his own endeavors, in *The Advancement of Learning* (1605) he called attention to Luther's work as reformer and noted the latter's attack upon the scholastic tradition on the basis of his "new discovery," one marked by the recovery of insight and understandings afforded by "ancient authors," understandings long neglected. In what represents — as far as the present writer has been able to discern — Bacon's sole reference to Luther in his philosophical writings, he commented:

86. *WFB*, vol. 4, p. 62 (lxi). Zagorin puzzles over this egalitarian strain in Bacon; see Zagorin, *Francis Bacon*, p. 85. It can be conjectured that Bacon saw the new life of the mind as a corollary to Luther's priesthood of all believers, especially in line with Calvin's later development of it. It is apparent that Bacon left himself open to a wide spectrum of others' views and gifts; see above, p. 193. Hawley comments on Bacon: "[F]or himself he condemned no man's observations, but would light his torch at every man's candle." Bacon was no intellectual elitist; he saw need for a broadening circle of critical thought.

87. *WFB*, vol. 4, p. 11.

88. *WFB*, vol. 4, p. 11.

89. See above, p. 209.

Martin Luther, conducted (no doubt) by an higher Providence, but in discourse of reason finding what a province he had undertaken against the Bishop of Rome and the degenerate traditions of the church, and finding his own solitude, being no ways aided by the opinions of his own time, was enforced to awake all antiquity, and to call former times to his succors to make a party against the present time; so that the ancient authors, both in divinity and in humanity, which had long slept in libraries, began generally to be read and revolved.[90]

Luther was a participant in a more general revival of learning and language skills that preceded him in the Renaissance. But Bacon nonetheless saw in Luther a level of radical intellectual/cultural criticism not previously achieved, certainly not in theological terms.[91] Luther's incorporation of the apostle Paul's Corinthians' perspective of the cross as the "foolishness and weakness" of God fostered in his theology a sense for the freedom of faith vis-à-vis the synthetic wedding of philosophy and theology characteristic of so much medieval scholastic thought.

In addition to Bacon's recognition of a precedent in Luther for wide-ranging philosophical-theological criticism, one can suggest that in Calvin, too, Bacon was exposed to criticism of the idol-framing propensity of the human mind. In an early section of the final edition of the *Institutes*, Calvin attacked what he regarded as the excessive use of visual images in the church and characterized the human mind "as a perpetual forge of idols."[92] In initially addressing the problem of "idols" in visual form, a commonplace of medieval religious life, Calvin understood such to be obstacles to the auditory word of salvation offered in the gospel. He saw the human mind to be the "forge" of such idols. Bacon, it can be suggested, developed his critique of idols as a liberation both of the understanding and of the senses, affording a means to enlivened percep-

90. *WFB*, vol. 3, pp. 282-83; see also p. 501.

91. It is important to recognize on this point the exception of William of Occam with his emphasis upon the will and command of God, a divine will establishing the call to human obedience, in contrast to a rational moral order fixed in nature and shared in by the human subject. Luther is different from Occam in seeing human life reoriented by God's gift of grace.

92. John Calvin, *Institutes of the Christian Religion*, trans. Henry Beveridge (Grand Rapids: Eerdmans, 1953), vol. 1, p. 97 (1.11.8).

tions of the "word" resident in "the book of nature." In his criticism of
the workings of the mind, as noted, Bacon never fell prey to thoroughgoing skepticism, one that would deny any truth and in effect "destroy
the authority of the senses and understanding." Rather, he declared, "I
proceed to devise and supply helps for the same."[93] Thus, he continued,
"The idols and false notions which are now in possession of the human
understanding, and have taken deep root therein, not only so beset
men's minds that truth can hardly find entrance, but even after entrance
obtained, they will again in the very instauration of the sciences meet
and trouble us, unless men being forewarned of the danger fortify themselves as far as may be against their assaults."[94]

One should not suppose, as some have, that Bacon in the end substituted his inductive, experimental approach in the sciences for a prior,
merely nominal religious sensibility and understanding. Rather, a sense
of God's transcendence in a perceivable orderliness of nature underlay
Bacon's confidence in the projected inductive-experimental method and
its promise of discovery of new truths, accompanied always with the essential concomitant of practical (technological) applications. In this regard it is important to note that the later Bacon-inspired Royal Society,
founded in 1660-1662 to advance the natural sciences, included inventors
as well as what might be termed theoreticians in its membership. To illustrate, it can be noted that Isaac Newton was accorded membership in
the society in 1672 for the development of the reflecting telescope, a
model of which he gave to the society, along with an explanatory paper.
This was fifteen years before Newton made his most notable intellectual

93. WFB, vol. 4, p. 53 (xxxvii).

94. WFB, vol. 4, p. 52 (xxxviii). Bacon envisioned here a continuing struggle even for a
newly idol-conscious perception of nature, one analogous to Luther's continuing struggle
against sin for the justified believer. Something similar to Luther is also found in another
Bacon aphorism when he remarks: "I . . . would have my doctrine enter quietly into the
minds that are fit and capable of receiving it; for confutations cannot be employed when
the difference is upon first principles" (WFB, vol. 4, p. 53 [xxxv]). For Luther, of course,
the "entrance" into minds, or in Luther's case "hearts," is the work of the Holy Spirit.

An additional note on McKnight's treatment of Bacon's "utopia" of the New Atlantis:
the governing elite of "Bensalem" saw it necessary to continue to send out its ships secre-
tively around the world to stay abreast of new insight and "discovery" that take place outside the bounds of the island "utopia." The message of Bacon's New Atlantis appears to be
that where religious controversy is resolved, many more, but clearly not all, scientific discoveries and inventions can be turned to human betterment.

contribution, the 1687 *Principia Mathematica*. Bacon saw in his proposed inductive method of natural knowledge a cornucopia of new inventions dedicated to the betterment of human life. He never doubted that this possibility was afforded by a beneficent Creator. In the *Novum Organum* Bacon wrote: "The beginning is from God: for the business which is in hand, having the character of good so strongly impressed upon it, appears manifestly to proceed from God, who is the author of good, and the Father of Lights."[95]

To achieve this bounty of future good, Bacon believed the separation of science from the philosophical tradition was essential. And he seems to have seen in Luther's break with scholasticism an anticipation of his own project. Bacon remarked: "[A]s things now are, to discourse of nature is made harder and more perilous by the summaries and systems of the schoolmen; who having reduced theology into regular order as well as they were able, and fashioned it into the shape of an art, ended in incorporating the contentions and thorny philosophy of Aristotle, more than was fit, with the body of religion."[96] Bacon entertained critical distance between the human and the divine, between immanent speculative processes and the Transcendent. He scorned "those who have taken upon them to deduce the truth of the Christian religion from the principles of philosophers, and to confirm it by their authority; pompously solemnizing this union of the sense and faith as a lawful marriage, and entertaining men's minds with a pleasing variety of matter, but all the while disparaging things divine by mingling them with things human."[97] He rejected as well the intrusion of religion into the sphere of natural philosophy, science. Of note here was his concern that conservative Christian clergy frequently obstructed the advance of scientific inquiry. Bacon complained:

> [C]ertain divines . . . are weakly afraid lest a deeper search into nature should transgress the permitted limits of sober-mindedness; wrongfully wresting and transferring what is said in holy writ against those who pry into sacred mysteries, to the hidden things of nature, which are barred by no prohibition. Others with more subtlety surmise and reflect that if second causes are unknown everything can more readily be referred to the divine hand and rod; a

95. *WFB*, vol. 4, p. 91 (xciii).
96. *WFB*, vol. 4, p. 88 (lxxxix).
97. *WFB*, vol. 4, p. 88 (lxxxix).

point in which they think religion greatly concerned; which is in fact nothing else but to seek to gratify God with a lie.[98]

Bacon saw a paired need, in theology and in science, for a separation from the binding suppositions of speculative thought. Natural philosophy, he argued, must be freed from the constraints of static philosophical categories in order that new scientific discoveries, such as the actual voyages of discovery in his own times,[99] might enlighten and freshly equip future generations for the betterment of the human condition. In criticism of the too-guarded, timid inquiries of his contemporary practitioners of science — and in words that closely parallel Thomas Kuhn's 1967 description of "normal science"[100] — Bacon observed:

> If there be any who have determined to make trial for themselves, and put their own strength to the work of advancing the boundaries of the sciences, yet have they not ventured to cast themselves completely loose from received opinions or to seek their knowledge at the fountain; but they think they have done some great thing if they do but add and introduce into the existing sum of science something of their own; prudently considering with themselves that by making the addition they can assert their liberty, while they retain the credit of modesty by assenting to the rest. But these mediocrities and middle ways so much praised, in deferring to opinions and customs, turn to the great detriment of the sciences.[101]

98. *WFB*, vol. 4, p. 88 (lxxxix); cf. also vol. 3, p. 219, where Bacon offers a comment on those who worry about "raveling too far into God's secrets." He writes: "For if they mean that the ignorance of a second cause doth make men more devoutly to depend upon the providence of God, as supposing the effects to come immediately from his hand, I demand of them, as Job demanded of his friends, *Will you lie for God as man will for man to gratify him?*" (italics Bacon's). Bacon on this point anticipated Dietrich Bonhoeffer's later twentieth-century complaint against a "God-of-the-gaps" theology, in which gaps in human knowledge about the world, e.g., the origins of life, are claimed as the special province of God. See Dietrich Bonhoeffer, *Letters and Papers from Prison* (New York: Macmillan, 1972), pp. 311-12. In different editions of Bonhoeffer's prison letters, see the letter of May 29, 1944.

99. Bacon was much taken with the voyages and discoveries of the European explorers; see e.g., *WFB*, vol. 4, p. 82 (lxxxiii).

100. See Thomas Kuhn, *The Structure of Scientific Revolutions* (Chicago: University of Chicago Press, 1960, 1970), pp. 10-34.

101. *WFB*, vol. 4, p. 16.

Bacon stands, in his own times, and even today, as an advocate of continuing, ongoing change in the realm of all human thought, not alone in the sphere of the sciences and technology. He was, however, much less prone to embrace change in received political institutions, for here he believed that "the reformation of a state in civil matters is seldom brought in without violence and confusion." Rather, he much preferred the pursuit of new knowledge because "discoveries carry blessings with them, and confer benefits without causing harm or sorrow to any."[102] Yet even in the realm of politics, he was a strong advocate for updating England's laws. He especially saw the need for revising its patent procedures to allow innovators to be the beneficiaries, profit-wise, of their own inventions. And it is possible to see in his proposal to have the English king, James I, serve as patron of the new inductive science a subtle critique of the tradition of the royal prerogative; for, as patron, the king would inevitably have to yield some prerogative to the initiators of the new knowledge.

Bacon is a key example of the ripple effect of the religious revolution that helped initiate the wide-ranging transformation in the attitude toward change that took root in the consciousness of Europe during the sixteenth/seventeenth centuries and gained further impetus with developments in the New World. Bacon concluded the "Plan of the Work," his project for the renovation of knowledge, with a prayer, a prayer for God's blessing upon an enduring, this-worldly human vocation:

> Thou, when thou turnedst to look upon the works which thy hands had made, sawest that all was very good, and didst rest from thy labours. But man, when he turned to look upon the work which his hands had made, saw that all was vanity and vexation of spirit, and could find no rest therein. Wherefore if we labour in thy works with the sweat of our brows thou wilt make us partakers of thy vision and thy sabbath. Humbly we pray that this mind may be steadfast in us, and that through these our hands, and the hands of others to whom thou shalt give the same spirit, thou wilt vouchsafe to endow the human family with new mercies.[103]

Bacon saw in the development of a new, disciplined knowledge of God's natural world and its technological applications the basis for

102. *WFB*, vol. 4, p. 113 (cxxix).
103. *WFB*, vol. 4, p. 33.

great new beneficial works in service to the human community. He believed such blessings were attainable "without causing harm or sorrow to any" — something, by contrast, he feared would result from efforts to force change in the political order or the fanning of religious controversy. On this point one can observe in Bacon a too-unquestioned expectation of the future benignancy of technological advance. This vision claimed credence for him in the face of what he saw to be brooding political and religious turmoil. His prophetic vision failed, however, in his inability to anticipate the quotient of power and ambition that would accompany the gains in technology or the social-political upheavals that would often follow in their train. Political and social problems remained to be addressed within the framework of the political order. But then, Bacon even here had a sense for the interwoven nature of the social fabric. Toward the end of the *Novum Organum,* in arguing for care in scientific observation, he remarked:

> Lastly, concerning the disdain to receive into natural history things either common, or mean, or over-subtle and in their original condition useless, the answer of the poor woman to the haughty prince who had rejected her petition as an unworthy thing and beneath his dignity, may be taken for an oracle — "Then leave off being king." For most certain it is that he who will not attend to things like these, as being too paltry and minute, can neither win the kingdom of nature nor govern it.[104]

Bacon's dedication of his major work to the king, James I, represented a gift of vision but also, at a remove, an implied check on the powers of monarchy and the royal prerogative.

If it can be charged that his vision of the benign nature of future technological innovation was too unquestioning, nevertheless his bold affirmation of freedom for, and in, the exercise of critical thought stands out as a statement, at a subtle remove, of justifying faith in the life of the mind. Though he never explicitly made a linkage of the Luther texts of Romans 1 and 1 Corinthians 1, the two texts seem implicitly joined in Bacon's thought — this to the furtherance of edification in the human community and attendant good works.

---

104. *WFB,* vol. 4, p. 108 (cxxi).

Chapter 6

A Theological Summary and Discussion/Interpretation

It was proposed in the opening chapter that one of the major problems in the Christian theological tradition of our time has been the loss of a sense of the transcendent God. Although this is a problem that can be traced to what intellectual historians describe as the transition from the medieval "Religious Age" to a modern, scientific "Age of Reason," a history briefly sketched in Chapter 2, the starting point for our discussion was the decline of the "Christ/culture" debate that has occurred over the half-century since H. Richard Niebuhr published his 1951 *Christ and Culture*. Much diverse theological discussion has ensued over the past fifty years with much new thinking and, from the perspective of the present writer, much unfulfilled promise. For example, in relation to the essentially sociological-theological categories set forth by Niebuhr in 1951, one can note that while those categories still shed light on the Christ/culture question they seem very much on the periphery of contemporary theological discussion. This is so, I believe, because the christological context and emphasis that characterized Niebuhr's post-liberal, Barth-leavened theological frame of reference has been eroded by a further decline in the sense of transcendence. Divine transcendence was a theme that Barth's theology notably recaptured in the disillusionment of World War I and the post–World War I European intellectual and theological world. The more recent decline in the sense of transcendence has been accompanied expectedly by a corresponding loss of a sense of subjective human limit: emotionally, rationally, and self-critically. In its stead has come a surge of subjective immediacy and widespread spiritual consumerism, a preoccupation, for example, with the cultivation of "spirituality," a word and phenomenon prevalent on the American religious scene and in the literature that responds to and helps shape the commercial market for that scene. Similar interests are found abroad as well. Religion as inwardness, akin to reader-response criticism in the literary world, has come to occupy overmuch theological interest and attention.

Theological Summary

Though Niebuhr never offered a thoroughgoing *theological* discussion of his five sociological types (to review: Christ against culture, Christ of culture, Christ above culture, Christ in paradoxical dialogue with culture, and Christ as transformer of culture), the point has been made that two of the latter three, those in Niebuhr's analysis especially rooted in the Reformation, embraced faith in an intervening, "unnatural" divine grace and the discovery of a newfound freedom in that faith. The medieval tradition of a "Christ above culture," one manifested in a hierarchical ecclesiastical rule over human life, drew heavily upon the "other world," life after death, as sanction for its this-worldly position of eminence and power. It has been argued that the struggle of Luther to elaborate a contrasting message of "the freedom of faith through grace" led him by steps to contest ecclesiastical claims of otherworldly sanctions and authority. He came to view those claims as humanly constructed restrictions upon God's forgiving presence to faith, with its accompanying call to responsible freedom as set forth in the biblical, gospel message. Luther affirmed the message of forgiveness and grace as the paramount, distinctive content of "the Word of God."

In conjunction with developments in Luther scholarship, especially the work of Ernst Bizer, Martin Brecht, and Lennart Pinomaa, the point has been made that Luther came increasingly to his fuller understanding of the gospel of grace (justification by faith) sometime after his lectures on Romans — and after posting the ninety-five theses of 1517. That he allowed in 1518 a salvation by humility[1] is an indication that he remained a step away from the more complete statement of justification set forth in the 1520 pamphlet *The Freedom of a Christian*. Especially significant

---

1. See above, pp. 105, 115.

in the latter writing — critically so in the view of the present writer — was Luther's linkage, in the final paragraph of that work, of justification by faith (Rom. 1:18) with the assertion of God's transcendence expressed in 1 Corinthians 1:18-25. This latter passage presents divine transcendence as confounding, in Christ's cross, all human knowledge and power, a "foolishness of God" that is wiser than men, a "weakness of God" that is stronger than men. For Luther this meant that the salvation offered by God in the cross was no mere add-on to, or completion of, a human knowledge purged of error. It represented, rather, a radical, divine disruption of the human scene with the offer of a divine love and forgiveness that human thought did not anticipate or conceive of independent of God's own self-disclosure. This understanding led Luther to characterize the human assumption of punishment and reward, the earning of merit, as little more than "superstition," a superstition extensively exploited by the medieval church. It has been proposed that Luther's linkage of justification with the "foolishness" of the cross in *The Freedom of a Christian* has not been sufficiently noted, that this linkage lies very much at the heart of Luther's appreciation of the freedom and sovereignty of the Word of God and its central message of forgiveness and justification.

It is possible to interpret this foolishness and weakness of God passage as an injunction to personal humility and a call to cultivate a subjective piety, a limited interpretation that Luther himself seems to have entertained for a while even after the October 1517 posting of the ninety-five theses. What helped open up this restricted hermeneutic of inward "spirituality" was, as suggested, Luther's encounters with the this-worldly realities of an ecclesio-centric otherworldliness, even though his later, increasing accent upon a "two kingdoms" teaching restrained its fuller development. It has been argued that the impact of discrete historical confrontations enlarged Luther's recognition and awareness of the critical this-worldly nature of God's "foolishness and weakness" in juxtaposition to the world's — and the church's — "wisdom" and "power."[2] In

---

2. In *The Interpretation of Cultures*, Clifford Geertz suggests that the concrete realities of the world set certain limits to the religious imagination. He writes: "[No] one, not even the saint, lives in the world religious symbols formulate all of the time, and the majority of men live in it only at moments. The everyday world of common-sense objects and practical acts is . . . the paramount reality of human experience — paramount in the sense that it is the world in which we are most solidly rooted, whose inherent actuality we can hardly

the aftermath of these encounters, Luther was called to play an increasingly Old Testament–like prophetic role vis-à-vis the ecclesiastical world of his own and previous times, a prophetic calling that, up to the time of Luther, had been largely co-opted and precluded by the medieval dictum that "obedience is the highest form of humility."[3]

The first of three events that moved Luther beyond the internalization of 1 Corinthians 1 to an increasingly concrete, this-worldly awareness of God's transcendence was his supposed "hearing" before Cardinal Cajetan in October 1518. There the obduracy of the papacy and its spokesperson, Cajetan, made it clear to Luther that there would be no open theological discussion of what was, for Luther, the commanding, central message of the Word of God. Cajetan made it plain to Luther that the papacy's primary interest was in obtaining the recantation of his previously expressed views and his unqualified obedience, thus calling for his silence on a Scripture-informed understanding of grace.

A second event came nearly seven months later at Leipzig, in June 1519. This was Luther's debate with John Eck and the latter's accusation that Luther was guilty of the "heresy" of John Hus, condemned by the Council of Constance in 1414-1415. After the debate, upon reading some of Hus's writings sent to him by two of Hus's followers who had attended the debate, Luther declared "We are all Hussites," thereby acknowledging and affirming views previously condemned — erroneously so, in Luther's view — by the medieval church.[4] Again, the need for a wide-ranging theological-historical criticism of the church, one theologically grounded in Scripture, impressed itself upon Luther and reinforced his previously undertaken reappraisal of church decretals begun in the aftermath of the Cajetan encounter.

Soon thereafter, in a third major unveiling of the presence of a

---

question (however much we may question certain portions of it), and from whose pressures and requirements we can least escape." Clifford Geertz, *The Interpretation of Cultures* (New York: Basic Books, 1973), p. 119.

It is proposed here that some of the realities of Luther's world, conjoined with his biblical focus, helped provoke new theological-historical insights and moved him out of the spiritual inwardness of his previous monastic frame of reference.

3. See above, p. 100, esp. n. 79.

4. In December 1999, in anticipation of the new millennium, the Vatican apologized for the Inquisition's condemnation and execution of Hus. Pope John Paul II praised Hus for "his moral courage." See *The Christian Century,* January 5-12, 2000, p. 13.

"Word" in relation to his contemporary world, Luther read and was fully persuaded by Lorenzo Valla's 1440 scholarly exposé of the forged nature of the "Donation of Constantine." That the medieval church had produced and exploited a false claim to earthly power in clear contradiction of "the weakness of God" confirmed for Luther that a counteragency, a demonic presence, had gained a foothold within the church and was at work to undermine the central message of free grace. The course of the two years that followed the posting of the theses against the sale of indulgences, originally rooted in pastoral concerns about a distortion of the message of forgiveness and its financial exploitation, directed Luther's struggle to a world wherein he saw the church as itself engaged in the pursuit and exercise of earthly as well as spiritual power and dominion. In Luther's view, the church had made, on a long-term basis, unwarranted claims to political power conjoined with false claims of control over the heavenly destinies of ill-informed people, a people whose subjection stemmed in major part from their susceptibility to the exploitation of otherworldly fears in ignorance of the Word of God.

The thrust of these evolving perceptions over the years between 1517 and 1520 were reinforced by Luther's recall and reappraisal of earlier experiences in his 1510 visit to Rome and led him to insist that the church reappraise itself vis-à-vis the cross and set limits to claims of power in its sacerdotal role of providing access to heaven. In this regard, during the years 1518 to 1520, Luther took special issue with the church's interpretation of "the keys of the Kingdom," the claim that what the church "bound on earth" was somehow bound also in the afterlife. Against this view, Luther argued that the forgiveness of sins was not so much a power, a prerogative, of the church hierarchy, to be meted out via penance to believers in quest of life after death, but a duty of the church to proclaim, to preach, as present grace to believers.[5] The debate about the keys and the assumed special power of a hierarchically structured church was not only a debate about the ultimate basis of authority in the church (Scripture versus papal office); it was a debate also about the substance of faith amidst the concreteness of present life in contrast to, and in tension with, common representations of punishments and rewards in the next life.

Especially telling in this theological revolution was Luther's insistence that Christian ethics was essentially oriented to this life and was

---

5. See above, pp. 88-91.

not a means of securing life in the next world. Luther's "ethics of grati-tude"[6] was a call for faith to live out a forgiveness at hand, in and for this life, a call freed from anxiety about acquisition of merit for the next. In this context Luther made the theologically radical point that sin is es-sentially unbelief, by which he meant that the unwillingness to live by God's forgiveness in Christ and the cross was nothing less than the rejec-tion of God's grace in preference for some form of human self-justification. Luther, in asserting the this-worldly nature of a faith-inspired ethics, argued for the creative, spontaneous freedom of the "law written upon the heart"[7] in contrast to inborn legalistic inclina-tions to seek merit, even when merit-motivated actions were projected through the church-administered aids (grace) of penance and eucharist. It was here that Luther situated his call for Christian "adulthood,"[8] here too that a distinctly Christian egalitarianism gained currency and conta-gion in a changing economic-social world. Luther's accent upon the call to trust in an encompassing unmerited grace on the grounds of a preached gospel, with its accompanying sense of the equal status of all believers, denied a privileged spiritual status for monastery and hierar-chy. Justification's grounding in the cross-event fundamentally chal-lenged the status-claims of spiritual and worldly wisdom and power, even when this point came subsequently to be imperfectly, unevenly per-ceived among many who followed in the Reformation tradition.

In these theological struggles and controversies, divine transcendence took on a previously unappreciated this-worldly significance. The hu-man disposition to consign a transcendent God to the "other world" and to embrace ritualized access to life after death was challenged by a transcendent Word inextricably bound up with a concrete, this-worldly cross-event. In this context, waiting upon an otherworldly "solution" to problems of injustice and inequality came, at times only by steps, to de-mand challenge. For many of the faithful, clearly not all, a continuing expectation of heaven was leavened by a this-worldly purpose and sense of responsibility. The peasants of Germany in 1525 grasped something of the new sense of here-and-now equality, but their resort to violence in

6. See above, pp. 99, 116.
7. See above, pp. 102-4. Again, the scriptural sources are Jeremiah 31:31-34 and He-brews 8:8-13.
8. See above, pp. 100-101. Cf. also p. 112 and Pannenberg citation.

pursuit of justice alarmed much of Europe and undermined their important statement. Such was certainly the response of Luther, who looked chiefly to grateful goodness and charity within established social structures as faith's proper response to grace. As a result, this aspect of the Luther bequest moved frequently in the direction of political quietism. Yet Luther's reform nonetheless loosed a peculiar new leaven of freedom and equality in Europe that was not to be contained within the bounds of fixed political and social orders. Luther's resistance to papal authority, especially his 1520 open letter to Pope Leo X,[9] which accompanied publication of *The Freedom of a Christian,* set forth a distinctive Christian this-worldliness that sparked continuing spiritual and intellectual unrest and contributed to opening up, often in other venues, a too-rigid ecclesiastical, social world.

This was the case because Luther's reform, as discussed above,[10] enlisted other voices committed to the gift of transcendent grace and freedom. Like Luther, the early reformer Martin Bucer addressed the problem of the need for reorientation in Christian ethics, an ethics no longer preoccupied with concern for otherworldly reward (or punishment). But, where Luther had spoken of a "law written upon the heart," the spontaneous and creative goodness generated by faith's acceptance of God's work of redemption in Christ, Bucer stressed a sense of the determinative nature of God's decision "for us." Like Luther, Bucer struggled with the self-turned-in-upon-itself — and thus with ethics — in undue individual concern for, and guardianship of, the soul. In a 1523 pamphlet Bucer urged that "no one should live for himself alone, but for his neighbor," certainly a central New Testament theme. But, in making reference to Romans 8 and Romans 9:1-3 (Paul's willingness to make sacrifice of his own salvation in Christ for the sake of the salvation of his Jewish brethren), Bucer pointed to God's prior steadfast decision "for us" in Christ, an "election" that allowed the believer to risk even his/her own understanding of salvation in service to the gospel and turn it to service of the well-being of the neighbor and the broader community, the "commonwealth."[11]

It was in the context of this "election," the sure promise of God's

---

9. See *Luther's Works* (Philadelphia: Fortress Press, 1955-1986), vol. 31, pp. 334-43.
10. See above, pp. 118, 120.
11. See above, pp. 126-28, 135-36.

love for the believer, that Bucer pressed beyond Luther's definition of social duty and encouraged a rational choice of and education in vocations, vocations judged worthy on the basis of their capacity to contribute to what was later to be phrased "the greatest good for the greatest number." This latter phrase was subsequently offered as a universal ethical maxim in the work of the eighteenth- and nineteenth-century English philosophers Jeremy Bentham and John Stuart Mill. But, in the sixteenth century, Bucer rooted moral duty in the individual's preparation for, and commitment to, a life vocation and not as an ethical maxim for case-by-case, ad hoc decisions. Unlike the inclination of Luther to accede to inherited or socially and economically determined occupations, Bucer encouraged definition and choice of vocation as an expression of this-worldly Christian responsibility for the well-being of the commonwealth. Though he by no means rejected Luther's "law written upon the heart," Bucer made room for its expression in vocation beyond the acceptance of the given economic-social order. Christian commitment in vocation moved, with Bucer, in the direction of more varied and rationally selective responses to electing grace. God's steadfast commitment to the salvation offered in Christ called for the choice of, and service in, *vocation* in furtherance of a greater social good. With Bucer — and this revised view of vocation — Christians were encouraged to live out employment in the world in ways beyond the limited medieval option of "vocation" as ecclesiastical/monastic commitments, offices at root devoted to the need of ministration of an otherworldly, life-after-death redemption. Rather, faithful Christians were called to vest their lives, individually and collectively, in service to "the greater glory of God" and thereby lend future shape to a perceived, increasingly malleable, social-political order. Again, not all new believers were so comprehending or committed, but new visions and energies were unleashed in the building of corporate life. The critique of absolute monarchy and an inherited social order was leavened and furthered by the inspiration and views of new forms of service opened to the laity.

John Calvin brought additional insight and vision to the contributions of Luther and Bucer in renewed understanding of God's transcendence and the call to this-worldly engagement and mission. While embracing the overarching message of justification and forgiveness as the basis for the Christian life, Calvin, even more so than Bucer, accented diversity in the believer's vocational options. He did this largely on the basis of his understanding of the church as "the communion of saints."[12] Drawing on the image of the interrelated parts of the body in Romans 12, 1 Corinthians 12, and Ephesians 4, Calvin affirmed the diversity of functions in service as essential to the well-being of the entire community of believers. He underlined the variety of spiritual gifts and choices of vocation within the believing community — and from thence, by extension, to the broader social order, whereas Luther looked rather to a seemingly co-equal social-political order in definition of vocation. All of this Calvin set within the compass of God's providential work in history, one that called for the believer's attentiveness to God's work, word, and will in every present era. In fundamental theological agreement with Luther and Bucer, but in distinctive qualification of otherworldly orientations, Calvin, as quoted earlier,[13] declared in his letter to Sadoleto that one "imbued with true piety" must "regard as insipid that long and labored exhortation to zeal for heavenly life, a zeal which keeps a . . . [person] entirely devoted to himself, and does not, even by one expression, arouse him to sanctify the name of God." Beyond each person's care for his/her soul lay commitment to God's will for the well-being of the neighbor and the social, corporate order.

Calvin's subsequent delineation of a "third use of the law," in development beyond Luther's emphasis upon its purposes and uses in restraint of evil and conviction of guilt, set forth the purpose of moving the community forward, making corrections and charting courses for new, realizable social goods "to the greater glory of God." Government was never envisioned, but especially not in Bucer or Calvin, as an enemy of the people in the sense of some present-day ideologies. Government, for Bucer and Calvin, was seen as a providential instrument not only for preserving order but also for communal growth and development. It demanded responsibility and stewardship in all ranks of the magistracy and citizenry. In his understanding of the "communion of saints," Calvin made room always for faithful edification in the speech of persons of varied gifts, even from those of assumed lesser intellectual acumen. In government also, room was to be made for correction and input from "below," from people in positions separate from those of chief magistrate or other established offices. As Calvin urged an educated clergy

---

12. See above, pp. 157, 163.
13. See above, p. 152.

and laity to keep themselves open to a word of God on the lips of fellow believers, so government ought to allow for an edifying "word" from lesser-placed officials and representative figures.[14] Calvin shunned the idea that the voice of the people was the voice of God, but he nonetheless affirmed the shared goals of a common life and the need to check, within the structures of government, abuses of power arising from sin-beclouded assumptions of personal prerogative.

The third use of the law in Calvin did not mean a "re-catholicizing" of Protestantism (law as a means of salvation)[15] but marked an effort to work toward forms of spiritual and social life better conforming to God's will for a more humane, interdependent human order.[16] Unlike Luther,

14. Calvin was more expansive in his theological critique of the "world's wisdom" than of the established structures of political power, an outlook enjoined by the Romans 13 passage, a view strongly affirmed by Luther. This was reflected also in the views of Francis Bacon. The specter of anarchy reinforced these views. In his commentary on 1 Corinthians 1:18-25, Calvin subjected both human learning and the exercise of political power to spiritual criticism but did not discount the human character and value of both, offering also very positive affirmation: "How greatly deserving of honour are the liberal sciences, which refine man in such a way as to make him truly human! Besides, what a great number of products they yield! [Cf. Bacon.] Who would not use the highest praise to extol statesmanship, by which states, empires and kingdoms are maintained? — to say nothing of other things! I maintain that the answer to this question is obvious from the fact that Paul does not utterly condemn, either the natural insight of men, or wisdom gained by practice and experience, or education of the mind through learning; but what he affirms is that all those things are useless for obtaining spiritual wisdom." *Calvin's Commentaries*, ed. David W. and Thomas F. Torrance, *The First Epistle of Paul the Apostle to the Corinthians*, trans. John W. Fraser (Grand Rapids: Eerdmans, 1960), p. 38; see also pp. 39-42. The concluding sentence in this section of the commentary reads: "[A]nyone can see quite clearly how improper it is to ascribe either foolishness or weakness to God, but it was necessary to use such ironic expressions in rebutting the insane arrogance of the flesh which does not hesitate to strip God of all His Glory." Rather than an "ironic" reading for this passage of Scripture, the present study puts forth that the cross is a too-often ignored expression of God's *historically grounded* transcendence and a revaluation of human values, this in the context also of the humanly inexplicable resurrection. On this latter point, see n. 67 below.

15. For this interpretation, one at variance with the view set forth in the present work, see Steven Ozment, *The Age of Reform: 1250-1550* (New Haven: Yale University Press, 1980), pp. 374-75. Positively, Ozment's discussion in his chapter "Marriage and the Ministry in the Protestant Churches," pp. 381-96, points up another of the "leavening" aspects of the Reformation.

16. On differences between Luther and Calvin on "the third use of the law," see Edward A. Dowey, "Law in Luther and Calvin," *Theology Today* 41, no. 2 (1984): 146-53.

Calvin believed that law allowed the possibility that one could press forward to greater shared life and equity in society, even as the believer recognized that he/she might likely fall short of consistent expressions of "spontaneous goodness" in Luther's sense. In other words, it was possible in vocation to believe and act counter to the self's sinful inclinations, that freedom from the law as a means of personal salvation contained within it, paradoxically, a freedom *for* the law as direction and promise of a more inclusive human future.[17] It became increasingly possible to view increased social equity as obedience, as "affirmative action," and not alone as a spontaneous, individualistic response of the heart.

In the English Reformation, the confluence of a number of distinctive forces and conditions made for patterns of change different from those on the Continent. In England, strains of Lutheran and Calvinist thought interacted with an indigenous Lollard tradition.

The gradual assimilation of Reformation perspectives, from biblical roots, leavened the hierarchically structured English church and was accompanied as well by developments in political governance. The persecution of Protestants during the brief reign of Mary Tudor (1553-1558), combined with the persecutions of the earlier Lollard tradition, along with the distinctive insular consciousness of the English people, helped steer a religious course that grew increasingly distant from Rome. The St. Bartholomew's Day Massacre in France (1572) reinforced imprinted memories of the rule of Mary Tudor and stimulated a religio-political concern to guard against arbitrary royal determinations in the relations of church and state. In an earlier 1552 letter to Archbishop Cranmer, Calvin set a tone for Puritan religio-political involvement. God, he wrote, "would by no means have those people inactive whom He Himself has placed on the watch."[18] This was of a piece with Peter Wentworth's later

---

17. André Biéler gives account of the "humanism" of Calvin, with emphasis on his economic teachings; see *The Social Humanism of Calvin*, trans. Paul T. Fuhrmann (Richmond, VA: John Knox Press, 1964). In a passage consonant with a major emphasis in the present work, Biéler writes: "[T]here is no real Christian life outside a visible community, however numerically and humanly feeble it might be. 'Because it can never happen,' says Calvin, 'that those who are truly persuaded that God is the common Father and that Christ is the only Chief and Head of them all, be not united among themselves in brotherly love to the end that they communicate together for their mutual progress'" (p. 19).

18. H. Robinson, ed., *Original Letters Relative to the English Reformation* (n.p.: Parker Society, 1847), vol. 2, p. 712; cited by Christopher Hill, *God's Englishman: Oliver*

words in Parliament when he declared: "Wherefore God for his great mercies sake, grant that we may from henceforth shew our selves neither Bastards nor Dastards therein, but that as rightly begotten Children, we may sharply and boldly reprove God's Enemies, our Princes and State; and so shall every one of us discharge our Duties in this High Office, wherein he hath placed us."[19] It was in this speech in 1575 that Wentworth also insisted, to Queen Elizabeth and her ministers, that issues of religious reform could not be reserved to the bishops and kept from discussion in Parliament, because, he pointed out, it was Parliament, not the bishops, that had instituted the religious settlement under Elizabeth. His opposition to the queen on these matters took him to the Tower — under Henry VIII it would likely have cost him his head. But Parliament recognized in Wentworth's words its own responsibilities and freedoms. It interceded with the crown and subsequently was able to welcome Wentworth again into its company.

Seventy years after Wentworth asserted Parliament's role in these matters, a further development of the argument was heard in the course of the English Civil War (1642-1648). In the 1647 debates at Putney on the subject of the fate of the captured king, Charles I, a historian noted, "[R]epresentatives of the rank and file [of the New Model Army] claimed that since 'the poorer and meaner of this kingdom . . . have been the means of the preservation of the kingdom,' 'the poorest man in England' had a right to choose his own government."[20] This later, more revolutionary statement went beyond the convictions and intent of Peter Wentworth and most Puritans of the earlier time. In fact, the Commonwealth, the republic, which was established as a result of the civil war — and later, the Protectorate under Oliver Cromwell — did not long survive the latter's death in 1658. The English monarchy was restored in 1660 under Charles II. But after the years of civil war, the years of the Commonwealth and the Protectorate, the power of the monarchy was never the same.[21] There is little question

---

Cromwell and the English Revolution (New York: Harper Torchbooks, 1972), p. 225; cf. Letters of John Calvin, Compiled from the Original Manuscripts and Edited by Jules Bonnet (New York: Ben Franklin, 1854, 1973), vol. 2, p. 347.

19. Quoted above, p. 184.

20. Christopher Hill, The World Turned Upside Down (New York: Penguin Books, 1975), p. 38.

21. Hill, in God's Englishman, pp. 253-76, discusses the impact of Oliver Cromwell and the years of the Commonwealth upon subsequent English history.

that the seeds of this English revolution took root subsequently in the fresh soil of the New World, nourished by the widespread exercise of vocation in local political assemblies and government offices throughout the Colonies. Importantly, the responsibilities of vocation at various levels of life helped breed a new, broader sense of citizenship.

Though not usually a subject among interpreters of Reformation theology, the story and contribution of Francis Bacon, with its wide impact upon later Western thought, has been presented in the present work against the background of the history of the English Reformation. In line with his assertion that "truth is the daughter of time," Bacon saw his life and work within a historical context. As quoted above, Bacon declared in the preface to the *Novum Organum*: "I am wont for my own part to regard this work as a child of time rather than wit. . . . But for this accident . . . I wish that if there be any good in what I have to offer, it may be ascribed to the infinite mercy and goodness of God and to the felicity of your Majesty's times."[22] In his early career Bacon devoted himself, in the first instance, to the pursuit of high office in government, a goal he subsequently achieved during the reign of James I. Bacon's father had filled the office of lord keeper of the seal for years during Elizabeth's rule, and Bacon saw himself following in such service in government. He made positive contributions in this political role, but throughout his official career he generally shunned calls for radical or major political reform. He rejected anti-monarchy measures, except as he subtly projected a gradual restriction of the power of the monarchy in his own proposal for royal sponsorship of, and subscription to, a council of scientific inquirers and inventors upon whom the monarch should properly depend for advice and appropriate guidance. In pursuit of political office Bacon relied heavily, often obsequiously, on the patronage of others. His political career ended in disgrace when he was impeached for bribery in 1621 and then removed from his position as lord chancellor. But in his intellectual pursuits and outlook he was fully his own person and saw, coming out of such labors, a greater, divinely inspired good.

As stated earlier, Bacon, in the course of his political career, at times expressed concern about his vocation in government, feeling he was better "called" to philosophical work than the exercise of high office. This uncertainty about his calling in politics is evidenced relatively early

22. Quoted above, p. 214.

in the dedication of the first edition (1597) of his *Essays*. The dedicatory letter to his older brother Anthony reads: "I sometimes wish your infirmities translated upon myself, that her Majesty mought have the service of so active and able a mind, & I mought be with excuse confined to these contemplations & studies for which I am fittest, so commend I you to the preservation of the divine Majesty."[23] In a later reflection, Bacon commented on his "wasted time in politics," though the later editor of his writings, James Spedding, discounted what he regarded as Bacon's overly negative assessment of his political accomplishments.[24]

Spedding was right to discount Bacon's too negative view of his work in government, but there can be no question that he himself saw his calling — and his greatest accomplishment, his greatest gift — in philosophical work as the framing of a new order of knowledge and the promise of great future social benefits. It is of note that Bacon also — not by happenstance — made reference to the apostle Paul's willingness to surrender his salvation for the benefit of his brethren, citing the Romans 9 passage along with Exodus 32:32 and describing it as "an ecstasy of charity and infinite feeling of community."[25] Bacon worked at this philosophical vocation over the course of his political career and published the *Novum Organum* while serving as lord chancellor. In the closing sections of that work, Bacon laid out his hope for human betterment, contrasting the promise of work in government with labors in a revised new science and its expected accompanying new technologies. In comparing the two callings, he wrote: "[T]he benefits of discoveries . . . extend to the whole race of man, civil benefits only to particular places; the latter last not beyond a few ages, the former through all time. Moreover the reformation of a state in civil matters is seldom brought in without violence and confusion; but discoveries carry blessings with them, and confer benefits without causing harm or sorrow to any."[26]

It is clear that Bacon lacked the political vision of many who came after him. Like Luther, he would have rejected the radical political re-

---

23. James Spedding, Robert L. Ellis, and Douglas D. Heath, eds., *The Works of Francis Bacon* (London: Longmans, Green, Reader & Dyer, 1853-1874), vol. 6, p. 523. Hereafter cited as *WFB*, with volume designation. I have frequently added Roman numeral section designations in parentheses.

24. *WFB*, vol. 14, pp. 378-81; cf. also pp. 569-71.

25. *WFB*, vol. 5, p. 7.

26. *WFB*, vol. 4, p. 113 (cxxix).

form of a Thomas Jefferson and other signers of the American Declaration of Independence, or the motto of the Great Seal of the United States: "Novus Ordo Seclorum," "the new order [political] of the ages." It may, of course, also have been the case that another time and place might have altered Bacon's political perspective. But for himself, in his own times, he saw the greatest contributions to the human future deriving from the practical results of science and technology, and only very marginally in a restructuring of government. With such an outlook, Bacon represented a departure from the perspective of Martin Bucer, who a hundred years earlier had declared work in government to be the highest form of Christian service, second only to the ministry of the preached Word. But the world had changed since the time of Bucer; and Bacon made for even greater change with his commitment to the acquisition of new knowledge and the work of invention. This new possibility of vocation — and Bacon's view of his own special vocation — was framed in the following words of the *Novum Organum*:

> Moreover I think that men may take some hope from my own example. And this I say not by way of boasting, but because it is useful to say it. If there be any that despond, let them look at me, that being of all men of my time the most busied in affairs of state, . . . and in this course [of writings] altogether a pioneer, following in no man's track, by resolutely entertaining on the true road, and submitting my mind to Things, advanced these matters, as I suppose, some little way. And then let them consider what may be expected (after the way has been thus indicated) from men abounding in leisure, and from association of labours, and from successions of ages: the rather because it is not a way over which only one man can pass at a time (as is the case with that of reasoning), but one in which the labours and industries of men (especially as regards the collecting of experiences) may with the best effect be first distributed and then combined. For then only will men begin to know their strength, when instead of great numbers doing all the same things, one shall take charge of one thing and another of another.[27]

27. *WFB*, vol. 4, p. 102 (cxiii). Though there is question that Bacon directly called to mind Calvin's understanding of the church as "the communion of saints," Calvin's view of the Christian community of faith projects an interchange of gifts of faith and spiritual capacities that build toward a more mature, fulfilling corporate, ecclesial future. Bacon's

Despite Bacon's belief that the record of his own extensive experiments, in the second volume of the *Novum Organum,* was an essential part of his overall work, the judgment of scholars has long since concluded that Bacon's scientific experiments lacked enduring merit. In a lecture in November 1961, marking the four hundredth anniversary of Bacon's birth, Virgil K. Whitaker offered the view that Bacon's record of experiments was without value. He then added: "It is a paradox that though Bacon set out to describe a philosophy of nature, he is always best in writing about man."[28] And, in his writing about man, Whitaker offered that "especially its Idols . . . become more enthralling and challenging with each rereading."[29]

What Bacon accomplished in his discussion of the "idols" was a new critical evaluation of the motivations, dispositions, and vulnerabilities of human thought. And this meant, at the same time, a requirement of ever-new openness in understanding and appraisal of the human condition and its knowledge traditions. In a way, the later work of Locke, Hume, Kant, Hegel, Marx, and Freud can be seen as applications and elaborations of Bacon's critique of inherited intellectual habits of mind. Of late, postmodernism and efforts at deconstruction follow in a train of criticism that seeks to think and see things in new light. Less apparent to many who inherit Bacon's critical mindset, however, is the theological dimension that informed his treatment of the idols, the fact that he chose to think of the problem in terms of idolatry. In this he expressed an unwillingness to view the world in other than humble, self-critical terms, a view of the world framed in awareness of a transcendent God whose works demanded human inquiry and participation as well as an active goodness and the actualization of an intellectual freedom afforded by grace, a freedom no less vital than Luther's freedom from works of the law.

That Bacon avoided addressing the exercise of political power with the same degree of critical questioning he displayed in analyzing human thought processes reflects his deep-rooted antipathy toward fanaticism and concern for social stability. He saw religion, at one level, as a guar-

---

view of the future scientific community is strikingly similar to Calvin's view of the nature and growth of the Christian faith community; see above, pp. 157, 162, 163, and n. 17, above.

28. Virgil K. Whitaker, *Francis Bacon's Intellectual Milieu* (Los Angeles: William Andrews Clark Memorial Library UCLA, 1962), p. 26.

29. Whitaker, *Francis Bacon's Intellectual Milieu,* p. 26.

antor of social order and the ultimate sanction for works of peace and charity. In the 1612 edition of the *Essays*, he noted the troubling phenomenon of contemporary religious controversy and offered a conflicted opinion about its origins. "The quarrels, and divisions for Religion, were evils unknown to the Heathen: and no marvell; for it is the true God that is the jealous God; and the gods of the Heathen were good fellowes. But yet the bonds of religious unity, are so to be strengthened, as the bonds of humane society be not dissolved."[30] Eight years later he described what he regarded as an alternative to political, religious strife: "[Mine is not] a trumpet which summons and excites men to cut each other to pieces with mutual contradictions, or to quarrel and fight with one another; but rather to make peace between themselves, and turning with united forces against the Nature of Things, to storm and occupy her castles and strongholds, and extend the bounds of human empire, as far as God Almighty in his goodness may permit."[31]

To be sure, Bacon's use, in this instance, of the metaphor of an "assault" upon nature differed from his more common image of "discovery." It jars a contemporary consciousness, one informed by awareness of the extent and dangers of the human abuse of nature. But here one should note that Bacon fashioned his vision, even with its martial imagery, as an alternative to the disheartening political-religious turmoil of his times and his prescient forebodings of such struggles still to come. It is argued in this study that Bacon's greatest contribution lay in explication of the deceptions and deficiencies of the workings of the human mind, afflictions he saw carrying over into the future. His contribution to critical thought lent force to the processes of change and helped lay the foundations of a distinctly modern mindset. It laid grounds for faith in new beginnings that moved out from its locus in religious reform and reinforced then-current inquiries into the spheres of nature and technological innovation, embracing as well human perceptions of the world as a whole.

In Luther, Bucer, Calvin, and Bacon, the reach of vocation beyond the restricted medieval concept of ecclesiastical and sacramental office served as a vital laicizing of vocation in and for the world. This had important grounds in an egalitarian gospel of redemption, the gift of a

30. *WFB*, vol. 6, p. 543.
31. Quoted by Whitaker, *Francis Bacon's Intellectual Milieu*, p. 27.

transcendent God who called faithful believers away from a world-denying otherworldliness, though still, to be sure, maintaining hope of life after death. The spiritual recovery, in the sixteenth and seventeenth centuries, of a sense of divine transcendence, the sense of a God who variously addressed the immediacies of present life, provided for many a vision and outlook capable of working critically with emerging economic and cultural forces in the building of a God-initiated — and sustained — human future. Some faith communities joined in commitment to shaping a culture of progress yet were also able to hold to the biblical tension of being "in the world but not of the world." One can discern at this point the theological underpinnings of H. Richard Niebuhr's dialectical/paradoxical and transformative types of the faith/culture relationship. One can observe, however, that when awareness of God's transcendence, a transcendence manifested in a cross, yielded ground to the more appealing belief in a divinely instituted rational natural order, faith "in the world but not of the world" gave ground to the "Christ of culture" described by Niebuhr.

It needs to be said that Christian piety and commitment continued powerfully in the life and structures of the medieval church, even as the leadership of that church resisted what it regarded as a reform from "outside," a reform carried through in diverse places such as Wittenberg, Strassburg, Zurich, Geneva, and London. In point of fact, in the mid-sixteenth century the church at Rome gained energies through its own internal reform and renewal, building upon increased, renovated disciplines in its spiritual life. The church at Rome held steadfastly to its sacramental system, a system capable of nurturing spiritual reverence and awe, a sense of sacred mystery, one that provided/provides its believers with longstanding satisfactions and assurances. Works of Christian love, sacrifice, mercy, and concern for the poor have marked its piety. The expansion of its mission into the New World and Asia during the sixteenth and seventeenth centuries testified to its then new-won vigor and reinforced its self-image — an image, however, that remained, in H. Richard Niebuhr's terms, a church "above culture" in an assumed role as overseer and guardian of human life on earth, guardian of culture in general. In the faith of its devoted believers, it continues to mirror this image with its continuous call to obedience, a justification by obedience, which, for many, continues to bear the solace and expectation of assured access to heaven.

Theological Interpretation and Reflections

In a review essay of a recent work on the thought of Reinhold Niebuhr, H. Richard's brother, the University of Chicago theologian David Tracy paid tribute to Niebuhr as "the finest American theologian since Jonathan Edwards, and perhaps the most profound religious realist in America since Abraham Lincoln."[32] The occasion for Tracy's essay was a book by Elisabeth Sifton, Reinhold's daughter, titled *The Serenity Prayer: Faith and Politics in Times of Peace and War.*[33] Sifton rejected at the start a passive, pietistic misuse of Niebuhr's widely used prayer, the prayer that implored God to "give us grace to accept with serenity the things that cannot be changed, courage to change the things that should be changed, and the wisdom to distinguish the one from the other." In the course of his essay, Tracy, a committed but not uncritical Catholic, observed that the Reformation, notably in the work of John Calvin, gave expression to a "sense of history replacing nature as the locus of God's covenantal presence."[34] In his positive reading of Niebuhr's work, Tracy offered no elaboration of the bases for this Reformed shift from nature to history as focus of theological interest and commitment. Our present study has sought to offer such explication in the Reformation emphases upon God's transcendence, the theological critique and qualification of otherworldliness, the "laicization" of Christian vocation, the confirmation and building of community, and the oft-neglected link between Christian freedom and critical thought (1 Cor. 1).

Awareness of God's transcendence is not a theological or historical constant. The sense and reality of divine transcendence cannot be humanly possessed, cannot be domesticated. Neither can it be experientially or ritually induced. Mystery can be ritually enshrined; but biblical transcendence escapes ritual. Martin Buber, the Jewish philosopher and theologian, made this point well in his 1923 *I and Thou* when he spoke of unanticipated "meetings," historical encounters in the divine/human relationship.[35] Earlier, in the nineteenth century, Søren

32. David Tracy, "God's Realist," *The New Republic,* April 26, 2004, p. 37.

33. Elizabeth Sifton, *The Serenity Prayer: Faith and Politics in Times of Peace and War* (New York: W. W. Norton, 2003).

34. Tracy, "God's Realist," p. 36.

35. See Martin Buber, *I and Thou,* trans. Ronald G. Smith (New York: Charles Scribner's Sons, 1958), pp. 109-12.

Kierkegaard struck a similar note in asserting the incommensurability of divine transcendence with philosophical, aesthetic, and ethical traditions. Kierkegaard, before Buber, spoke of a human-God relation in the categories of "I and Thou." In matters of faith, reason, and God's transcendence, Kierkegaard greatly impacted later twentieth-century theological discussion with the summary judgment, pervasive throughout his writings, that "[m]erely to obtain the knowledge that God is unlike him, man needs the help of God; and now he learns that God is absolutely different from himself."[36] Kierkegaard came to this judgment with the correlative insight that "deepest down in the heart of piety [read also 'spirituality'] lurks the mad caprice which knows that it has itself produced its God."[37]

Through a major portion of the twentieth century the Swiss theologian Karl Barth offered provocative testimony to such a transcendent biblical God. Barth spoke out on behalf of a "Word of God" in Scripture that broke through the modern, self-assured scholarly investigations into the origins and "religion" of the Bible, offering theological critique of nineteenth-century biblical criticism on the basis of the Bible's own witness to a transcendent, redeeming God. On this basis, Barth also engaged the post–World War I political world and struggled against the National Socialist regime in Germany prior to and throughout World War II. In the aftermath of that event, he offered criticism also of what he perceived to be many self-righteous assumptions on the part of the West during the first decades of the Cold War.[38]

In the perspective of sixteenth- and seventeenth-century theological perceptions of God's transcendence, the question is asked — again — whether it is possible to move from a starting point in questions about "man," humankind, to the question about God, whether it is possible to begin with an affirmation of some innate affinity between the human and the divine and conclude with an understanding consistent with the God witnessed to in Scripture and reaffirmed, if only at times, in sober

36. Søren Kierkegaard, *Philosophical Fragments*, trans. David F. Swenson (Princeton: Princeton University Press, 1946), p. 37.

37. Kierkegaard, *Fragments*, pp. 35-36.

38. For Barth's political/theological perspective during the first decade of the Cold War, see "Between the Firing Lines," in Eberhard Busch, *Karl Barth: His Life from Letters and Autobiographical Texts*, trans. John Bowden (Philadelphia: Fortress Press, 1976), pp. 381-86.

theological interaction with historical events. One is faced ever again with the question of a natural theology, a knowledge of God implicit in the world and accessible to reasoned thought by each person. It is the case — the likely case — that for most people it is the natural order, the creation, that best defines the beginning point for an idea of divine transcendence, God's lordship. Yet, in taking this course, people inevitably carry over subjective judgments that give rise to personal worldviews and tend simultaneously to delimit God's transcendence.

An example can perhaps be offered from church practice in a number of contemporary mainline Protestant churches where revision of the longstanding liturgical form "Father, Son, and Holy Ghost" has been replaced by "Creator, Christ, and Holy Ghost" in the interest of gender equity. With this substitution the thought is expressed that by replacing "father" with the gender-neutral "creator" one is better assured of the equality of the sexes. But with a starting point in "creation," in a natural world of the experiencing human subject, one places the same human subject in a defining role, subtly so, of the first-order Subject: "God." Every person's assumed experience of existence in a world becomes the point of departure for accommodation then of a "Christ" and a "Holy Ghost." One has to ask if there is not a likely second step from this starting point simply to "Jesus" and then also to whatever one can make of a felt "Holy Ghost" or "Holy Spirit." At least in the old formula there is some sense that it is the child, in human terms, who identifies the parent ("Father"), counter to the very natural expectation that the other parent would be the one more able to do that (cf. Mark 3:31-35). It is at least noteworthy that two of the four New Testament Gospels omit reference to a birth narrative, suggesting that a logic deriving from the natural order is not, after all, determinative for faith, a point-of-faith-viewing suggested by the account in the first chapter of Genesis of a seven-day creation narrative giving priority to a historically given law as the framework for the coming-to-be of the natural world. And one must ask in this context if the prologue to the Gospel of John, the creation through the Word and the Word then made flesh, is not better understood as a subordination of nature to the Jesus/Christ story (the world did not know Christ through "wisdom") rather than as a mandate to winnow the philosophical and other religious traditions for the proper conceptualization of nature's "God."

In the 1998 papal encyclical *Fides et Ratio* ("Faith and Reason"), restatement is offered of the long-term Catholic teaching of natural theology in response to the perceived current temper of relativism, scientific positivism, and nihilism as primary characteristics of the contemporary thought-world. With an introduction of "know yourself," the encyclical argues that "the more human beings know reality and the world, the more they know themselves in their uniqueness, with the question of the meaning of things and of their very existence becoming ever more pressing."[39] The encyclical contends that the more one matures in an awareness of selfhood-in-a-world, the more one ought to conclude with the question of God.[40] A critical point in the argument involves the assertion of the unity of truth — scientific and theological — through elevation of Aristotle's rule of "non-contradiction" in logic and human communication to a metaphysical principle, a step impelled not alone by Plato and Aristotle's effort to surround themselves with a rational, ordered world, but one adopted theologically also by the medieval church in exposition of the "Word made flesh" passage of John 1.[41] The encyclical asserts that the truths of natural theology are not those of a fully operative autonomous reason but those guided by a theologically informed, faith-informed reason under charge of the church, with a call for obedient acceptance by persons who would fulfill the innate human quest for truth, especially those who have not exercised an inquiring, philosophical bent of mind. As stated in the encyclical, the move toward an all-encompassing, "absolute" truth "is

39. *On the Relationship between Faith and Reason: Fides et Ratio* (Washington, DC: United States Catholic Conference, 1998), p. 3. Though this encyclical bears the imprimatur of Pope John Paul II, it appears to reflect primarily the theological work of the then Cardinal Ratzinger, now Pope Benedict XVI.

40. *Faith and Reason,* p. 4. It probably does not need to be pointed out that a philosophical alternative to that being proposed in the encyclical is the sense of absurdity that can also attach to the emergent consciousness of the self in a world, as, for example, in the thought of Heidegger, or in Albert Camus's *The Myth of Sisyphus.* In the realm of popular culture, this latter view found frequent expression in Berkeley Breathed's "Opus" comic strip, especially the strip of December 20, 2006.

41. On interpretations of John 1, see Rudolf Bultmann, *Theology of the New Testament,* vol. 2, trans. Kendrick Grobel (New York: Charles Scribner's Sons, 1955), pp. 63-69, esp. p. 64; Karl Barth, *Witness to the Word: A Commentary on John 1,* trans. Geoffrey W. Bromiley (Grand Rapids: Eerdmans, 1986 [1925, 1933]), pp. 73-75; Karl Barth, *Church Dogmatics* I/2, *The Doctrine of the Word of God,* trans. G. T. Thompson and Harold Knight (Edinburgh: T. & T. Clark, 1956), pp. 150-51.

attained not only by way of reason but also through trusting acquiescence to other persons who can guarantee the authenticity and certainty of the truth itself [i.e., by and through the Catholic hierarchy]. There is no doubt that the capacity to entrust oneself and one's life to another person and the decision to do so are among the most significant and expressive human acts."[42]

While it would seem that there are two courses that can be followed to an absolute truth, one via reason and one via "trusting acquiescence" to the church's teaching, even the former course is subject to the guidance and correction of the church, for "[d]eprived of what Revelation offers, reason has taken side tracks which expose it to the danger of losing sight of its final goal."[43] The encyclical goes on to assert:

> The word of God reveals the final destiny of men and women and provides a unifying explanation of all that they do in the world. This is why it invites philosophy to engage in the search for the natural foundation of this meaning, which corresponds to the religious impulse innate in every person. A philosophy denying the possibility of an ultimate and overarching meaning would be not only ill adapted to its task, but false.[44]

It concludes:

> Reflecting in the light of reason and in keeping with its rules, and guided always by the deeper understanding given them by the word of God, Christian philosophers can develop a reflection which will be both comprehensible and appealing to those who do not yet grasp the full truth which divine Revelation declares. . . . A philosophy in which there shines even a glimmer of the truth of Christ, the one definitive answer to humanity's problems, will provide a potent underpinning for the true and planetary ethics which the world now needs.[45]

Along with the compassion and benign concern present throughout most of *Fides et Ratio*, one must remark that in its claim for the univer-

42. *Faith and Reason*, p. 50. Cf. Calvin on this; see above, pp. 146-47.
43. *Faith and Reason*, p. 73.
44. *Faith and Reason*, p. 120.
45. *Faith and Reason*, p. 148.

sal validity of natural theology one discerns the theological-epistemological grounds for H. Richard Niebuhr's delineation of the "Christ above culture" category in his typology of Christian social ethics. Absent in *Fides et Ratio* is an appreciation for the critique of reason essential to understanding God's transcendence in the "offense" and "foolishness" of the cross (1 Cor. 1:18-25). At this point one is prompted to ask whether, in its claim to authoritative oversight of culture via natural theology, the Catholic tradition has not laid claim to a philosophical-ethical equivalent of the "Donation of Constantine," a "donation" from the essentialist thought-world of Plato and Aristotle, albeit "adapted," not forged as in the original "Donation."

Counter to this theological borrowing from Aristotle — and from Stoic natural law — stands Bacon's declamation against the idols of the theatre, with its suggestion that the human mind is continually impelled to fashion its own "coherent" world — or "stage," in Bacon's terms.[46] Among many others who contest a static *rational* framework for thought and being, Paul Tillich argued that "reality as a whole . . . is not the whole of reality,"[47] by which he meant that reality as a structured, rational whole is called into question in its encompassing sufficiency by the existentially, creatively new, brought to expression in and through the particular, the engaged human self, under inspiration, in Tillich's case, of an energizing "Power of Being." Tillich's *kairos* moments, both collective and individual, were later in his thought subsumed under the category of "New Being."[48]

If the Reformation statement of faith emphasized a recovered appreciation for the transcendence of God, it did so in the first instance in the context of a new appreciation for the Word of God expressed and found

---

46. See above, p. 211.

47. Paul Tillich, *Systematic Theology* (Chicago: University of Chicago Press, 1950), vol. 1, p. 18; see also pp. 19-26.

48. For an account of a substantive 1923 exchange between Tillich and Barth on the matter of divine transcendence, see my *Tillich: A Theological Portrait* (Philadelphia: Lippincott, 1968), pp. 35-64; and on Tillich's later shift of emphasis to "New Being," see pp. 94-100 in that same volume. As an affirmed "philosophical theologian," Tillich was himself largely committed to a form of natural theology arising out of the German philosophical idealist tradition, though one at variance with the Aristotelian-Thomistic school of thought. For a brief discussion of the major philosophical presuppositions of Tillich's system, see the present writer's article titled "The Presuppositions and Fault Lines of Tillich's System," in the former Czech journal *Metanoia* 6, no. 3 (Fall 1996): 104-18.

in Scripture. Here Luther's breakthrough to an understanding of justification by faith was formative and expansive. It was germinal in bringing to the fore the message of free grace, a proclaimed forgiveness beyond priestly prescriptions of penance. It was germinal in establishing in grace a basis for human equality beyond all natural considerations: "[I]n Christ there is neither Jew nor Greek, there is neither slave nor free, there is neither male nor female" (Gal. 3:28). This brought a "priesthood of all believers" from the sphere of an afterlife to the here-and-now of earthly existence. And, in linking the gospel of forgiveness/justification to the "foolishness" and "weakness" of God manifested in the cross, Luther introduced a qualification of otherworldly orientations/expectations of judgment beyond death. As outlined above,[49] Luther contested the church's claim to hierarchically administered "keys of the kingdom" and assumed custody of access to heaven. Rather, he saw the gospel of forgiveness conveyed through a Word preached[50] in the language of the people, a Word from Scripture rendered with new translations into accessible languages. In the stead of an ethics motivated by fear of eternal punishment and hope of reward, Luther saw ethics grounded in the response of gratitude for the grace of justification and reconciliation, one expressed through, and with, a newfound this-worldly freedom.[51]

University of Chicago theologian Brian Gerrish shed light on this understanding of Reformation theology in the present situation when he wrote a 2003 article on "sovereign grace." He wrote in criticism of much

---

49. See above, pp. 88-91.

50. Gerhard O. Forde accents the vital role of preaching in Luther's hermeneutics; see "Law and Gospel in Luther's Hermeneutic," *Interpretation* 37 (July 1983): 240-52.

51. Oswald Bayer, a recently retired German theologian at Tübingen, offers helpful discussion of Luther's understanding of Christian freedom in an article "Freedom? The Anthropological Concepts in Luther and Melanchthon Compared," *Harvard Theological Review* 91, no. 4 (1998): 373-87. Bayer writes: "Freedom from self-justification is . . . not accomplished through the law. It is achieved solely through the gospel by which God's Spirit turns the heart around in faith and renews it. The renewal effected by the gospel frees a person so that he or she is able to live in . . . a secularity *(Weltlichkeit)* which . . . is no longer burdened and crushed by the desire for eternity and the demands of salvation" (p. 386). In *Living by Faith: Justification and Sanctification* (Grand Rapids: Eerdmans, 2003), Bayer makes the point that justification by faith, though one among other Christian doctrines, represents nothing less than the substance of the gospel. On this point, see also Karl Barth, *Church Dogmatics* IV/1, *The Doctrine of Reconciliation,* trans. G. W. Bromiley (Edinburgh: T. & T. Clark, 1956), pp. 321-23.

contemporary "spirituality" in a "church which offers reassurance without judgment, Christian education without the call for conversion; or seeks to rally the resources within us rather than pointing us to the resources outside us; or misconstrues the resources — as though they lay only in Christ's teaching and example, not in his victory over sin and death and his power to heal our sickness."[52] In thus speaking of "sovereign grace" — what might also have been termed "the grace of the sovereign God," Gerrish offered a quotation from Luther's *Lectures on Galatians:* "This is the reason why our theology is certain: it snatches us away from ourselves and places us outside ourselves."[53] In the perspective of the prophetic meaning of the cross set forth in our preceding discussion, it might be added that this Reformation theology transposes the believer into an altered, "resurrected" world where faith is called to engagement in awareness of God's transcending foolishness and weakness — always in the face of the world's assumed wisdom and power.

Martin Bucer's linkage of personal commitment to God's objective decision "for us" in the cross of Christ (Rom. 8:35-37) with the apostle Paul's expressed willingness to "be accursed and cut off from Christ" (Rom. 9:3) gave further statement to faith in the sovereign grace of God.[54] The association of the two passages had special significance for Bucer in the context of the threat of death that attended the early preaching of the evangelical message; but, as suggested previously, it had wider applications in the understanding of vocation for all who shared awareness of the "priesthood of all believers" and the "laicization" of vocation that followed from it. Extension of this insight followed in Calvin's argument, advanced against Cardinal Sadoleto, that preoccupation with the salvation of one's own soul does not move one beyond obsession with self. As put by Calvin and quoted previously, "[I]t certainly is the part of a Christian . . . to ascend higher than merely to seek and secure the salvation of his[/her] own soul."[55] What Bucer and Calvin argued is that the willingness to surrender one's assumed human grip on "eternal salvation" for a purpose of God in this life brought one simultaneously into reliance on the "objective," transcendent love of God

---

52. Brian Gerrish, "Sovereign Grace: Is Reformed Theology Obsolete?" *Interpretation* 57 (January 2003): 56.

53. Gerrish, "Sovereign Grace," p. 57.

54. See above, pp. 126-28.

55. Quoted above, p. 145.

promised in Romans 8:35: "Who shall separate us from the love of Christ?" The latter is a love that calls into question the believer's tendency to clutch tightly his/her "salvation," so that the believer can address in its immediacy God's guiding love to the neighbor.[56] For Calvin, especially, this "predestination" had the capacity to edify faith's "reason" in its this-worldly tasks and commitments. It afforded a "peace" and freedom "that passeth understanding." Fanaticisms, even barbarisms, deriving from expectations of rewards in an afterlife are displaced by charities in this life, underwritten and sustained by God's own enduring commitment and promise to us.

What Calvin brought to the theological table in addition to this point shared in part with Bucer was his understanding of neighbor in relation to community. Rather than seeing the neighbor primarily, if not exclusively, as an object of charity, Calvin saw the relationship of believing neighbor to neighbor in terms of reciprocity, a recognition that God's gifts of grace are marked by diversity as well as by the shared grace of God's redeeming love and justification. Calvin's understanding of the church as "the communion of saints" was pivotal here. It is an expression, a conclusion, not only of his affirmation of the transcendence of God but of the priesthood of all believers. The latter, for Calvin, is clearly *not* a license for every believer's individual autonomy, rooted in each person's supposed innate knowledge of God, joined often with awareness of one's own existence, an awareness of God independent of the cross, even when supposed only as precursor to knowledge of a redemptive message. Rather, for Calvin, the priesthood of all believers was

---

56. There is a hint of this later development of thought in Luther's *Ninety-Five Theses*, where, in the twenty-ninth thesis, Luther attacked the church's teaching about purgatory, a place of satisfaction for unrequited sins. He cited the legend of the saints Severinus and Paschal who, in purgatory, surrendered their own transfer into heaven so that others in purgatory might gain theirs. Luther, in characterizing this story as "legend," was offering a "demything" of purgatory by questioning a singular commitment to redemption of everyone in purgatory. Luther suggested this while at the same time rejecting the otherworldly efficacy of the purchase of indulgences. (The current papacy has very recently sought to resuscitate the teaching of indulgences; see the *New York Times*, February 10, 2009, pp. 1, 19, sec. A.) Bucer and Calvin in their later interpretations of the two Romans passages directed faith from envisioning rewards in heaven to the daily tasks posed by the conditions of the neighbor, an involved movement of faith from the "other world" to this world as the proper occasion for responsibility and decision in the context of God's sovereign grace, an involvement of joint effort in addition to individual works of charity or merit.

viewed in relation to each one's Spirit-inspired gift of faith, coming always as a gift to the community as well, calling for openness to the Spirit's gift of faith to others in community. For Calvin, the "communion of saints" is a community of growth in the Spirit, growth in charity but also in graceful insight and edification, a shared growth in grace. In the "communion of saints" there is the shared faith in "God for us" but also a sharing in the special, individual gifts of the Spirit. As elaborated above,[57] Calvin built upon the metaphor of the physical body: "No member has its function for itself, or applies it for its own private use, but transfers it to its fellow members; nor does it derive any other advantage from it than that which it receives in common with the whole body. Thus, whatever the . . . [believer] can do, [that individual] is bound to do for . . . [the] brethren, not consulting . . . [individual] interest in any other way than by striving earnestly for the common edification of the church."

Accompanying this theological understanding of the church, Calvin, in his reforming measures, contributed to the design of a church polity, an ecclesiastical structure, that not only guarded against the abuse of concentrated power in a hierarchy, but remained open to shared edification arising from within the "communion of saints." An intermixture of lay and clerical power in the governance of the church; elective positions in its governance; provision for appeal to the judicatories and governing bodies of the church; a concerted effort to establish the independence of the church over against dominance by state authorities — these were marks of Calvin's ecclesiology that survived his own frequently overzealous efforts to reform the morals of the city of Geneva and to guard the orthodoxy of a Scripture-based, civic-wide confession of faith. It remained for others coming after Calvin to develop more fully, in less troubled political times, the potential of some of Calvin's own theological insights. Some of this leavening found expression in the English Reformation, but also, importantly, in a "new," "virgin" world where an increasingly widely shared experience of governing gave rise to new designs of governance and self-governance.

At a later troubled time in Europe, after the tragic Nazi years, Karl Barth described a Christian leavening of the political order and a direction for Christian political activity:

57. See above, p. 157.

Since the Church is aware of the variety of the gifts and tasks of the one Holy Spirit in its own sphere, it will be alert and open in the political sphere to the need to separate the different functions and "powers" — the legislative, executive, and judicial — inasmuch as those who carry out any one of these functions should not carry out the others simultaneously. No human being is a god able to unite in his own person the functions of the legislator and the ruler, the ruler and the judge, without endangering the sovereignty of the law. The "people" is no more such a god than the Church is its own master and in sole possession of its powers. The fact is that within the community of the one people (by the people and for the people) definite and different services are to be performed by different persons, which, if they were united in one human hand, would disrupt rather than promote the unity of the common enterprise.[58]

Barth, with insights garnered from Calvin's understanding of the church as the "communion of saints," elaborated on the fellowship of believers as a *polis,* a social-political body, that moves beyond "both individualism and collectivism."[59] For Barth, Christian ethics in its social dimensions — dimensions essential to any ethics grounded in justification — is informed by the this-worldly life of the justified fellowship of the faithful. As Barth stated in 1931, the church's duty is to "preach forgiveness and no obedience but that which springs from forgiveness."[60] This is an ethic that serves the civil community in furtherance of the ends of freedom, equality, and justice for its citizens. Thus he wrote in 1946: "The adult Christian can only wish to be an adult citizen, and he can only want his fellow citizens to live as adult human beings."[61]

The meaning of adulthood implies the development of a thoughtful and critical outlook on life in all its manifestations. Justification is an

58. Karl Barth, *Community, State, and Church: Three Essays,* with an Introduction by Will Herberg (Garden City, NY: Anchor Books [Doubleday], 1960), pp. 175-76.

59. Barth, *Community, State, and Church,* p. 174. In his Introduction, Herberg offers a critique of Barth's view of the relationship of church and state (see pp. 35-37); but, to the mind of this reader, Herberg fails to understand how deeply Barth's thought is embedded in the here-and-now interrelationships of the justified and sanctifying ("edifying") community of the faithful (Calvin) — hardly a relationship of a simple "above" and "below."

60. Rolf Joachim Erler and Reiner Marquard, eds., *A Karl Barth Reader* (Grand Rapids: Eerdmans, 1986), p. 22.

61. Barth, *Community, State, and Church,* p. 174.

imprint upon the heart, as Luther maintained. But it also engages the mind and affords edification, as Calvin taught. Faith in justification yields the counterintuitive awareness that our value as persons inheres finally in God's love for us and not in our innate or self-perceived "righteousness." Especially off-setting is the message of the cross, a message that "offends" us in our rational constructs of God. Calvin pointed up the compulsive inventiveness of the human mind in framing idols and described the mind as "a perpetual forge of idols." And Bacon carried Calvin's appraisal of the mind's potential for self-delusion further by elaborating on its capacity to shape worlds for itself on the basis of abridged, confining perspectives adapted to human comfort levels — not physical, sensory images but idols of tribe, cave, marketplace, and theatre, with the latter representing grand schemes designed to afford the self "rest" in its own domesticity. Numerous such natural theologies congruent with humankind's varied spiritual propensities continue into our time, inclusive as well of those constructed most recently on the basis of scientific advances in the fields of microbiology and neuroscience.

Bacon, years ago, addressed a world of upheaval and change, one marked by expanding human awareness of its boundlessness and increasingly taken by its own competence in exploration of that world. He shared in this awareness of his times but also stopped to note the limits of the mind in interpreting that world. The human mind, he observed, was particularly — one could say, inordinately — prone to bring to its view of the natural environment, history as well, the baggage of social place, individual conditioning, commercial involvements, along with an encompassing framework or worldview. He warned that even if forewarned of this tendency toward illusory, comfort-assuring coherence, the human mind would continue to be plagued by its domesticating compulsions. Aware of this ingrained habit of mind in religious adherents as well as in those committed to commercial and artistic pursuits, he was concerned that the community of believers might seek to shun new inquiry into the world around it for fear that they might somehow dishonor God. As Bacon better expressed it: "Some surmise and reflect that if second causes are unknown everything can more readily be referred to the divine hand and rod; a point in which they think religion greatly concerned; which is in fact nothing else but to seek to gratify God with a lie."[62] Such fearful

62. Quoted above, pp. 217-18.

piety, one can note, is apparent still in our contemporary world in the efforts of some to counter evidence for evolution with a fabricated "creationism" and an ideological biblicism. For Bacon, as suggested, at issue in a self-critical approach to knowledge about the world, one inclusive of history and philosophical postulates, was the hope and expectation that accessible in the order of nature was a knowledge potential that could/would yield great new charities in technological advances. In face of the bitterness of the religious disputes of his day, Bacon believed that a reformed, reconceived examination of the natural order would bring forth great new material benefits for humankind, benefits free from conflict and human hurt.[63]

Of course, a problem is posed by this assessment of the role for critical thought in the freedom and redemption afforded by justification. The problem is posed by allowance that the mind, attuned to presumptions of "wisdom" and "power," can itself be turned back upon faith in God. Atheism and a secular relativism are altogether possible. At that point there looms a "dark night in which all cats are gray."[64] Yet, whatever "conclusions," if any, may be drawn at this point, they are always also subject to the biblical critiques of "wisdom" and "power," critiques of the finality and self-sufficiency of human reason. Paradoxical as this is, it remains the case that as God in Christ, professed in faith, has been exposed to the *world's* judgment at the cross, the world has been simultaneously brought under *God's* judgment upon its presumptive wisdom and power. It is also the case that here the believer is not left alone in paradox, without edification in movement beyond the world's wisdom. An understanding nurtured in faith remains and is an essential part of the life of faith. Citation of words by Barth is again apt. He speaks of a "transition" that comes in the life and thought of the believer with the response of faith to God in the Christ event:

> The power of the transition is the power of this particular divine seeing and thinking and speaking [in the totality of the Christ event]. Its effect is, therefore, something that takes place to and in the reason of each one. It is a receiving in which the divine seeing and thinking and speaking in Jesus Christ finds its response in a

63. See above, pp. 219-20, 234.
64. A metaphor borrowed from Barth.

251

human, Christian seeing and understanding and knowing, in an awakening and enlightenment of the reason. . . . In virtue of this power . . . [the person of faith] will be one who sees and understands and knows. If it did not have this effect, it would not be this power. It is not, therefore, the power of a blind and formless and inarticulate and irrational stirring, nor that of a blind and formless incitement or even pacification of an irrational and inarticulate excitement or even peace. There are other forces that have effects of this kind. All religions bear testimony to this fact.[65]

But here one can also ask Barth — along with his many edifying theological insights — whether in his concern to exposit the possibility/actuality of revelation via the Word of God he does not at times seem to overshadow in his thought the sense for a living God whose sovereignty and transcendence are manifest in the weakness and powerlessness of Jesus' death on the cross. The nature of God's transcendence in the *cross* is a question more crucial by far than that of Bonhoeffer's charge against Barth of a "positivism of revelation."[66] Barth was concerned, early on in his historical situation, to preserve the integrity of the church's biblical message against its diminution, or dissolution, through the inroads of liberal, post-Enlightenment philosophical suppositions, a struggle that Barth continued against the attempted political-theological subversion of the German Evangelical Church by the Nazis before and throughout World War II. It is fundamental that the Word of God be understood as other than a word spoken by humankind to itself, as Barth maintained; but there is also a work and service of Christian edification to be found

65. Barth, *Church Dogmatics* IV/2, p. 313.

66. See Dietrich Bonhoeffer, *Letters and Papers from Prison*, enlarged edition, ed. Eberhard Bethge (New York: Macmillan, 1972), p. 286. Barth took note of this criticism by Bonhoeffer but questioned the further criticisms that Bonhoeffer felt followed from it; see Busch, *Barth: His Life from Letters*, p. 381. Despite some shared accents with Bonhoeffer's later theological writings, the *Letters and Papers* and *Ethics*, the present writer has raised questions about the continuity and fundamental consistency of his theology; see David Hopper, *A Dissent on Bonhoeffer* (Philadelphia: Westminster Press, 1975), and an article: "Bonhoeffer, Barth, and the Problem of Immediacy," *Metanoia* 3, no. 4 (1991): 214-21. The concluding "Kierkegaardian" critique of Barth in this article has been revised and rejected in David Hopper, "If Kierkegaard Had Read Calvin . . . ," an unpublished paper read at the "Fifth International Kierkegaard Conference" at St. Olaf College, Northfield, Minnesota, June 13, 2005.

in exposition of the historical leavening of culture suggested in H. Richard Niebuhr's categories of the dialectical and transforming impact of Christian social ethics.

The present writer has suggested that the seventeenth-century figure of Francis Bacon is an important, largely unrecognized subject in this regard, unrecognized because of his lack of perceived theological status. Barth mentions Bacon *not once* in the entirety of his multivolume *Church Dogmatics* (9,185 pages), yet Bacon played a major role in the maturation of the critical mind in Western history. If Barth wrote that "[t]he adult Christian can only wish to be an adult citizen, and he can only want his fellow citizens to live as adult human beings," surely one can suggest that the adult Christian should want to be a thoughtful believer and, in turn, want his/her fellow human beings to be critically thoughtful as well. This should mean, for adult Christians, that they not, in Bacon's terms, "seek to gratify God with a lie," but that they share, as Bacon suggested, in the continuing acquisition of knowledge about the world. Bacon sought to enlist curiosity about the world in service to the world, an alternative that he offered to what he saw as unending religious controversy, with forebodings of religion-inspired warfare and terror. There is no lack of statements of personal faith by Bacon throughout his written works, statements that expressed affirmation of God's transcendence and his own sober humility, a humility synonymous with openness to new truth and, correspondingly, in rejection of forms of human knowledge paraded as eternal verities.

Bacon contributed greatly to the emergence of a culture of change, not least to the rise of the belief in progress and to the change in the attitude toward change. This belief, which took root in the West, has since taken on wider though perhaps more limited expression elsewhere among the world's peoples and cultures. Convinced as Bacon was that "truth is the daughter of time," he would have welcomed correction in some of his own hopes and perceptions. He had expected, as indicated, that the technologies developed out of an empirical, new order of knowing, with fresh inquiry into "the book of nature," would yield great new charities for humankind and afford respite from destructive controversies. Much in this realm has transpired as he had hoped. So great has been the technological advances in virtually all day-to-day activities that the world has become very much dependent upon technology for its own survival. Yet, in considering what Bacon had hoped for technology, one must ask if he did not also ignore early signs of its corruption by political, economic power, or at least its potential for such. If Bacon was sensitive to the continuing threat of delusion and self-projection in human thought processes, his own stated hopes for technology seem at times blind to the dangers of its possible actual abuses. In the course of development, as modern societies have become increasingly dependent upon technology as their virtual lifeblood, they have also become ever more vulnerable to disruptions in the complex interconnections of economic and political life. This has meant that, with this development, modern societies have also become more anxious, more concerned, about economic uncertainties and strategic threats to transportation and communication infrastructures, as well as to the persistence and threatening proliferation of nuclear and other weapons of destruction in the hands of ideologically driven governments or disaffected dissident groups.

What Carl Becker once hoped for in regard to the gradual rationalization of human thought processes in adjustment to technology has not come to pass, even though much current hope centers upon the communication and educative potentials of computer technology and the Internet. Identity politics and ideologies, now often religion-inspired, have gained potency through these same means of communication. New life has been breathed into old, historic resentments, a charge that can be brought even against the present work. Whether the dissemination of positive new knowledge and the capacity for critical self-knowledge can keep pace with potent enmities seems at times in question. The rivalry over a this-worldly political/cultural future during the decades of the Cold War was checked by the thought of mutual nuclear destruction. Hope survived. What is troubling in the present historical situation is that otherworldly expectations can unleash defiant disregard for the current interdependencies of our actual world. And recent decades have brought additional concerns in growing awareness that global warming poses urgent threats to a sustainable world order. The current major economic crisis deepens concern for social-historical progress.

Reaffirmation, rediscovery, of God's sovereign grace nurtures a hope that goes beyond our current diminished hopes and heightened anxieties. It calls into play a new — yet not so new — form of Christian witness. It can perhaps even elicit a form of "martyrdom" that is prepared to subordinate its otherworldly hopes and expectations in order to sharpen commitments and duties in preserving a threatened creation. It can work with fresh vigor to restore greater equity in the social order in the face of an often conscienceless, "free-market" global economy. As argued in the foregoing disquisition, such a life-faith draws upon the grace, the justification, of a sovereign God whose transcendence is manifested in a cross — and an equally confounding resurrection.[67]

67. Barth offers observation on the confounding nature of the resurrection, the witness to which as found in the New Testament lies within the believing community. Barth writes: "We cannot read the Gospels without getting the strong impression that as we pass from the story of the passion to the story of Easter we are led into a historical sphere of a different kind. . . . Whether we take the accounts of the resurrection appearances in detail or put them together, they do not give us a concrete and coherent picture. . . . Rather we are confronted by obscurities and irreconcilable contradictions, so that we are surprised that in the formation of the canon no one seems to have taken offence at them or tried to assimilate the various accounts of this happening which is so basically important for the New Testament message. . . . The appearances cannot, in fact, be separated from the formation and development of the community (or of the original form of the community as the narrower and wider circle of the apostles). It was in them that this formation and development took place. None of them is represented as having occurred outside this context." Barth continues: "It is beyond question that the New Testament itself did not know how to conceal, and obviously did not wish to conceal, the peculiar character of this history, which bursts through all general ideas of history as it takes place and as it may be said to take place in space and time. There is no proof, and there obviously cannot be any proof, for the fact that this history did take place (proof that is, according to the terminology of modern historical scholarship)." Barth, *Church Dogmatics* IV/1, pp. 334-35.

Index of Names

Albert, Prince Consort of Queen Victoria, 38
Althaus, Paul, 104n.90
Aquinas, Thomas, 4, 131
Aristotle, 31, 80, 105, 192, 210, 217, 242, 244
Asad, Talal, 65-68
Augustine, 5, 11, 96, 107, 148
Aurelius, Marcus, 45

Bacon, Anne, 204-5
Bacon, Anthony, 205, 234
Bacon, Francis, xi-xiii, 26-27, 35, 49, 164-65; impact of his thought (Richter), 189-90; as Lord Keeper, Lord Chancellor, 190-91; impeachment, 190-91; personal library, 192; on the "idols," 192, 203, 209-13, 236, 250, Calvin on . . . , 215; "truth as daughter of time," 193, 197, 202, 204, 214, 253; *Observations on a Libel,* 193; mediation of church controversies, 197-98; on English church reform, diversity in church order, 199-202; "book of nature," 202-3, 203n.71; inductive, empirical method, 208, 212, 236; relationship to Elizabeth I, 213; reference to Luther, 214-15; rejects "honoring God

with a lie," 217-18; on vocation, 233-36
Bacon, Nicholas, 176, 193, 204-5; Lord Keeper under Elizabeth, 190; on church reform, 177, 178-79; on reform of English law, 177-78
Bainton, Roland, 70; on Luther's near-death experience, 70
Barth, Karl, ix-x, 7, 9, 25-26, 62n.1, 168n.2, 221, 240, 248-49, 251-53, 255n.67
Beard, Charles, 37-39, 43
Becker, Carl, 37, 39-53, 139n.40, 254
Bergson, Henri, 13
Bizer, Ernst, 114-17, 222
Bonhoeffer, Dietrich, 9-10, 210n.89
Brecht, Martin, 72, 78, 120, 222; on Luther's "theology of humility," 101
Brooks, Harvey, 57
Buber, Martin, 239-40
Bucer, Martin, xii, xiii, 118, 120-23, 205, 227-28; relationship to Luther, 120-22, 133, 135-36; *Das ym selbst niemant . . .* ("Instruction in Christian Love"), 124-33; on vocation, 126-30; on creation, 131-33, 136-37; on community, 132; to England (1549), 135, 137; on marriage, divorce, 136-37; on education of women, 137

257

Bultmann, Rudolf, 9
Bury, J. B., 27-40

Cajetan, Cardinal, 224
Calvin, John, xii, xiii, 5, 67, 118, 137,
    228-29, 246; *Institutes of the Chris-
    tian Religion,* 138; and Bucer, 138,
    151-53, 157-58; Geneva and William
    Farel, 138, to Strassburg, 139; in de-
    fense of reforming ministry, 144; on
    hearing the Word, gift of Spirit, 146;
    on edification, 146, 154, 157, 160,
    229; on humility and obedience, 146;
    on "communion of saints," 147, 156-
    57, 229, 231n.7, 247; on tradition,
    148-50; on purgatory, 148-49; on
    Lord's Supper, 149; on "justifica-
    tion," 150-51; "ethics of gratitude,"
    150; "election," 151, 152-53; on voca-
    tion, 153-54; on the "keys," 153-54;
    "foolishness of the cross," 155-56;
    different from Luther, 158; "third
    use of the Law," 158-59, 161; on gov-
    ernment, 159-61, 201, 231; on the law,
    161-62; (see below, "priesthood of
    all believers," under Luther)
Carson, Rachel, 13
Cobb, John, 14-15
Comte, Auguste, 34-35, 36
Condorcet, Antoine-Nicholas, 34
Copernicus, Nicolaus, 29
Cox, Harvey, 10-12, 21
Cranmer, Thomas, 172, 175, 231
Cromwell, Oliver, 232
Cromwell, Thomas, 170-71

Darwin, Charles, 17, 35-36
Descartes, René, 28-30
Dickens, A. G., 187-89
Diderot, Denis, 23-24
Durkheim, Emil, 12, 65

Ebeling, Gerhard, 85
Eck, John, 71, 86, 105, 224

Edward VI, 171-72, 174
Elizabeth I, 176-86; papal bull against
    Elizabeth, 180; Catholic rebellion
    (1569), 181; and opposition Puritan
    party, 183-86; Spanish armada, 182-83

Feuerbach, Ludwig, 17
Fichte, Johann G., 17
Fontenelle, 30-31
Francis of Assisi, 13
Franklin, Benjamin, 16, 188
Franklin, Josiah, 16, 188
Freud, Sigmund, 17, 62, 236
Fuhrmann, Paul, 125n.13, 129n.23

Galileo, 17, 29, 30
Geertz, Clifford, 58n.59, 62-66, 223-
    24n.2; definition of religion, 62; cri-
    tique of Geertz (Asad), 65-69
Gerrish, Brian, 245-46
Greschat, Martin, 125, 131
Griffin, David, 14
Gustafson, James, xi, 3n.3

Hawley, William, 193, 214n.87
Hegel, Georg W. F., 18-19, 36, 236
Henry VIII, 169, 173-74, 180; divorce,
    question of heir, 169; Henrician reli-
    gious reform, 170, 173; supreme au-
    thority in English church, 171
Hume, David, 40-41, 47n.37, 236
Hus, John, 92, 93, 173, 224; Luther
    on . . . , 93-94
Huxley, Aldous, 53-56
Huxley, Thomas, 36

Iggers, George, 56
Isaacson, Walter, 16

Jefferson, Thomas, 189, 235
Jonas, Justus, 69, 120

Kant, Immanuel, 55, 236
Kepler, Johannes, 29, 30

Index of Names

Kierkegaard, Søren, 18, 69, 239-40;
Fear and Trembling, 69
King, Martin Luther, Jr., 11
Kuhn, Thomas, 218

Langer, Suzanne, 63
Luther, Martin, xii, 61, 67, 70; his
death (Oberman treatment), 68-69;
earlier near-death experience, 70;
hearing at at Diet of Worms (1521),
71-73; justification by faith, 72, 126,
102, 104; letter to Charles V (after
Worms), 73; on the ban (excommunication), 75; inner sphere of conscience and faith, "two kingdoms"
teaching, 76, 76n.22, 110-11, 128n.22,
223; *Address to Christian Nobility /
I Cor.* 1:18-25, 79-80, 95, 106, 108-9;
Ninety-five Theses, 88; I Cor. 1:18-25,
79-80, 95, 97, 104, 223; on "the
keys," 81, 88-92, 225, 245; "theology
of cross," 82, 95n.69, 104n.90, 116-
17; *Anfechtungen*, 83; relation with
von Staupitz, 83-85; Leipzig debate
with Eck, 86-93; Heidelberg Disputation (1518), 90, 104; *Freedom of a
Christian*, 93, 101-2, 107-8, 129n.23,
222; *Babylonian Captivity*, 95-97,
107, 116; "ethics of gratitude," 99,
130, 156n.62, 226, 245; Jer. 31:31-34,
102-3; "law and gospel," 103-4, 116;
priesthood of all believers, 109-10
(see below, "Priesthood of all believers"); Peasants Revolt (1525), 110-
11, 113; "tower experience," 113-16;
the "breakthrough," on Bucer, 133

Malinowski, Bronislaw, 62
Marx, Karl, 17, 236
More, Thomas, 170

Namier, Lewis, 23
Newton, Isaac, 31-32, 216-17

Niebuhr, H. Richard, xi-xii, 2-8, 16-17,
19-20, 69, 221-22, 238
Niebuhr, Reinhold, 11, 239

Oberman, Heiko, 68-71, 81, 90, 101,
115, 120

Pannenberg, Wolfhart, 111-13
Parsons, Robert, 194
Pauk, Wilhelm, 114, 125
Pinomaa, Lennart, 115, 156n.62, 222
Plato, 18, 31, 242
Pole, Cardinal Reginald, 175-76

Robinson, John A. T., 9-10
Rupp, Gordon, 114-15n., 116
Russell, Bertrand, 14, 45

Sadoleto, Cardinal Jacopo, 139, 246;
on otherworldly salvation, 146,
Catholic reform with Pole, 175
Saint-Pierre, Abbé de, 33-34
Schoenberger, Cynthia, 77
Seymour, Edward (Duke of Somerset),
171
Socrates, 18-19
Spencer, Herbert, 35
Staupitz, von, 83, 85, 86-88, 99
Stuart, Mary, 180
Stubbs, John, 185

Tillich, Paul, 9-10, 21, 64n.5
Tracy, David, 239
Troeltsch, Ernst, 5-7, 17, 21, 24, 109,
162-64
Tudor, Queen Mary, 174-76, 231

Valla, Lorenzo, 20, 81, 225; see "Donation of Constantine"
Voltaire, 40

Weber, Max, 5, 16, 62, 65, 130
Wentworth, Peter, 183-85, 231-32
White, Lynn, Jr., 12-13, 26

259

Whitehead, Alfred North, 13
Winner, Langdon, 55
Winstanley, Gerard, 32
Winthrop, John, 162
Wolsey, Cardinal, 170
Wood, Gordon, 15-16
Wright, David, 125

Wyclif, John, 92, 173

Zagorin, Perez, 191, 209; on Bacon's "idols," 214
Zell, Matthew, 124
Zwingli, Huldreich, 133

Index of Subjects

Anthropology, 2, 48, 62-68
Autonomy, concept of, 17-18, 21

Caesaro-papism, 173-74
Calling, doctrine of, 16, 234; see also
  "Vocation"
Cold War, 8, 52, 244, 254
Communion of saints, xi, xii; see same
  under "Calvin"
Copernican revolution, 29-30
Consciousness, human, 62
Counter-culture, 11
Culture, religion and culture, 1-2, 63;
  see also "Typology"

Deconstruction, 18-19, 236
Devil, Luther and . . . , 69, 95, 105
Diet of Worms, 71-72, 105, 112
Disillusion, 46-48, 58-59
Donation of Constantine, 81-82, 94-95,
  174, 225, 244

Edification, xiii; see same under "Cal-
  vin"
Encyclopedia, encyclopedists (French),
  33-34
English Reformation, 168-69; under
  Henry VIII, 169-71; under Edward
  VI, 171-72; under Elizabeth I, 178-79;

Puritan protest, 179, 183, 184; grow-
  ing criticism of monarchy, 187
Enlightenment (French), 23-24, 28, 40-
  43, 48, 65, 66; spokesmen for . . .
  (philosophes), 40-44, 47-48
Environmentalism, Earth Day, 13
Equality, 98, 109-11, 118
Erastianism, 174
Ethics (and progress), 39
"Ethics of Gratitude," 99, 150, 226
Eucharist, 97-98; Calvin on Lord's
  Supper, 149
Evolution, 38; see also "Darwin"
Exhibition of London (1851), 38, 52

"Faith and Reason," 1998 papal encyclical, 241-44
Freedom (Christian), 98, 101, 103, 111,
  118, 245n.51
French Revolution, 4, 46

Geneva, 138, 159; letter of Sadoleto to
  Genevans, 138; governance in . . . ,
  139; reply of Calvin published
  in . . . , 151
Grace, xiii, 102-3, 111, 245-46
Great Depression, 58

Holocaust, 58

Immanence, divine, 13
Industrial Revolution, 24

Justification by faith, 72, 76, 114-15; see same under "Luther"

"Keys of the kingdom," 81, 88-92

Martin Marprelate controversy, 135-36
Maturity, spiritual — and adulthood, 100-101, 110-12, 118-19, 249-50
Medieval system of salvation, 76, 139-40n.40
Multiculturalism, 1-2, 18

National Socialism (Nazism), 25, 58, 240
Neo-orthodoxy, 9

Obedience, 100, 142; . . . and humility, 142
Ontological anxiety, 62
Otherworldliness, xii, 24, 61, 69-70, 91-92, 145, 226, 229; Sadoleto on . . . , 141

Peasants Revolt, 110-11, 113, 198, 226
Positivism, 45
Pragmatism, 8
Priesthood of all believers, 109-19, 245-47; see same under "Luther"
Progress, concept of, xii, 21-22, 27-29, 32, 36-37; social-political idea of . . . , 32-35, 49-50, 56-59; distinct from evolution, 38-39
Providence (divine), 28-29, 36-37, 195, 199, 201
"Puritan party," under Elizabeth, 183, 185

Reformation, 66, 107, 187-89; see "Luther"

Regensburg Colloquy, 133-34
"Religion," 1-2, 61-65, 67
Renaissance, xii, 27, 42, 167, 215
Revelation, 13
Russian Revolution, 45

St. Bartholomew's Day Massacre (1572), 181-82, 185, 189, 206-7, 231
Schmalkaldic League, 125, 134
Scientific Revolution, Copernican . . . , 29-30, 66
Secularism, 10-11
Social gospel, 8
Soviet Union (USSR), 58
Spain, 182, 195
Strassburg, city of, 123-25, 135, 139, 151

Technology, 38, 48-53, 55-58
Theology, 2, 7-9, 14-15; natural theology, 102-4, 104n.90, 242-44
Thirty Years War, 46, 207
This-worldliness, 24, 98, 101, 108, 111-12, 128, 145, 168, 226-27
Tolerance, ix-x
Tradition (custom), 96, 107; Calvin on . . . , 148
Transcendence, divine, x, xii-xiii, 7, 13-14, 61, 96, 107, 117, 165, 188, 217, 226, 236, 247
Trent, Council of, (1545-63), 134, 179-80
Truth, xi, 210, 242-44; "truth as the daughter of time"; see same under "Bacon, F."
Typology, types of Christian social interaction, xii, 3-7, 20, 67-68

Vietnam War, 11, 55
Vocation, 109, 127-30, 188-89, 228-29, 237-38; see "Calvin" on same

World War I, 43-47, 49, 51, 58, 221, 240
World War II, 8-9, 25, 52, 54, 240